Dynamic Simulation
of
Physical Distribution Systems

Dynamic Simulation of Physical Distribution Systems

DONALD J. BOWERSOX

OMAR KEITH HELFERICH   EDWARD J. MARIEN

PETER GILMOUR   MICHAEL L. LAWRENCE

FRED W. MORGAN, JR.   RICHARD T. ROGERS

1972
MSU Business Studies

Division of Research
Graduate School of Business Administration
Michigan State University, East Lansing

ISBN: 0-87744-112-X
Library of Congress Catalog Card Number: 72-619501
© 1972 by the Board of Trustees of Michigan State University
East Lansing, Michigan. All rights reserved

PRINTED IN THE UNITED STATES OF AMERICA

A SCIENTIFIC INVESTIGATION is not the cold-blooded, straightforward, logical process that texts proclaim. It's an adventure. Sheer scientific excitement arises from the unexpected event, from the obvious assumption that's very wrong, from the hunch that pans out, from the sudden insight, and from the invention that covers the unanticipated procedural gap. The fact is that as organizations took form before our eyes, their struggle determined ours.

Chapman, Kennedy, Newell, and Biel,
Management Science, April 1959.

CONTENTS

List of Figures 11
Foreword 13
Preface 15

1 Research Perspective 19
    Research Orientation 20
    Research Procedure 22

2 System Model Conceptualization 25
    Situation Analysis 25
    Experimental Factors 26
      Target Variables 29
      Controllable Variables 32
      Uncontrollable Variables 33
    Total LREPS Conceptual Model 34
    Dynamics 38
    Summary 39

3 LREPS Solution Approach 40
    Physical Distribution Problems and Model Classification Scheme 40
      General Techniques 43
      Unifying Dimension 46
      Behavior of the Model 47
      Environmental Inputs 49
    Review of Selected Models 50
      Kuehn and Hamburger 51
      Shycon and Maffei 53
      Ballou 56
      Forrester 58
      Carrier Air Conditioning Company 61
      Packer 62
      Ballou 64

Solution Approach Specifications   65
   Physical Distribution Problem Statement   66
   General Research Requirements   68
   Model Operating Limits   69
   Model Capabilities   69
Summary   70

4 LREPS Mathematical Model   71

Design Methodology   71
   Mathematical Model: Philosophy   71
   General Design Considerations   77
   Special Design Considerations   78
Mathematical Model   82
   Supporting Data System Activities   83
   Demand and Environment   84
   Operating System Activities   91
   Report Generator System   127
Summary   134

5 LREPS Computer Model   135

Design Approach: Computer Model   135
   Design Requirements   136
   Design Methodology   137
   LREPS Programming Language   138
Computer Model   145
   System Linkages   147
Operationalizing LREPS   152
   LREPS Versions   154
Computer Model Evaluation   156
   Evaluation of GASP IIA   156
   Model Building Procedures   157
   Software and Hardware Features: Minimize Reprogramming   158
   Software and Hardware: Efficient Processing   158
   Model Output   159
   Compatability among Computer Systems: FORTRAN Version   159
   Computer Size Requirements: FORTRAN Version   160
   Operating System Requirements: FORTRAN Version   161
   Computer Compatibility and Size Requirements:
     COBOL Version   162
   Preliminary Model Validation Results   164
Summary   164

6 Validation   165

Philosophy and Process of Validation of Computer
   Simulation Models   165

Literature Review   168
    Cohen   168
    Bonini   169
    Clarkson   170
    Balderston   171
    Forrester   171
    Amstutz   173
Design of LREPS Validation Procedure   175
    Validation Procedures   175
    Types of Validation   176
Validation Techniques   178
    The Chi-Square Test   178
    Theil's Inequality Coefficient   178
    Spectral Analysis   179
    Regression Analysis   179
    Correlation   179
    Analysis of Variance   180
    The F Distribution   180
    Multiple Comparison   180
    Multiple Ranking   180
    Sequential Analysis   181
    The Kolmogorov-Smirnov Test   181
    Response-Surface Analysis   181
    Factor Analysis   182
    Graphical Techniques   182
Validation Results for LREPS   182
    Long-Term Stability   183
    Output Versus Historical   183
    Sensitivity to Model Assumptions   184
Summary   185

7 Experimental Design   187

A Review of Existing Simulations: Their Design and Analysis   188
    Cohen   188
    Forrester   189
    Balderston   190
    Cyert   190
    Bonini   191
    Kaczka   192
    Tuason   193
Key Considerations in Experimentation   195
Strategic Planning: Designing Experiments   196
    Objectives of Experimentation   197
    Factor Characterization and Specification   197
    Response Variables   199
    Measurement Techniques   199
    Experimental Design Alternatives   201

Tactical Planning: Running Experiments   204
　Starting Conditions   204
　Stochastic Convergence   205
Summary   206

8 LREPS Utilization   208
Introduction   208
　Applications—Physical Distribution (LREPS-PD)   212
　Applications—Marketing (LREPS-MK): Product Forecasting   220
　Applications—Financial (LREPS-F)   224
LREPS Research and Development   227
　R&D: Applied Systems Planning   227
　R&D: Basic Research   231
Summary   232

Appendix 1: Data Base Information   237

Appendix 2: LREPS System Activity Flowchart   247

Appendix 3: Example of LREPS Report Output Format   259

Appendix 4: Overview of Functions in LREPS—Finance   265

Notes   271

Selected Bibliography   281

LIST OF FIGURES

Figure		Page
1–1	LREPS Systems Design Procedure	23
2–1	Echelons of the Physical Distribution Network	27
2–2	General Description of Simulated Situation	28
2–3	Summary of Experimental Factor Categories	29
2–4	Order Cycle: Reorder and Customer	31
2–5	LREPS Systems Model Concept	35
3–1	Physical Distribution Problem Classification Scheme	41
3–2	Physical Distribution Model Classification Scheme	41
3–3	A Classification of Systems Analysis Techniques and Their Attributes	44
3–4	A Heuristic Program for Locating Warehouses	52
3–5	Simulation Test of a Particular Warehouse	55
3–6	Organization of Production-Distribution System	59
3–7	Simulation and Adapted Forecasting Applied to Inventory Control	63
4–1	A Five-Stage Iterative Modeling Process	75
4–2	Format for Activity Analysis—General Plan	76
4–3	Format for Activity Analysis in LREPS	79
5–1	Criteria for Selecting Predominant Computer Programming Language	139
5–2	LREPS Total Computer System Flowchart	146
5–3	Exogenous Input Preparation	148
5–4	Operating System's Interface with Input/Output	149
5–5	Report Generator System	150
5–6	LREPS Operating System Linkages	151
5–7	LREPS Operating System Input/Output Flowchart	153
5–8	One-Year Validation Results	163
8–1	Representative Information Output LREPS	210
8–2	Total Cost—Illustration I	214
8–3	Order Cycle Time—Illustration I	214

8–4	Total Cost—Illustration II	216
8–5	Order Cycle Time—Illustration II	216
8–6	Relationship Distribution Centers to Order Cycle Time—Illustration III	218
8–7	Percentage Orders Filled in 5.0 Average Order Cycle Days—Eight Warehouse Configuration—One Year—Illustration III	218

FOREWORD

This monograph describing the Long-Range Environmental Planning Simulator represents a major contribution in the fields of marketing and logistics management. It is laudatory not only for its content but also for the many contributions it has made to the Graduate School of Business Administration, the student body, and the faculty.

The reader is best able to judge its substantive and intellectual content. There are, however, many contributions which, although more subtle, are equally as important as the basic work. First are the insights provided concerning the interface between the market affairs of the corporation and the logistical support of those activities. From the very beginning measurements of the geographic market density, the variations in channel coverage, and the possible shifts in market opportunities through time were considered in planning the current and future product flows needed to service markets. Second, the introduction of dynamic simulation in place of comparative statics in physical distribution models represents a major breakthrough for corporate policy formulation. Third, the opportunity provided by the Johnson & Johnson Domestic Operating Company to the faculty and graduate student body of the Department of Marketing and Transportation Administration cannot be measured in any objective way. This project could not have been undertaken without the sponsorship of Johnson & Johnson. Of course, financial sponsorship was essential, but is in no way the most important part of the relationship. Few companies have the wealth of data and the willingness to share it with an educational institution. Not only was the project made possible by the excellent managerial information system of the sponsor but also the willingness of the Johnson & Johnson management to collect additional data where they did not exist before. The continuous working relationships established throughout the project have been superb. It is unique in the long sought private sector/educational relationship. The Johnson & Johnson Domestic Operating Company is to be commended for its willingness to enter such a project when only minimal assurances of success could be provided at the beginning, as well as for the continued interest, support, and collaboration of its management in the conduct of this research.

Donald A. Taylor, Chairman
Department of Marketing and
Transportation Administration
Graduate School of Business Administration
Michigan State University

PREFACE

The Long-Range Environmental Planning Simulator reported in this monograph is the product of team research. The nature of the LREPS research project was sufficiently complex to require the services and talents of a number of highly qualified individuals. With the exception of myself, all persons directly involved in the research and development of LREPS were students at Michigan State University. The primary purpose of the research project was to enrich the academic experience of this group of students. While naturally any team research reflects the joint contribution of all associates, the overall design of the LREPS project provided ample opportunity for demonstration of individual creative and theoretical accomplishment. The six doctoral students who completed LREPS join me as co-authors of this monograph. To date, five have completed doctoral dissertations based on LREPS and the final dissertation is in process.

In particular, I wish to comment on the extraordinary contributions of Omar Keith Helferich and Edward J. Marien. Dr. Helferich served as overall Project Director. Dr. Marien directed the computerization of the LREPS model. Each of these two dedicated individuals expended their time and energies far beyond what could normally be expected of students, and without their dedication LREPS would not be a reality.

As of this writing, Dr. Helferich is Director of Logistics Research and Planning, Systems Research Incorporated, Lansing, Michigan; Dr. Marien is Assistant Professor of Marketing, Wisconsin State University; Dr. Peter Gilmour is with the Department of Economics, Monash University, Victoria, Australia; Dr. Michael L. Lawrence is Assistant Professor of Finance, School of Business, University of Missouri; Dr. Fred W. Morgan, Jr. is Assistant Professor of Marketing, Miami University; and Richard T. Rogers is in the department of Brand Management, The Proctor & Gamble Company.

Many students worked part-time on the LREPS project. Among those who made significant contributions in the areas of modeling and programming were Dr. Kanti Prasad, Gerald Brown, John Dean, and Barry Press.

The administration of Michigan State University made the project possible by providing the support necessary to work effectively. In particular, Dr. Kullervo Louhi, Dean of the Graduate School of Business Administration, and Dr. Donald A. Taylor, Chairman of the Department of Marketing and Transportation Administration, provided constant support and encouragement to all concerned with the LREPS project. In addition, the team expresses appreciation to Dr. Dole A. Anderson, Director of the Division of Research, who provided the necessary space to headquarter the LREPS project and who is assisting in the distribution of results by publishing this report. Finally, the LREPS team expresses its appreciation to Felicia Kramer, who devoted countless hours to preparation of the monograph manuscript.

Research of the scope necessary to develop LREPS, in addition to the time and talent of those noted above, requires a great deal of financial support. As a dialogue of contemporary times, it is becoming increasingly necessary to seek financial support from outside the academic community in order to assist capable students in their educational programs. The subject research was fully funded from the private sector, including appropriate payments to the University for overhead, administration, faculty salary, and computer facilities. The topic of the research was of sufficient depth to classify the effort as basic research as opposed to problem solving. The sponsor firm agreed to provide confidential information and invested substantial resources in manpower, travel, and communications in addition to the grant which supported the research effort.

Confidential reports dealing with the results of experimentation and specific operation of simulations related to the sponsor's business have been provided under separate cover. The sponsor agreed to a general reporting of the aspects of the research which represent synthesis and expansion of the fields of physical distribution, modeling, simulation, and dynamics while retaining the right to the specific simulation model and analysis related to the details of their firm. The combined content of this monograph and the supporting thesis reports have been completed with this commitment in mind.

In final analysis, sponsorship is secondary to cooperation. All concerned with the development of LREPS were constantly impressed with the high quality of continued cooperation received from the executives of the Johnson & Johnson Domestic Operating Company. In particular, we wish to acknowledge the assistance of Herb Stolzer, John Varley, Graham Brush, Jr., and Bill Partipilo, who were in fact members of the research team.

In excess of thirty calendar months, fifty man years, over three hundred years of simulated business operations, and thousands of dollars of research support have been invested in LREPS. The focal point—physical distribution planning—has yielded most expected and many unexpected results. However, one singular thought has been discussed over and over by the research team. Namely, the potential for understanding business operations available from simulated experimentation remains in its infancy. We sincerely hope that the reporting of the LREPS research represents a small step forward.

Donald J. Bowersox, Professor
Department of Marketing and
Transportation Administration
Graduate School of Business Administration
Michigan State University

1

RESEARCH PERSPECTIVE

This monograph reports research completed on the subject of physical distribution planning at the Graduate School of Business Administration, Michigan State University. The objective was to design and program a dynamic simulator capable of replicating a firm's physical distribution system over a long-range planning horizon. The resultant model simulates physical product and communication flows between the manufacturing and multiple operational echelons that constitute the physical distribution system. The simulation model is called LREPS, an acronym for Long-Range Environmental Planning Simulator.

The LREPS model contains a number of unique features not integrated in other existing physical distribution simulators. First, LREPS is a comprehensive model of physical distribution operations which integrates physical facilities, order processing, inventory, material throughput, and transportation as a system capable of total cost and customer delivery performance measurement. Second, the structure of LREPS is dynamic allowing a variable time-planning horizon with sufficient feedback to ensure that future consequence of any earlier system change is fully considered. Third, the model is structured to cope with inventory planning and facility location on a simultaneous basis thereby integrating the temporal and spatial aspects of system design. Fourth, LREPS simulates multiple order cycles within a physical distribution network on a probabilistic basis and in an echeloned structure thereby introducing the realism of staging and performance delays. Fifth, LREPS is modeled on a universal basis thereby allowing the model to be efficiently applied to different enterprise situations. In addition, flexibility is provided within any given simulated structure such as the introduction of new products or the examination of alternative channels of distribution. Finally, LREPS is structured on an environmental basis which allows experimentation between the boundary of the firm and critical external factors that influence performance. This particular feature expands the strategic value of the model beyond system design to include contingency planning capabilities.

RESEARCH ORIENTATION

During the past several years techniques of system simulation have gained widespread application to a variety of business problems. Simulation is a process in which a given situation is replicated within a computer. In terms of business planning, the situation simulated may replicate a firm as it normally functions or it may postulate operations once major changes are introduced. The main usefulness of simulation is that management is able to estimate consequences of alternative courses of action prior to final commitment.

To the extent that simulated activities can be projected into the future, long-range planning capabilities are introduced. Long-range planning deals with the futurity of today's decisions with respect to the most probable estimate of future conditions. As such, long-range planning is concerned with. Where are we going? (strategic planning), and How do we get there? (operational or implemental planning). P. F. Drucker defines long-range planning as follows:

> It is a continuous process of making present entrepreneurial (risk-taking) decisions systematically and with the best possible knowledge of their futurity, organizing systematically the efforts needed to carry out these decisions, and measuring the results of these decisions against expectations through organized, systematic feedback.[1]

The power of simulation is that it allows present risky decisions that have long-range implications to be projected into the future under an unlimited combination of potential operating and competitive conditions.

Simulation does not in any analytical sense produce an optimum or best answer to a planning problem.[2, 3] As such, simulation does not enjoy the precise mathematics of an analytical model. In compensation, simulation models are not limited by rigorous constraints and related simplifying assumptions characteristic of analytical models. A simulation model can be constructed without careful quantification of relationships between particular variables, since such relationships can be derived from output observations over a series of controlled simulation runs.[4] Thus complex planning problems can be confronted with the numerical procedures of simulation without the limitations of analytic models. In terms of problem solving, simulation is an approximation technique which must rely upon a number of trial replications in order to isolate from among the options tested the most satisfactory plan.

Somewhat analogous to simulation, physical distribution has attracted considerable management attention over the past few decades. In a popular sense, physical distribution is concerned with the complex task of getting the right combination of products to the right customers at the correct time to accomplish a successful transaction.[5]

Because physical distribution deals with several measurable attributes, it is a prime candidate for quantitative analysis. The essence of physical distribution is physical product flow. The products under consideration constitute entities capable of exact measurement. Product flow concerns rate, which is capable of measurement with respect to direction, level, and velocity. The geography of physical distribution is concerned with spatial distribution of demand and the associated problems of fixed facility locations and transportation. Providing a consistent standard of customer service concerns levels of advanced inventory commitment and customer order-cycle times. Both the spatial and temporal aspects of physical distribution performance, similar to the physical product flow, are capable of exact measurement.

However, from these fundamental and measurable attributes of physical distribution, very complex systems have emerged in the American economy. Physical distribution is an integrative field which strives to merge transportation, inventory allocation, warehouse operations, order communications, and materials handling together into a single performance system. From a cost viewpoint, each part or component of physical distribution is subordinated to the system's total cost of performance.[6,7] Thus it makes little difference how many dollars management budgets or spends on a specific part of physical distribution as long as the total cost of all parts in consort are controlled to plan.

The degree of customer service that a specific physical distribution system is consistently capable of providing is a vital marketing concern. As a result, total distribution cost is only relevant within the constraint of desired customer service. The quality of customer service provided by a physical distribution system is an integral part of total marketing effort, and, appropriately, the design of a physical distribution system should be planned within a firm's marketing strategy.

Most firms have a wide range of alternatives in the design of a physical distribution system. Unfortunately, many existing systems have evolved over time without initial design or major redesign. The opportunity is to redesign and implement a system which provides a competitive advantage in terms of cost and service capabilities.

While the objectives of physical distribution planning can be simply stated, the design of systems to accomplish the stated objectives constitutes a complex problem. To date, a number of different quantitative techniques have been applied to physical distribution system design.[8] As a general statement, past applications have failed to accomplish three desirable objectives: (1) full integration of spatial and temporal relationships in a total system design, (2) sufficient detail in structure to allow planning of an individual physical distribution component design while retaining a multiechelon and multichannel format, and (3) incorporation of sufficient realism into the model to evaluate the impact of operational dynamics upon design.

The LREPS research was initiated to provide a more useful planning tool for physical distribution. In terms of long-range planning the model is of the strategic variety. Its primary focus is upon how the physical distribution system should be structured over time. Because LREPS is a continuous model with respect to a planning horizon, a suggested implemental plan is generated to accommodate each solution. The term *long-range* is defined to encompass problem evaluation which extends beyond a single year's operation. For the LREPS model, long-range is synonymous with the planning horizon, which can be set to represent any number of years. The model's task is to replicate integrated physical distribution operations over the selected planning horizon. The researchers' and planners' task is to design an experimental structure for model utilization.

RESEARCH PROCEDURE

The overall research design for the LREPS model is flow diagrammed in figure 1–1. The content of this monograph is planned

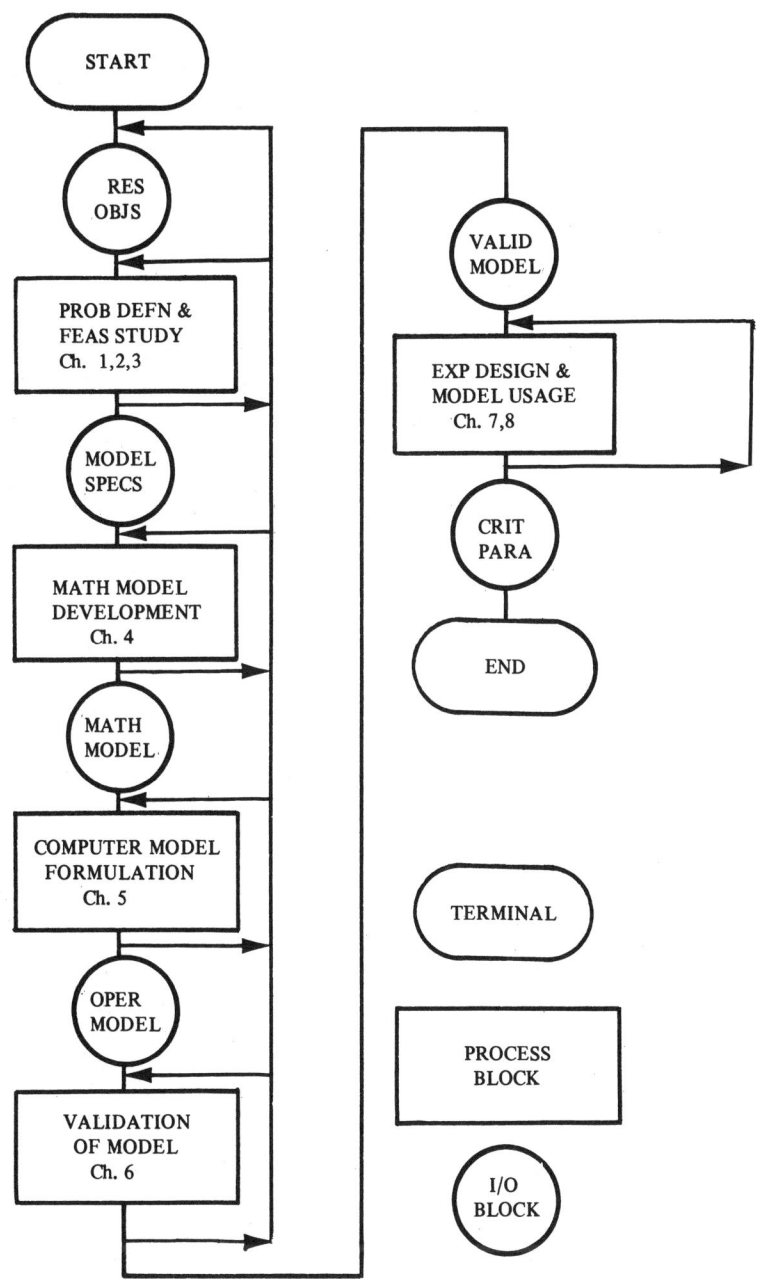

Figure 1-1
LREPS Systems Design Procedure

around the research steps completed in the design and development of the model.

Chapter 2, "System Model Conceptualization," introduces the scope and range of the physical distribution system modeled. Initially, the research situation is presented by a description of the type and echeloned arrangement of the physical distribution network modeled.

Emphasis is placed on the universality of the model by means of a conceptual overview of its experimental capabilities. Next, the conceptual model and its three major systems are generally described. The final section discusses the dynamic aspects of the system model.

Chapter 3, "LREPS Solution Approach," presents the logic followed in selecting the solution approach for LREPS. The nature of physical distribution problems and related solutions are classified on the basis of variables. Next, a review of several simulation models which have selected characteristics of interest to the research is presented. Finally, the solution technique selected—simulation—is discussed.

The LREPS mathematical model is presented in chapter 4. The design methodology used to develop the model is described, followed by a discussion of the transformations (equations) employed in key areas of the model.

Chapter 5, "LREPS Computer Model," presents the overall philosophy and procedures that guided the development of the LREPS operational model. An overview of the operational computer model is presented with references to appendices for examples of the data base, system flowcharts, and typical management report formats. The final section provides a brief evaluation of the operational LREPS model.

In chapter 6, "Validation," a general philosophy of validation of computer models is presented, followed by a discussion of validation techniques. The procedure used to test the validation of LREPS and the nature of results are also presented in the chapter.

Chapter 7 is devoted to experimentation. The approach to simulated experimental design and methods available to analyze results of sets of computer runs are presented.

The final chapter is devoted to LREPS utilization. To date, over 300 years of simulated business operations have been completed using the LREPS model. Past and current applications utilizing LREPS for systems planning are discussed. The final section presents potential areas of utilization for applied and basic research.

2

SYSTEM MODEL CONCEPTUALIZATION

This chapter is concerned with the conceptual aspects of the LREPS model. The first section, an analysis of the research situation, describes the type and echeloned arrangement of the physical distribution network modeled. The second section presents a conceptual overview of the inputs, outputs, and operational components of the total system model. The third section discusses the three-staged nature of the LREPS conceptual model. The final section examines the dynamic aspects of the conceptualized system model.

SITUATION ANALYSIS

The general nature of the physical distribution system model is that of a manufacturing firm which produces and distributes on a national basis a multiple-product line through either marketing middlemen or company facilities. The LREPS system model structure consists of three echelons which can be arranged in a variety of different product flow channels from point of manufacturing to geographical point of demand satisfaction. Figure 2–1 illustrates the echelon structure of the model, which is discussed below.

The initial echelon of the model is manufacturing. The manufacturing control center (MCC) produces either a complete or partial product line which is automatically placed in an adjoining replenishment warehouse (RC). All product flow reorders to the second echelon are supplied from the RC.

The second echelon consists of distribution centers (DC) and consolidated shipping points (CSP). The primary function of the second echelon is to provide inventory replenishment and product delivery to satisfy customer service requirements. Three different types of distribution center alternatives exist at the second echelon. A primary distribution center (PDC) functions within the model as a full-line regional distribution center. A second type of distribution center is classified as a remote facility (RDC) in a sense that it services a limited market area within a region on a full-time basis. If the remote distribution center inventories less than a full product line it becomes the third type of distribution center (RDC-P). At the second echelon level the alternative of consolidated shipping points (CSP) also exists. The CSP does not stock inventory. Rather it serves as a geographical point where customer orders can be consolidated for purposes of transportation economies with subsequent break-bulk and local delivery.

The third echelon consist of customer locations. Specific customers can be identified on an individual basis, or, when desirable, agglomerated demand units (DU) can be employed. In mass marketing applications the 560 geographic ZIP sectional center areas are grouped into 400 geographic DUs. Hub cities of these 400 DUs serve as points of simulated customer demand.

The flexible structure of echelon arrangement allows the simulation of a variety of different physical distribution systems both with respect to echelons and alternative product flow paths. The range and scope of the simulated situation allows a wide variety of combinations with respect to product, market, and competitive profiles in addition to components of the physical distribution system. A general description of the simulated situation is presented in figure 2-2. As illustrated, the model can be defined more specifically as one involving: (1) unlimited conditions of product, market, and competitive profiles; (2) multiple facility locations in an echeloned arrangement; (3) multiproduct, multilocation inventory; (4) multiecheloned communication network; (5) multiecheloned transportation capability; and (6) varied material handling capability. The next section presents a conceptual overview of the total system model.

EXPERIMENTAL FACTORS

The experimental capabilities of the LREPS system model are classified on the basis of input and resultant output variables in figure

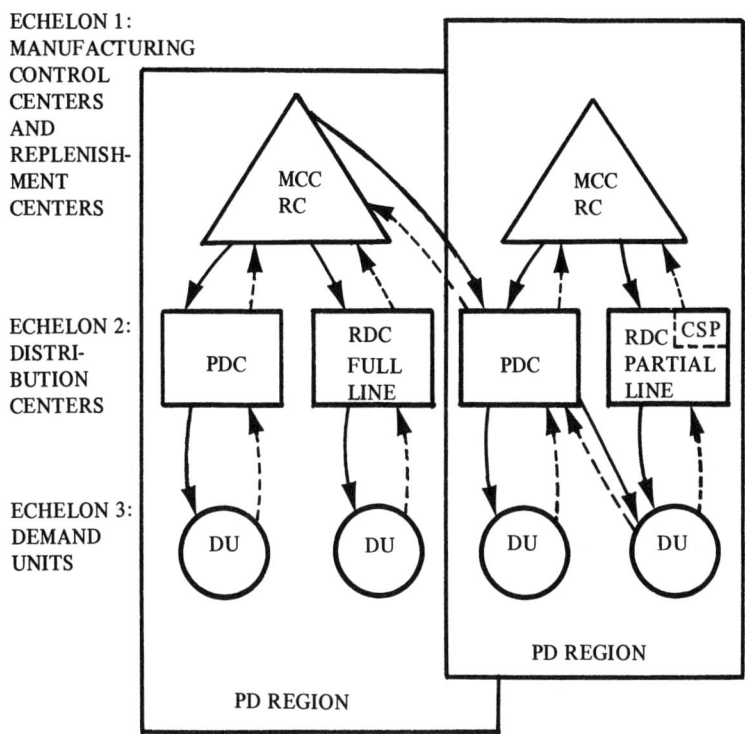

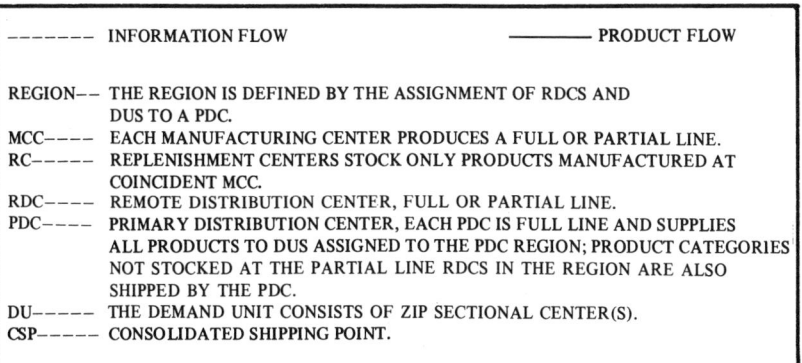

Figure 2–1
Echelons of the Physical Distribution Network

Figure 2–2
General Description of Simulated Situation

Physical Distribution System
  Manufacturing Control Centers (MCC)
    Multilocation
    Each produces full line or less
    Each product is produced at more than one location

  Replenishment Centers (RC)
    Multilocation
    Each stocks all products manufactured at adjacent MCC

  Distribution Centers (PDC) (RDC)
    Multilocation
    Full line—primary DC (PDC)
    Full or partial line—remote DC (RDC)

  Consolidated Shipping Point (CSP)

  Transportation
    Common carrier—truck, rail, air
    Private and contract truck

  Inventory
    Reorder point, replenishment and hybrid at RC, PDC, and RDC

  Communications
    Computer, teletype, mail, telephone

  Material handling
    Automated or manual

Product Profile
  Multiproduct line
  Actual or pseudo
  New or existing
  Key product groups by class of trade

Market Profile
  Order characteristics—actual or pseudo
  Multicustomer classes of trade
  Individual or agglomerated demand
  Total U.S. market

Competitive Profile
  Multicompetitors

2-3. Input variables are grouped as controllable and uncontrollable depending upon the degree of design influence enjoyed by the model users. The level, state, and flow relationships of the model are determined by the value of input variables which establish system boundaries, operational relationships, and, therefore, define the experimental range of the model. The output variables, classified as target, provide a measure of performance, given alternative physical distribution system configurations. The value of target variables results from model manipulation of a predetermined set of controllable and uncontrollable variables. Each category of variable is discussed below.

Target Variables

Target variables are endogenous to the system model. T. H. Naylor et al. describe the operational relationship between input and output variables as follows:

> Endogenous variables can be best defined as the dependent or output variables of the system and are generated from the interaction of the system's exogenous and status variables according to the system's oper-

Figure 2–3
Summary of Experimental Factor Categories

Target Variables (Output)
  Sales distribution
  Customer service
  Physical distribution system costs
  Physical distribution system flexibility

Controllable Variables (Input)
  Order characteristics
  Product mix
  New products
  Customer mix
  Facility network
  Inventory policy
  Transportation
  Communications
  Unitization

Uncontrollable Variables (Input)
  Marketing environment
  Technology
  Acts of nature

ating characteristics. Exogenous variables are the independent or input variables of the model and are assumed to have been predetermined and given independently of the system being modeled. Exogenous variables can be classified as either controllable or uncontrollable. Controllable or instrumental variables are those variables or parameters that can be manipulated or controlled by the decision makers or policy makers of the system.[1]

The major target variables of concern in physical distribution planning are sales distribution, customer service, cost, and flexibility.

In order to specify and control the geographical distribution of sales in a simulated situation, the model measures product sales by individual or grouped customer units, distribution centers, sales regions, total market, and a variety of other spatially oriented points. In addition, sales are accumulated and measured between locational points in the system. Such interpointal measures enable the evaluation of the practicality and alternatives for transporting products from one point to another. Various types of sales measures are incorporated in the model to accommodate different situations. For example, measurement is in dollars for one type of analysis and cases, line items, or weight for another type of analysis.

The essential physical distribution function is to service customers. The quality of customer service provided by a given system can be measured in terms of speed and consistency. Thus customer service is defined as a temporal sphere of operation. Customer service measurement in the model is oriented to the elapsed time required for a customer to receive a product once an order is placed on the system.

Figure 2-4 illustrates the temporal measures of the customer order and internal reorder cycles of the model. Each order cycle accumulates times associated with the following activities:

order transmission
order processing
shipment preparation
time delays due to stockout
shipment dispatch
transportation
time delays related to capacity or in-transit operations

These time elements can be accumulated to measure the speed and consistency of a given physical distribution system's customer and reorder cycles.

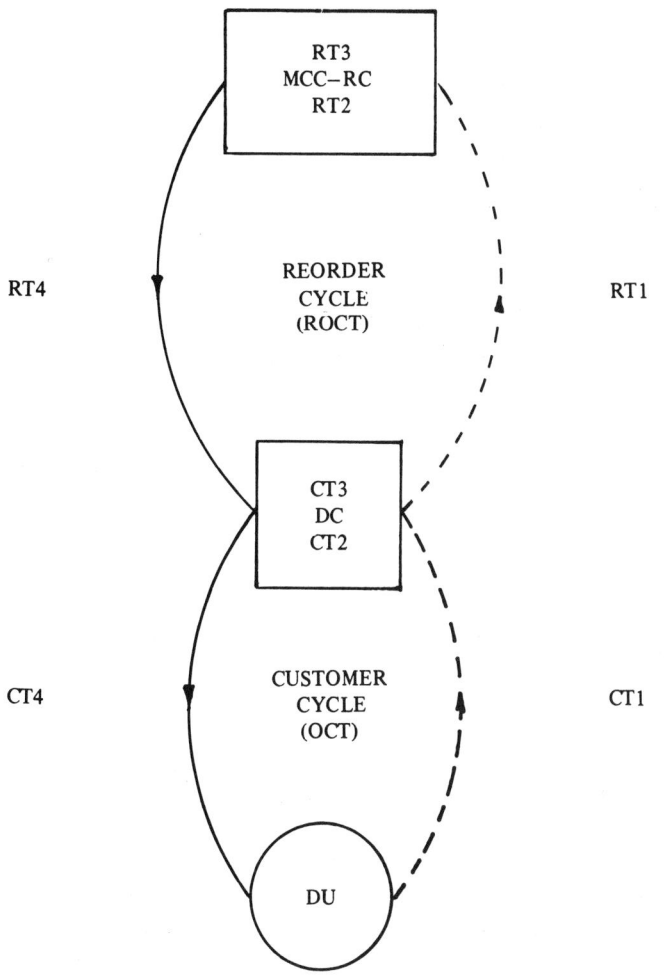

REORDER CYCLE
RT1: REORDER TRANSMITTAL
RT2: REORDER PROCESSING & PREPARATION
RT3: SHIPPING POLICY DELAY
RT4: INBOUND TRANSIT

CUSTOMER ORDER CYCLE
CT1: ORDER TRANSMITTAL
CT2: ORDER PROCESSING & PREPARATION
CT3: STOCKOUT DELAYS
CT4: OUTBOUND TRANSIT

Figure 2–4
Order Cycle: Reorder and Customer

In terms of conceptualization, a simulation model may be structured as probablistic or deterministic with respect to order-cycle times. In a deterministic model the time required to perform a specific task may be changed; however, once assigned, it remains constant during a simulated run. For example, a shipment between two locations will always take the same amount of time with no chance of delay. In a probabilistic model the value of a specific relationship is random with different times being experienced for a specific occurrence based upon probability distributions. The LREPS system model is probabilistic with respect to all echelons of customer and reorder cycles.

A final point concerning service is the recognition that customer order and internal reorder cycles are dependent in operation. Activity and performance in the reorder cycle will influence inventory availability for the customer order cycle. Likewise, the frequency and nature of customer order-cycle experience will influence reorder-cycle requirements. Compounding the performance impact of this interrelationship is one of the primary features of an echeloned systems model.

The speed and consistency of customer service must be measured with respect to the total cost of attainment. Total physical distribution cost includes the cost of transportation, communications, materials handling and packaging, holding inventories, and the cost of operating and maintaining facilities. Tradeoffs in costs between and among the above activities must be analyzed to test alternative levels of customer service. The LREPS model is capable of testing a system design which provides a specified level of customer service for a specific period of time and designs that incorporate changing levels of desired customer service across the planning horizon.

The final target variable measured is the flexibility of alternative distribution plans given changes in the internal and external business environment. The essential measure of flexibility is the ease with which alternative system designs can accommodate optimistic or pessimistic changes in the model's controllable or uncontrollable inputs. The system model target variable related to flexibility measures adaptability to change.

Controllable Variables

Controllable inputs include a combination of factors that are under the direct control of management. One type of controllable variable concerns operational factors that do not directly fall under physical distribution. Included are such items as the mix of products offered for sale, the customers or market segments serviced, the characteristics of the orders that are submitted to the distribution division for servicing, plus the introduction, deletion, and changing of the total product line. Although these factors are generally beyond the scope of physical distribution, they have a major impact on the performance of the distribution system. The system model is capable of testing the sensitivity of alternative plans to various arrangements of these factors.

More directly concerned with physical distribution system design are the facility network for distributing finished goods, the means of order entry, processing and preparation, the policies concerning the dispatching of customer shipments, the policies and procedures for controlling the levels of finished goods inventories, plus the means of transporting goods among suppliers, distribution centers, and customers.

By varying the options and alternative methods of combining the controllable variables, different distribution system designs can be measured with respect to target variable accomplishments. The LREPS model is capable of processing different levels for a set of controllable input variables and also includes the capability of modifying the set of controllable input factors over time.

Uncontrollable Variables

The input variables of the system model considered outside the direct control of the firm are classified as uncontrollable. The three main categories of uncontrollable variables are the marketing environment, technology, and acts of nature.

The marketing environment external to the firm creates the arena for physical distribution operations. Shifts in customer demand determinants between geographic locations plus changes in the absolute level of demand within a defined market area can have serious effects on distribution system performance. In addition, cost-of-living and relative increases in cost factors can have a substantial impact on planned distribution operations. Testing the sensitivity of distribution plans to varying assumptions concerning rates and levels of change in the environment is a basic capability of the LREPS model.

Another uncontrollable factor affecting physical distribution performance is the state of technology associated with the factors controllable by the firm. Advancement in the technological state of transporting goods, materials handling and packaging, communications, and distribution center operations are incorporated within the system model in order to evaluate the sensitivity and flexibility upon target variables.

The final uncontrollable input category is concerned with the broad area of acts of nature. While acts of nature are highly unpredictable, they are disruptive events which must be considered in the design of distribution systems. Such events as tornadoes, floods, wildcat strikes, or subversive activities can be scheduled at any specific point in simulated time to test the flexibility of the system and to aid managers in the establishment of contingency plans.

The range and scope of the LREPS model was illustrated in figure 2-3, which lists the most critical variables structured in the model. Experimental analysis utilizing LREPS can be planned around three sets of variables. For any specific experimental design, a given variable can be selected for analysis with the resultant impact upon all other variables, and total system performance can be measured and evaluated over the planning horizon.

Target variables represent the output of a given configuration of controllable and uncontrollable variables for the model. Model performance is measured by the resultant values of target variables. Controllable variables constitute the level, state, and flow relationships between different critical parts of the model. Controllable variables for any given experimental arrangement represent input which is predetermined with respect to initial value and model reaction range. The level and state of the controllable variable can be manipulated by LREPS users. Uncontrollable variables are given and are beyond the control of model users once a specific experimental run is initialized in the sense that impact upon performance cannot be controlled by model users.

TOTAL LREPS CONCEPTUAL MODEL

The dynamic simulator is a three-stage model as illustrated in figure 2-5, "LREPS System Model Concept." The total model is segregated into Supporting Data, Operating, and Report Generator Systems. The Supporting Data and Report Generator Systems are off-line while the Operating System constitutes the on-line computer portion of the LREPS model.

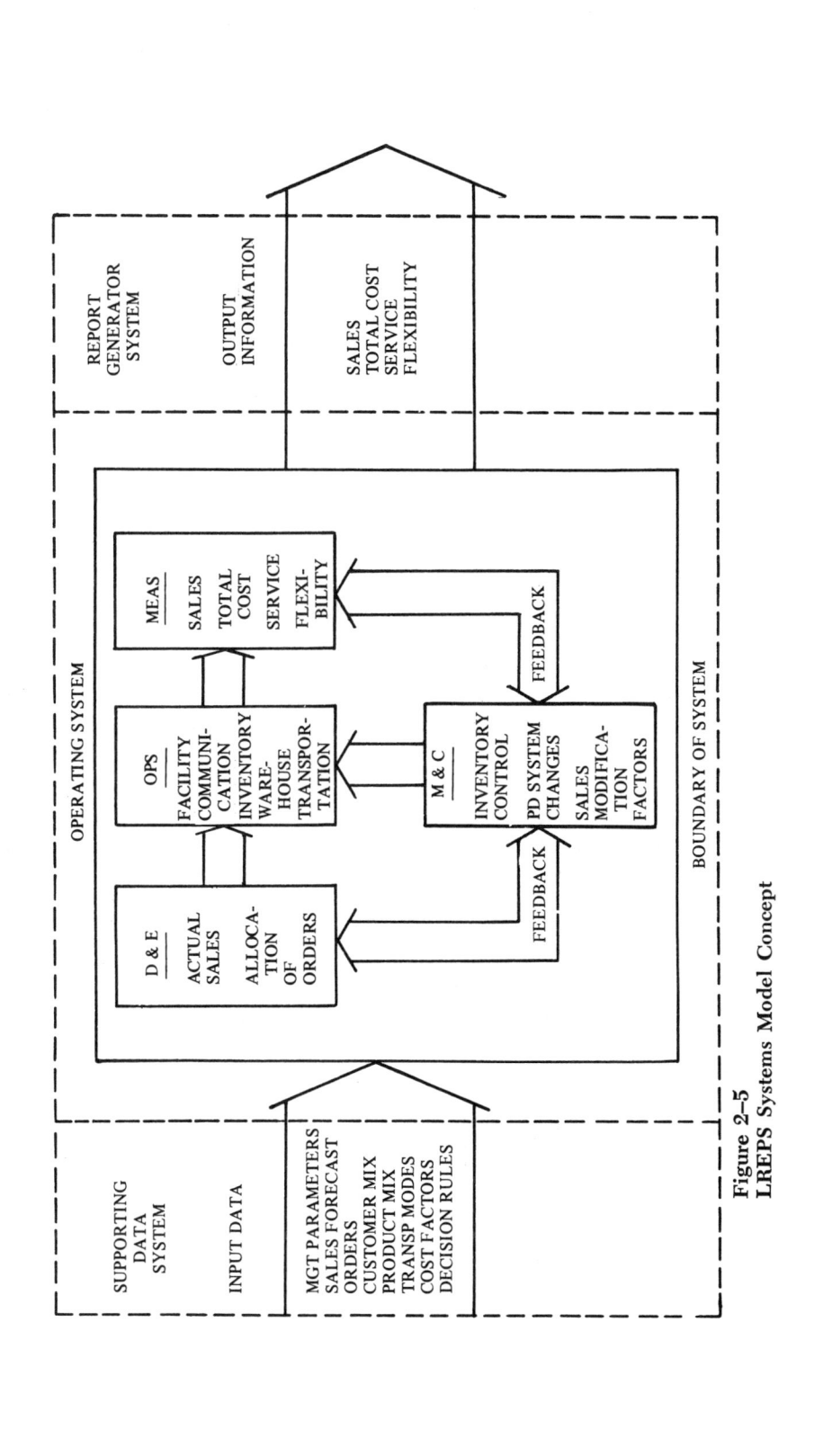

Figure 2-5
LREPS Systems Model Concept

The purpose of the Supporting Data System is to analyze, prepare, and reduce the exogenous inputs for a set of simulation runs or experiments. In addition, changes scheduled in experimental factors during a simulation run are introduced by the Supporting Data System. For each different application of LREPS, a unique Supporting Data System information loading must be generated.

The second stage of LREPS, the Operating System, simulates the operation of the physical distribution network. The second stage consists of four overlapping subsystems which form the integrated physical distribution model. The four subsystems, as illustrated in figure 2-5, are the Demand and Environment Subsystem, Operations Subsystem, Measurement Subsystem, and the Monitor and Control Subsystem.

The Demand and Environment Subsystem generates and assigns customer orders to agglomerated demand units. Stratified random samples of products and orders are selected and stored on magnetic tape. The sample of customer orders is used to develop a matrix of summarized blocks of orders. Simulated order generation consists of randomly selecting blocks of orders from the order matrix to satisfy the daily sales for each demand unit. The overall sales forecast is allocated to demand units on the basis of correlated independent market variables.

During this order generation step "pseudo" orders, with different order characteristics, can be added to the order matrix to test the effect of various levels of demand from different classes of customers, or the effect of changing buying patterns for existing classes of customers. In addition, the pseudo order matrix allows the introduction of new products to test the effect of significantly different products on system performance and design.

The output of the Demand and Environment Subsystem, allocated customer orders by demand unit and its assigned distribution center, serves as the input to the Operations Subsystem. Each demand unit is assigned to an in-solution distribution center based on a criterion such as minimum distance, minimum transit time, minimum transportation cost, or some other heuristic rule.

The Operations Subsystem processes simulated customer orders through the physical distribution system. Fifty products are tracked in detail to serve as the basis for product flow measurement. The order cycle between each demand unit and its servicing distribution center is replicated with appropriate time estimates for all phases of processing. Time estimates are based upon standards plus a variable or reliability element selected from a probability distribution. The sum of the averages of order transmission time, order processing and preparation time, stockout delay, shipment policy delay, and shipment transit time is defined as the average normal customer order-cycle time with variations in performance being measured in terms of standard deviation.

As orders are processed at each distribution center, inventories of tracked products are reduced. If inventory is insufficient the product is backordered or the order is cancelled. As inventory reorder points or periods are reached at the distribution center, multiple-product replenishment reorders are dispatched to the next echelon in the system. Once again, appropriate time delays are introduced to add realism. The range of inventory policies available in the model includes a daily reorder point, optional replenishment, and a hybrid system which is a combination of the reorder point and replenishment methods. The information for the tracked products is extrapolated to represent the total product line.[2]

The Measurement Subsystem is concerned with developing the cost, sales, service, and flexibility measures for the orders processed. Total cost is measured on the basis of cost parameters and mathematical transformations related to each component of the system. Fixed facility investment cost by size and type of facility is based upon an annual depreciated amount. Throughput costs for each distribution center are calculated using regression equations with different cost factors based upon size and location of the facility. Communication costs are calculated using regression equations where the independent variables are the number of orders and lines processed. Inventory carrying and reorder cost are calculated for all nodal and pipeline inventories. Inbound transportation costs to distribution centers are calculated on the basis of freight rate tables. Outbound freight rates from distribution centers to demand units are calculated from sets of regression equations based on distance.

The Monitor and Control Subsystem through feedback compares the desired levels of sales, cost, and service against levels achieved by the system. Modifications to the physical distribution system state, for example, addition or deletion of distribution centers and modified forecast sales, can be automatically activated in the simulation model. The Monitor and Control Subsystem contains a facility location algorithm which provides for expansion of capacity at initial or new locations as necessary and/or addition and deletions of locations as required. In essence, the Monitor and Control Subsystem functions as the timing and command center for executing the simulator.

The third and final stage of the simulator is the Report Generator System. This stage is designed to convert raw data output of the model into desired research or management report format. The Report Generator functions off-line and can easily be modified with respect to data-base display.

DYNAMICS

A characteristic of the conceptualized model was to introduce feedback relationships that would allow the relationships between controlled variables to internally adjust within the simulator on the basis of performance. To meet this requirement, the structure of the operating system of LREPS was designed on a dynamic as opposed to a static basis. The literature contains varied definitions and opinions concerning what attributes constitute a dynamic structure. The LREPS system model has four specific attributes that meet all known requirements for a dynamic structure.

First, the model is oriented to a variable time planning horizon. Thus, system design is traced in terms of a sequence of decisions over the horizon with different physical distribution system design structures at different points in simulated time. Transitions between system structural arrangements are made as necessary to meet desired levels of target variable performance.

Second, LREPS is time-interval dependent in the sense that deficiencies from one period related to inventory, facility network, and future sales are linked on a recursive basis through feedback mechanisms. For example, future period sales are linked to previous period performance in the sense that a reduction (increase) in simulated sales can occur as a result of poor (high) customer service by the physical distribution system.

Third, a location algorithm is included in LREPS which adds to the dynamic nature of the model, since periodically, through the planning horizon, facilities are evaluated to determine if expansion, additions, or deletions are in order. Two location routines are structured in the model. The first is heuristic with some aspects of the algorithm being similar to the Kuehn and Hamburger model.[3] The second option, under development, is an on-the-fly linear programming routine, to solve a point-in-time analytic solution to the location problem. Once a location is selected for expansion or addition, it is scheduled into solution after a time delay for normal construction and startup. A deletion is handled in a similar manner with an appropriate time delay for closing down the facility.

Fourth and finally, the changes in exogenous variables over a long-run planning horizon are another form of dynamics. The LREPS model is capable of simulating the effect of changing, within the planning horizon of an experimental run, environmental factors such as transportation rates, transportation technology, customer mix, product mix, and so on. This aspect of dynamics, the ability to measure the effect of a changing of the environment in which the real system operates, is frequently neglected by systems designers.

SUMMARY

In summary, this chapter presented the conceptual nature of LREPS which led to selection of the solution approach and subsequent development. The initial section described the business situation modeled with respect to echelons and scope of physical distribution system components, product, market, and competitive profiles. The experimental capabilities of the model were then presented in a coverage of critical input and output variables. Of central importance to the desired system model was the discussion of the interdependence and probabilistic nature of customer order and internal reorder cycles. Next, the total LREPS conceptual model was described in terms of the Supporting Data, Operating, and Report Generator Systems. Finally, the desired dynamic nature of model relationships was reported.

Given this general overview of the model, the next step in the research consisted of the development of the solution approach for model development, which is the main concern of chapter 3.

3

LREPS SOLUTION APPROACH

Earlier chapters presented an overview of the LREPS model and described the experimental nature of the simulator. In the actual research process the selection of a simulation solution approach was not finalized until the system model had been conceptualized and a review of alternative approaches completed. In this chapter the process used to select simulation as the solution technique is reported. The steps involved were: classification of planning approaches and models, review of existing physical distribution models, and description of the solution technique selected for the LREPS project.

PHYSICAL DISTRIBUTION PROBLEMS AND MODEL CLASSIFICATION SCHEME

There are many potential classification schemes for physical distribution planning problems and models. The purpose of developing a classification scheme is to aid in the review of models presented in the literature that are potentially applicable to the LREPS design criteria. Figure 3-1 presents the problem definition (independent) variables used to classify planning problems. All physical distribution planning problems can then be defined in terms of the following independent variables: physical distribution component structure both number and type, the planning horizon, and the influence of current decisions on future decisions in the model. As illustrated in figure 3-2, dependent variables are used to define and classify the solution approach. The dependent variables used for the model are: the type of technique, the unifying dimension, the behavior of the system, and the environmental inputs.

Figure 3–1
Physical Distribution Problem Classification Scheme

Problem Definition
The Independent Variables

1. Type and number of physical distribution components
    Single component
    Multicomponent
    All components
2. Planning horizon
    Short range (operational)
    Long range (strategic)
3. Influence by previous decisions
    Nonsequential
    Sequential

The independent variables selected to define the physical distribution planning problem of this research were introduced in chapters 1 and 2. Using these independent variables, each physical distribution model presented in the literature can be first classified according to the problem solved in terms of the number of physical distribution components and the type of components included in the problem statement. Each problem thus would be classified as either a single component, multicomponent, or total physical distribution system (all components).

Figure 3–2
Physical Distribution Model Classification Scheme

Approach to Solution
The Dependent Variables

1. Type of technique
    Analytical (optimization)
    Heuristic (simulation)
2. Unifying dimension
    Spatial (distance or location)
    Temporal (time)
3. Behavior of system model
    Static
    Dynamic
4. Environmental inputs
    Fixed over planning period
    Variable over planning period

The independent variable, planning horizon, refers to the period of time, usually five to ten years, over the period of problem consideration. For this variable the problem can be classified as either a short-term (operational) planning model with considerations for one to two years or a long-range (strategic) planning horizon where consideration is frequently five to ten years.[1]

The third and final independent variable used in the classification scheme is the dichotomy nonsequential versus sequential. This variable is used to classify a physical distribution planning model relative to the influence of current decisions on future decisions made in the model. C. Hadley describes a sequential decision problem as

> a problem which involves making two or more decisions at different points in time, and which has the property that the later decision(s) may be influenced not only by the previous decisions, but also by some stochastic parameters whose values will actually have been observed before later decisions are made.[2]

The key difference between sequential and nonsequential decision problems is that future decisions in sequential problems may be based partially on information known in the future but unknown at present. One of the frequent approaches to the solution of sequential decision problems uses the functional equation technique of dynamic programming.[3]

The dependent variable type of technique refers to the general approach, either analytical or heuristic, that is primarily used for planning. In this research, analytical is defined to include such mathematical techniques as linear programming, or dynamic programming. Heuristic techniques are nonoptimizing including such modeling techniques as simulation, which may or may not incorporate analytical (optimization) techniques to handle subsets of activities or components within the total model.

The second dependent variable, the unifying dimension, refers to the orientation of the model in developing measures of cost and/or service. The unifying dimension of a model is classified as spatial if the cost and/or service developed are based on location or transit time. If the model uses order-cycle time as the measure of physical distribution system performance, the model is classified as temporal or time oriented.[4]

The third dependent variable, the behavior of the model, refers to a classification of static versus dynamic. A dynamic model is defined as one where information feedback control loops provide time-varying interactions within the model.[5]

The fourth and final dependent variable, environmental input, is the set of operating forces that influences physical distribution policy and is external to the firm. The environmental forces are summarized by D. J. Bowersox as: industry competitive structure, market differentials, network of service industries, legal structure, and economic forces.[6]

In terms of physical distribution planning it appears that a clear relationship exists between independent and dependent variables. Definition of the problem in terms of simultaneous treatment of component structure, planning horizon, and influence of past decisions requires that a solution approach capable of handling all dependent variables be utilized. The research team's conclusion was that dynamic simulation was the best general solution approach.

As background for the reader, the investigation leading to the selection of dynamic simulation is reported below. Each of the dependent variables is reviewed in terms of the relationship to independent variables.

General Techniques

In terms of general techniques there is support in the literature that suggests that complex business planning problems must be solved with heuristic models, such as simulation, since mathematical analysis has not been capable of yielding general analytical solutions. The alternative, an experimental approach with the real system, is frequently too costly in time and money.[7, 8, 9]

A paper by M. A. Geisler and W. A. Steger considers alternative techniques in logistics systems analysis.[10] After classifying logistics systems, the authors present a classification of systems analysis techniques and their attributes as illustrated in figure 3-3. The objectives of systems analysis as stated by Geisler and Steger are to: determine their operating characteristics, study their completeness and consistency, evaluate new policies and procedures, and do sensitivity testing.

The object of selection from among systems analysis techniques, according to the authors, is to find the one technique that best deals with system characteristics in achieving the purpose of the analysis. The authors further state that

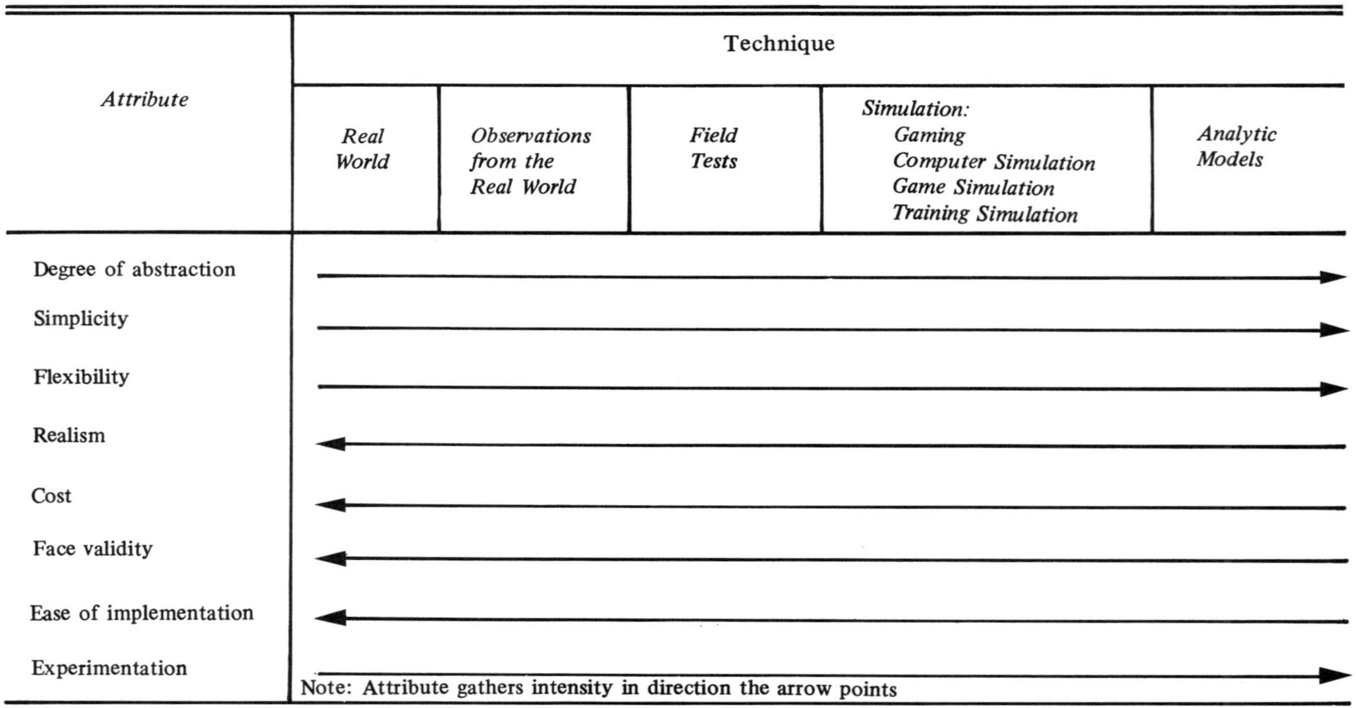

Attribute	Technique			
	Real World	Observations from the Real World	Field Tests	Simulation: Gaming, Computer Simulation, Game Simulation, Training Simulation	Analytic Models

Attributes (arrows indicate direction of increasing intensity):

- Degree of abstraction →
- Simplicity →
- Flexibility →
- Realism ←
- Cost ←
- Face validity ←
- Ease of implementation ←
- Experimentation →

Note: Attribute gathers intensity in direction the arrow points

SOURCE: M. A. Geisler and W. A. Steger, "The Combination of Alternative Research Techniques in Logistics Systems Analysis," in *Operations Management: Selected Readings*, edited by G. K. Groff and J. F. Muth (Homewood, Illinois: Richard D. Irwin, Inc., 1969).

Figure 3–3
A Classification of Systems Analysis Techniques and Their Attributes

simulation plays a very important and central role in the spectrum of techniques used, particularly in dealing with those facets of a system that are not now or may never be subject to a high enough degree of abstraction to lend themselves to analytical treatment.[11]

The conditions affecting choice between heuristic and optimizing models are discussed by A. A. Kuehn.[12] The value of optimizing models, he believes, is that the computational method leads to the best possible solution or set of solutions of the problem statement. This is in contrast to heuristic methods, which as a general rule do not guarantee reaching the optimal solution or solution set. Furthermore, heuristic methods do not provide an indication as to whether or not the optimal solution has been obtained. According to Kuehn, the value of heuristic methods can be stated in terms of complexity, size, and cost. First, heuristic methods can be used to solve much more complex problems than can be treated by existing optimizing models. Second, heuristic methods can be used to solve much larger problems than those which can currently be solved on existing computing equipment with the available optimizing models. Finally, heuristic methods can economically solve problems which could only be solved at prohibitive cost by available optimizing models.

Kuehn also states that he believes that heuristic and optimizing models will be integrated into individual programs. For example, heuristic methods might be used to develop advance starting points for subsequent analysis by optimizing models, or the latter might be used merely to determine when an optimal solution has been reached. He makes the important point that "even greater integration is likely insofar as optimizing algorithms are incorporated as subroutines within heuristic programs."[13]

Bowersox discusses the degree of optimization that a firm should seek in physical distribution systems design:

> The design of an optimal system is a noteworthy objective, but one that is never achieved. Even if an optimum system could be conceived, it is doubtful that construction and overall implementation could be completed in sufficient time to enjoy the perfect arrangement.[14]

Thus, according to Bowersox, the system study should serve as a guide to evaluate and modify specific segments of existing physical distribution systems, to serve as a blueprint. A successful systems analysis thus requires a flexible model that produces "satisficing" solutions after consideration of changing patterns of customer demand, corporate objectives, technological developments, and competitive actions.

M. K. Starr states that there is

> a definite relationship between the concept of long-range planning (where the subsystems are time sequentially interdependent) and the acceptability of sub-optimation. Similarly, for master planning (where the subsystems are interacting units of an extensive organization) suboptimizing methods must be accepted in order to achieve the highest possible level of systems analysis.[15]

The above literature review supports the concept that the solution to a total physical distribution systems design problem for long-range planning requires the use of heuristic, suboptimizing solution techniques.

Unifying Dimension

The second dependent variable is referred to by J. L. Heskett in expressing concern about the overemphasis on the use of spatial aspects: "undue, misplaced emphasis on spatial matters in physical distribution has prevented effective measurement of physical distribution activity and the development of truly valid system planning methods."[16] The unifying dimension must be "time":

> Time rather than distance will be the unifying dimension of an integrated model for helping plan and control a logistics system. This model—adapted to each company's special needs—will combine elements of a temporally oriented location model with an inventory model to produce information for planning purposes and a set of devices for the control of various elements of a company's logistics system.[17]

The two major cost areas, transportation and inventory, according to Heskett, have not been fully integrated in physical distribution analysis to date:

1. Location models have been spatially oriented to date, while inventory models have and will always be temporally oriented.
2. A physical distribution system can be described completely for analytical purposes only in terms of its inventories, but not in terms only of its transportation elements.[18]

He states that the majority of models for location analysis, such as center-of-gravity, linear programming, and heuristic, have been spatial rather than temporal.[19, 20] One exception he noted was Bowersox's use of transit time in location of analysis.[21]

In contrast, Heskett believes that inventory models do not have spatial orientation. The relevant time is not transit time between inventory locations, but rather is the order-cycle time from point of order transmittal to, and through, the distribution supply point and back to the point of delivery. His reasons for "time" as the unifying dimension can be summarized as follows:

1. Neither time nor cost necessarily bear close relationship to distance.
2. There is low relationship between order-cycle time and distance.
3. Spatially oriented models lack relevance because their primary objective has been cost minimization based on weighted distance, which has little to do with profit maximization.

Time-oriented models, he says, allow consideration of the order-cycle time and consistency; these two determinants of demand (revenue) plus cost relationships incorporated in a model allow the capability for profit maximization objectives.

In summary Heskett concludes:

> If an integrated, accurate method of analyzing and controlling physical distribution systems is to be developed, time instead of space will be the relevant unifying dimension to be used.[22]

> A system can be viewed most productively as a set of actual or potential inventory cells linked and partially determined by time-transit time for those inventory cells in network links, order-cycle time for those cells at network nodes.[23]

The above literature review indicates that a planning model for the total physical distribution system should include inventory control and the development of measures of the total order-cycle time.

Behavior of the Model

The third dependent variable to be reviewed refers to the static versus dynamic nature of the model. The review previously presented in this chapter suggests the use of a heuristic solution technique and temporal orientation for complex problems such as integrated physical distribution systems. Therefore, the literature review here concentrates on the sequential versus nonsequential requirements of the problem.

R. A. Howard discusses the use of the optimizing technique, dynamic programming, for solving certain types of sequential decision problems. He characterizes a sequential problem as "a problem in which a sequence of decisions must be made with each decision affecting future decisions."[24] He further states that "We need to consider such problems because we rarely encounter an optimal situation where the implications of any decision do not extend far into the future."[25]

R. H. Ballou discusses this problem in the context of a warehouse location model.[26] The shifting of market demand patterns and changing economic conditions can create many static, maximum-profit distribution centers over time. He states that in considering the possible multiple optimal distribution center location alternatives, the question is "what combination of these alternatives should be chosen to maximize cumulative profits from location for a given planning period?"[27] Ballou believes the decision problem is to determine the distribution center location plan, including the initial locations and all subsequent locations and/or relocations, so that cumulative profits from the decision stages are maximized for the entire period in which the distribution centers are needed, the planning period. In summarizing his ideas on the importance of considering the sequential problem he says: "The point is that existing models, although sophisticated, lack a certain amount of scope, especially for providing solutions that indicate the optimum location pattern over time."[28]

J. W. Forrester treats the time-varying (dynamic) behavior of organizations, which he defines as industrial dynamics.[29] The foundation for his industrial dynamics is the concept of information-feedback systems: "An information-feedback system exists whenever the environment leads to a decision that results in action which affects the environment and thereby influences future decisions."[30]

Various other authors also have used dynamic programming and other techniques to solve what have been referred to as dynamic planning problems, optimal time-staged decisions, sequential decision problems, or time-varying interaction systems. [31, 32]

The above brief review suggests that the sequential decision problem or time-optimal staging problem requires a dynamic approach.

Environmental Inputs

The fourth and final dependent variable is concerned with the operating forces that influence physical distribution policy.[33] The factors which represent environmental inputs are subject to change over the period of interest, the planning horizon. The magnitude of the change is thus a function of the rate of change and the length of the planning horizon.

As reported by Bowersox, there are a number of factors that have an impact upon effective physical distribution management. These include: geographic shifts, new product development, transport and unit loading, international marketing, competition, and channel pressures.[34]

P. Kotler and R. L. Schultz refer to this problem also:

> The American marketing system is a huge, complex network of marketing firms and facilities. . . . It operates within an economic system characterized by a high rate of product innovation, multiple instruments and channels of marketing communication and persuasion, and constantly evolving patterns of buyer wants, attitudes, and behavior.[35]

These two authors present a review of the various marketing simulation models for studying complex marketing problems related to environmental changes in advertising, price, new products, and market share.

The time dimension of long-range planning varies considerably, but as discussed by G. A. Steiner it is not at all unusual to find in industry today long-range projections of economic environment, customer demand for products, or new technology extending ten to twenty years in the future.[36]

Forrester, in referring to the challenge to top management in long-range planning, states that "the challenge lies in how today's decisions will affect the time interval between five and twenty years hence."[37]

J. F. Magee points out that it is reasonable to consider using a static model, not allowing for change of the environmental inputs, if the anticipated rate of change of the market is low enough and the flexibility of the physical distribution system great enough that a static model is useful.[38] For many other circumstances, however, he states:

We must take a dynamic view of the distribution system:
1. Because change in the system may be expensive and laborious.
2. Because anticipated future needs may be inconsistent with present needs.
3. Because we may not be able to see the future too clearly.[39]

There is little argument that today's market is dynamic and subject to continuous change. In fact, various authors have stated that the only thing constant is change itself. The physical distribution system operates within the environment of, and functions to serve the demands of, the marketing system. The inputs to a physical distribution long-range planning model must therefore be able to reflect the continuous change in the marketing environment and other external operating forces which determine the operating boundaries for the distribution system. It is thus apparent from the literature that long-range planning models for physical distribution must be dynamic in terms of providing for modification of environmental inputs.

The literature reviewed suggests that for the physical distribution problem defined in this monograph, which is a multiechelon, total physical distribution system (all components) with sequentially staged decisions over a long-range planning horizon, the types of models that would be of greatest assistance are heuristic models with optimization techniques incorporated within. The model should, in addition, be dynamic rather than static, with time as the unifying dimension rather than distance, and with capacity for changing the environmental inputs of the model.

The literature review makes evident that no existing model is capable of satisfying the LREPS conceptual requirements. The following section reviews in summary form the state of the art of physical distribution planning models.

REVIEW OF SELECTED MODELS

A recent review of applications of quantitative methods to physical distribution is presented by Ballou in which he discusses transportation models, inventory models, location models, warehousing analysis, merchandise layout, and dock requirements.[40] The techniques used in these models include linear programming, dynamic programming, network flow, and simulation. General reviews of quantitative techniques applied to physical distribution are also presented by Magee,[41] and by D. J. Bowersox, E. W. Smykay, and B. J. La Londe.[42]

Other books, monographs, and the like, also available in the literature, review the total range of possible quantitative techniques that have been applied to physical distribution system and/or component analysis and design.[43] In this monograph, however, only those models in the literature that appear to be useful for the development of a total physical distribution model are reviewed.

The models selected for review include: (1) a planning model to determine the geographical pattern of warehouse locations by A. A. Kuehn and M. J. Hamburger, (2) a multicomponent physical distribution model by H. H. Shycon and R. B. Maffei, (3) a dynamic programming model to find the optimal solution to the multiperiod location problem by Ballou, (4) a model of an industrial system developed by Forrester, (5) a combination linear programming and simulation model for physical distribution planning by Carrier Air Conditioning Company, (6) a multiproduct inventory model by A. H. Packer, and finally, (7) a multicomponent model with primary emphasis on inventory.

Each of these models is presented in the above order in terms of the problem-solution relationship of independent-dependent variables previously defined.

Kuehn and Hamburger

Several models have been developed that involve transportation and location but not inventory control. Kuehn and Hamburger developed a planning model to determine the geographical pattern of warehouse locations which would be most profitable to a company.[44] Figure 3-4 defines the model in terms of a general flow diagram. In the model marginal cost of warehouse operation is equated with transportation cost savings and incremental profits resulting from more rapid delivery. The problem includes screening and evaluation of alternative warehouse locations for a fixed set of exogenous inputs which define transportation costs as proportional to distance. Warehouse operating costs and opportunity costs associated with shipping delays are then used to estimate cost savings for addition of warehouses. The primary physical distribution components not considered are inventory and communications.

The planning horizon as developed in the problem is short range since the exogenous input is fixed. However, long-range considerations could be introduced using different exogenous input levels.

Figure 3-4
A Heuristic Program for Locating Warehouses

1. Read in:
   a) The factory locations
   b) The M potential warehouse sites
   c) The number of warehouse sites (N) evaluated in detail on each cycle, i.e., the size of the buffer
   d) Shipping costs between factories, potential warehouses, and customers
   e) Expected sales volume for each customer
   f) Cost functions associated with the operation of each warehouse
   g) Opportunity costs associated with shipping delays, or alternatively, the effect of such delays on demand

2. Determine and place in the buffer the N potential warehouse sites which, considering only their local demand, would produce the greatest cost savings if supplied by local warehouses rather than by the warehouses currently servicing them.

3. Evaluate the cost savings that would result for the total system for each of the distribution patterns resulting from the addition of the next warehouse at each of the N locations in the buffer.

4. Eliminate from further consideration any of the N sites which do not offer cost savings in excess of fixed costs.

5. Do any of the N sites offer cost savings in excess of fixed costs?

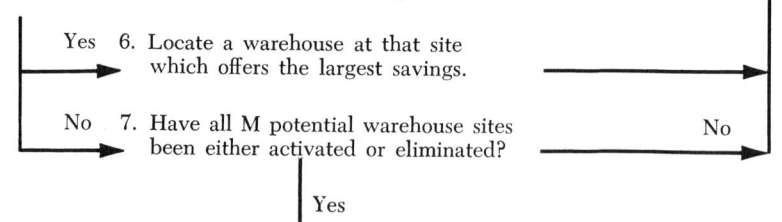

   Yes 6. Locate a warehouse at that site which offers the largest savings.

   No 7. Have all M potential warehouse sites been either activated or eliminated?   No

   Yes

8. Bump-Shift Routine
   a) Eliminate those warehouses which have become uneconomical as a result of the placement of subsequent warehouses. Each customer formerly serviced by such a warehouse will now be supplied by that remaining warehouse which can perform the service at the lowest cost.
   b) Evaluate the economics of shifting each warehouse located above to other potential sites whose local concentrations of demand are now serviced by that warehouse.

9. Stop

SOURCE: A. A. Kuehn and M. J. Hamburger, "A Heuristic Program for Locating Warehouses," *Management Science* 9 (July 1963).

The problem as defined is nonsequential, since only one set of decisions is made at a point in time. The problem does not involve time-varying interactions or decision stages over time. The general approach to developing a model for the problem selected was simulation rather than analytical. The authors state that

> the linear programming algorithms available for optimizing the routing of shipments in multi-plant, multi-destination systems cannot, in the current state of knowledge, be applied directly to the more general problem of determining the number and location of regional warehouses in large-scale distribution networks.[45]

The model is spatially rather than time oriented, since it does not allow the development of the total order cycle and a measure of the consistency of service.

The system behavior is static rather than dynamic according to the previously stated definition of dynamic models. In this model there are no situations that change over time, and no information feedback control systems. The model simulates at a point in time the activity that has occurred during a total previous operating period. There is no simulated calendar or passage of time within the model and therefore no feedback control loops can be developed.

The environmental or exogenous inputs are fixed for each simulated year. These inputs could be modified to simulate a different point in calendar time, for example, a future year. Thus the model could also be helpful as a long-range planning tool.

In summary, the Kuehn and Hamburger planning model does not consider the inventory component, is nonsequential, and is primarily a short-range planning model. It, therefore, does not provide an answer to the problem defined in this monograph. The Kuehn and Hamburger model, however, does serve as an excellent guide for the development of the location algorithm in the Monitor and Control Subsystem of the LREPS mathematical model.

Shycon and Maffei

In the multicomponent model developed by Shycon and Maffei, the problem is to combine the best features of direct plant-to-customer distribution with those of a national warehousing network.[46] Analysis is made to determine the number, size, and location of warehouses and processing locations which would properly serve customers at a minimum cost nationally. The flow of the Shycon and Maffei model is illustrated in figure 3-5.

As in the Kuehn and Hamburger model, this model includes elements of the transportation-warehouse operations, and location components. The authors state:

> It takes into account each of the important factors involved in the operation of a distribution system: transportation rate structures, warehouse operating costs, the characteristics of customers, demand for products, buying patterns of customers, costs of labor and construction, factory locations, product mix and production capacities, and all other significant elements. These factors, taken together, make up the distribution system.[47]

The model, however, does not include the inventory control or communications components of the physical distribution system.

The model, according to the authors, was designed to represent a complex, high-volume national distribution system with thousands of customers. Thus they state that the model makes provision for—

1. each customer's order sizes, his ordering patterns, the various types of shipments he receives, and his product mix;
2. handling the costs of the various kinds of shipments made such as: carload, less-than-carload, truckload, less-than-truckload, and various shipment sizes within the lower classifications;
3. variation in warehouse operating costs such as: labor costs, rentals, taxes for different geographic areas;
4. the many different classifications of products which Heinz manufactures, the alternative factory source points for each of these products, and the factory capacity limitations on each;
5. the knowledge of where these relationships differ, so that adjustments to cost and volume estimates might be made.[48]

Initially, the model was developed for short-range planning, but, as the authors stated, the customer demand data, product data, cost data, and the like could be changed to reflect long-range effects in the environment. Some of the possible uses of the model for long-range planning are given by the authors. These include: (1) distribution cost studies for different combinations of customer classification schemes; (2) locational studies to determine the effect of shifts in customer type or location, factory relocation; (3) studies related to changes in product mix, customer consumption patterns, product capacity at

Figure 3–5
Simulation Test of a Particular Warehouse

Preprocessing Run
(To eliminate the volume of shipments that go directly from factories to customers and hence will not effect the warehouse distribution system)

1. The computer is programmed for the preprocessing run. It is given detailed instruction as to what it should do with the customer information that it will receive.

2. Information on every customer in the national Heinz distribution system is fed into the computer.

3. The computer tests each customer to determine whether his volume of purchase is sufficient to justify direct shipments from factories.

4. A. If a customer's volume justifies shipments directly from the factory, the computer lists each such customer separately, according to the type of product he orders and the volume of his orders.

Test Run
(To determine the costs of distribution under various warehouse location configurations)

   B. At this point the computer retains the volume of customer orders which are not shipped directly and must go through the warehousing system.

5. First, the computer has fed into it a new program which tells how to compute costs on the basis of the information which it will receive in step no. 6.

6. Next, the following information is processed by the programmed computer.

   A. The results from the preprocessing run (i.e., the customer volume that flows through the warehousing system) which were retained in the computer in step no. 4.

   B. The particular warehouse location configuration that is to be tested.

   C. The freight rates, warehouse operating costs, taxes, etc. that make up the costs of the particular geographical areas in which the proposed warehouses are located.

7. *The Computer Issues the Results:*
   The costs of distribution for the Heinz company under the tested warehouse location configuration.

SOURCE: H. H. Shycon and R. B. Maffei, "Simulation—Tool for Better Distribution," in *Readings in Physical Distribution Management*, edited by D. J. Bowersox, B. J. LaLonde, and E. W. Smykay (New York: The Macmillan Company, 1969), pp. 243-60.

factory locations; and (4) studies related to changes over time in annual volume, or product line.

The final independent variable to consider is nonsequential versus sequential. The model is nonsequential in that only a single set of decisions are simulated. Decision stages over time are not considered.

The general solution approach selected by Shycon and Maffei provides further support for the relationship previously suggested that total physical distribution problems require heuristic solution techniques. The Shycon and Maffei model does not develop a measure of the total order cycle and service dependability and thus is spatially oriented rather than time oriented according to the definition previously presented. The behavior of their model is static rather than dynamic, since there is no simulated passage of time in the model. Recursive equations or information feedback control loops are therefore not possible. The environmental inputs are fixed for a given simulation run for one year. The major emphasis of the model is thus not to test the effects of a changing environment over a long-range planning horizon. However, as previously stated, various changes in environmental inputs do make the model suitable for testing the effect of any assumptions for a given future year.

In summary, the Shycon and Maffei model does not consider the inventory or communications component, is nonsequential, and is primarily a short-range planning model. It cannot, therefore, provide the answer to the LREPS conceptual system. The model, however, does include the essential elements which influence warehouse location. It thus provides background for development of the LREPS mathematical model.

Ballou

Ballou considers the question of what combination of multiple optimal warehouse location alternatives should be chosen to maximize cumulative profits from location for a given planning period.[49] In this model the mathematical technique, dynamic programming, is used to find the optimal solution to the multiperiod location problem. Ballou states that

> a physical distribution system can be conceptualized as several inventory storage points (nodal points) interconnected by a transportation network (links). Location of inventories or location of warehouse fa-

cilities, transportation service choices, and inventory-level alternatives are the three major decision areas that concern the physical distribution manager about the design of a distribution system.[50]

In treating only the location problem independently of other alternatives, Ballou states that an upper limit is established on the profits that the distribution system can generate, due to the fact that one degree of freedom in overall system design is lost.

The concern in this model is to determine the location plan that describes when and where relocation should take place throughout the planning period. This plan is established at present time (time zero) for the entire planning horizon and is the optimum plan based on the problem statement and the forecasted revenue and cost levels. The model provides an example of a multicomponent model that considers the sequential decision problem. Ballou states in this regard that "existing models, although sophisticated, lack a certain amount of scope, especially for providing solutions that indicate the optimum location pattern over time."[51]

The basic elements of transportation and location are considered in the model developed by Ballou. Inventory, warehouse operation, and communications are not, however, included in the problem definition. The planning horizon is primarily short range for the model as presented in the literature. As in the two previous models, however, the inputs could be modified to reflect long-range estimates of environmental factors. The problem as defined by Ballou states that future decisions are to be influenced by previous decisions. Thus the problem does investigate the multiperiod or sequential decision problem.

The solution technique found to be appropriate by Ballou was dynamic programming in which

> the best location plan is found by recasting the problem into a sequence of single-decision events. Then, according to Bellman's Principle of Optimality: in a sequence of decisions, whatever the initial decision, the remaining decisions must constitute an optimum policy for the state resulting from the initial decision.[52, 53]

The dynamic programming technique is an analytical technique for finding a warehouse location-relocation plan that will yield maximum cumulative profits for a given planning horizon.

The unifying dimension for this dynamic programming model is spatial even though delivery time is used as a basis for measuring service. As indicated previously by Heskett, transit time alone does not make a model time oriented. The model must also develop a measure of the total cycle time, and a measure of service consistency.

In summary, the model developed by Ballou is basically a location model with transportation costs and transit time used as the basis for measuring system performance. A key component, inventory control, however, is not considered. The model considers the sequential decision problem and thus provides a useful framework for developing this aspect of the LREPS mathematical model. The model is dynamic in the sense that it uses a completely recursive system of equations to solve the multiperiod problem. It solves the multiechelon decision problem.

Forrester

The model of the industrial system developed by Forrester attempts to match production rate to rate of final consumer sales.[54] The process of production and distribution, according to Forrester, is the central core of many industrial companies. A recurring problem is to match the production rate to the rate of final consumer sales. Forrester states that "it has often been observed that a distribution system of cascaded inventories and ordering procedures seems to amplify small disturbances that occur at the retail level."[55]

The model developed by Forrester, as shown in figure 3-6, deals with the structure and policies within a multiechelon distribution system. Flows of information, order, and materials are required to define the model. Three types of information are required: the organizational structure, delays in decisions and actions, and the policies governing purchases and inventories.

The organizational structure includes the nodes or echelons at which inventory exists: the factory, distributor, and retailer. Delays in flows of orders (information) and flow of goods are necessary to determine the dynamic characteristics of the system. Three principal components are defined by Forrester: orders to replace goods sold, orders to adjust inventories upward or downward as the level of business activity changes, and orders to fill the supply pipelines with in-process orders and shipments.

The physical distribution components included in the industrial dynamics production-distribution simulator are: transportation, inven-

FACTORY

FACTORY
WAREHOUSE

INVENTORY
NODE

DISTRIBUTORS

INVENTORY
NODE

RETAILERS

INVENTORY
NODE

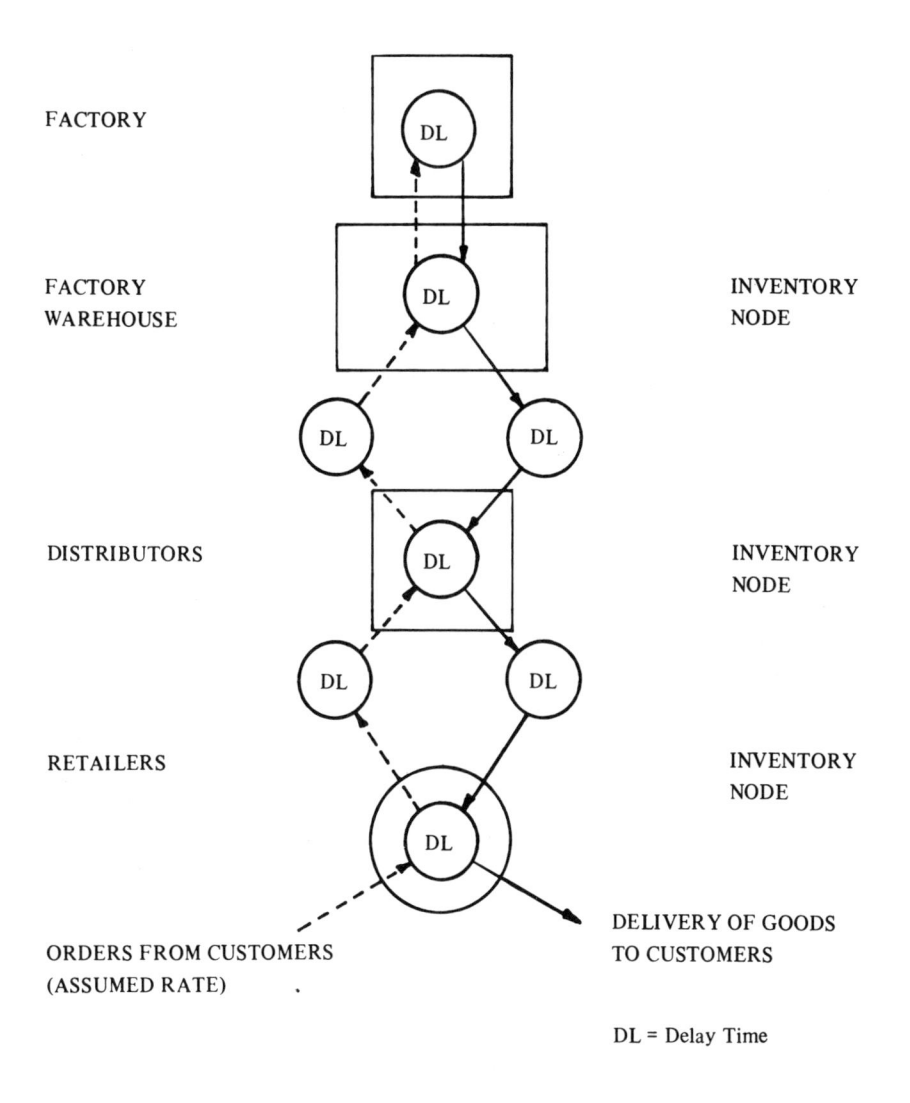

ORDERS FROM CUSTOMERS
(ASSUMED RATE)

DELIVERY OF GOODS
TO CUSTOMERS

DL = Delay Time

SOURCE: J. W. Forrester, Industrial Dynamics (Cambridge, Massachusetts: The M.I.T. Press, Massachusetts Institute of Technology, 1961), p. 22.

Figure 3–6
Organization of Production-Distribution System

tory, communications delays, a fixed set of locations, and warehouse or unitization.

The organization structure is a single factory, and single factory warehouse, and multidistributors and multiretailers. The distributors and retailers are each represented by a single location in the model. Aggregate increases and decreases in sales are assumed. Therefore, this model should be considered a single product type model. The problem as stated is thus one of total physical distribution system components for a single channel, single supply source, with multi-echelon inventory nodes.

The model as developed is a "closed" system. Inputs are initialized as rate equations. Since the model is not presented as a decision-making tool, there is no reference to a planning period horizon for decision making. The response of simulation runs to various changes in inputs is measured for dynamic effects on system variables in terms of one to three years. The period of influence could therefore be considered short range or long range. The problem as stated is sequential since the objective is to examine possible fluctuating or unstable behavior arising from the principal structural relationships and policies over time.

The general solution approach used by Forrester is heuristic. He makes the point that mathematical analysis is not powerful enough to yield general analytical solutions to situations as complex as the total physical distribution system. Forrester constructs a mathematical model of the industrial system that tells how the conditions at one point in time lead to subsequent conditions at future points in time. The behavior of the model is observed, and experiments are conducted to answer specific questions about the system that is represented by the mathematical model. The name *simulation* is often applied to this process of conducting experiments on a model rather than attempting the experiments with the real system. Forrester states that simulation consists of "tracing through, step by step, the actual flows of orders, goods, and information, and observing the series of new decisions that take place."[56]

The unifying dimension in the model is time. As previously stated by Forrester, in order "to be able to determine the dynamic characteristics of this system, we must know the delays in the flows of orders and goods."[57] The behavior of the model is dynamic in the sense that it consists of information-control loops and deals with time-varying interaction.

The model developed by Forrester presents observations and results of experimentations related to the dynamics of the total physical distribution system. It thus provided valuable insight in developing the dynamic aspects of the LREPS mathematical model.

Carrier Air Conditioning Company

The model developed by the Carrier Air Conditioning Company uses a combination of simulation and linear programming for a physical distribution system.[58] The problem as defined includes elements of transportation, inventory, warehousing, communications, and location and thus is a total physical distribution model.

The planning horizon is not stated, but it appears that the model is run using activity levels for one operating year. It could be considered short range or long range, since the model inputs could and apparently have been modified to simulate different markets, customer demand, production schedules, freight rates, shipping modes, delivery times, inventory costs, warehouse rates, and handling rates.

The problem as discussed in the article and illustrated in the input/output forms appears to be nonsequential. The decision maker requests the proposed physical distribution system he wishes to measure. The combination simulation and linear programming model then is used to develop the costs and a customer service level for the requested inputs.

The general solution approach, as previously stated, is heuristic with the optimization technique, linear programming, incorporated in the model. The unifying dimension appears to be spatial rather than processing and transit time, and the percentage of market within a time oriented. The model incorporates a measure of the time of order number of days. However, as previously defined, to be considered temporal the overall time dimension must include the use of unit inventory control, transit time, order processing times, delays due to stockouts, and the like to develop the only true "temporal" measure—the total order cycle. Merely reporting a transit time and/or order processing time does not make the model time oriented.

The model could be dynamic within the simulation of a given year. However, it does not appear to be dynamic over the planning horizon, which requires information-feedback loops or recursive equations. The model is short range in the sense that it simulates one year at a time. The effect of changes in environmental inputs could, however, be tested for any given future year which would provide long-range capabilities.

In summary, the Carrier Air Conditioning Company model includes elements of all of the components of the physical distribution system. The problem, however, does not consider the sequential decision problem, the unifying dimension is spatial rather than temporal, and the model is primarily oriented toward short-range planning. The model does present an illustration of the integration of a heuristic technique for general overall solution with analytical techniques incorporated for analysis of individual components. In this case, linear programming is used to solve the location problem within the constraints of the general solution provided by the simulation model.

Packer

The next two models reviewed in this section emphasize the inventory component. The first, by Packer, is primarily a single component model since it considers basically only the inventory component.[59] The problem, as Packer defines it, concerns a company that manufactures tow classes of inventory. One is subject to deterministic demand, and the second includes overhead inventories, such as components, which are probabilistic demands. The objectives are to determine the most effective parametric values for use in exponential smoothing formulas and to quantify the benefits resulting from the application of proposed inventory decision rules. The general program is outlined in figure 3-7.

The problem as defined is a multiitem, single echelon stochastic demand inventory problem. It is thus a single component problem. As implied by Packer, the planning horizon of the problem could be considered either long range or short range. The emphasis as written, however, is short range. The problem is sequential in that future decisions of when to order and the amount to order are a function of previous decisions.

The solution approach selected by Packer was that of adaptive forecasting and statistical determination of safety stock. This is a technique suggested by R. C. Brown.[60] These techniques consist of using the exponential smoothing method for estimating demand, and establishing the level of safety stock based on the past success in estimating demand. A heuristic-simulation solution technique is used to seek numerical solution to the two problems defined. Packer states that "considering the large number of items involved it appeared unrealistic

Figure 3–7
Simulation and Adapted Forecasting Applied to Inventory Control

The program generally functions as follows:

1. The values, switches, etc., are initialized.

2. The demand for the month is read.

3. A new forecast is made.

4. If any previous orders are due (lead time has expired since last order), incoming stock is added to the quantity on hand.

5. Any back orders unfilled from last month are filled.

6. The stock available is compared with a newly calculated order point.

7. If the order point equals or exceeds the stock available, an order quantity is calculated and the order is placed.

8. Sufficient stock is "issued" to meet current demand; a back order is established if current demand exceeds the stock available.

9. Under one option, detail relative to each month's activity is written. Under the second option, only summary totals are produced. For either option, program returns, reads the next month's demand, and repeats the loop from Step 2.

10. When the end of the simulated period (2 years) is reached, summary totals are written listing: (*a*) the average inventory in units and dollars; (*b*) the number of stockouts, demands, and orders; (*c*) the service percentage (in terms of both demands made/demands filled and quantity demanded/quantity filled); (*d*) safety and alpha factors; and (*e*) the average forecast error.

11. When all the items in the sample have gone through the above program, a summary report is run listing the following for each inventory class for the simulated period: (*a*) average inventory investment, (*b*) total and average orders placed per item, (*c*) total and average stockouts per item, (*d*) the number of sample items in the group.

12. If any more "knob" cards are present, the parameters are changed according to those cards and the entire process begins again.

SOURCE: A. H. Packer, "Simulation and Adaptive Forecasting as Applied to Inventory Control," *Operations Research* 15 (August 1967): 670.

to attempt to achieve an optimal policy for any of the individual items."[61] His decision to some extent was based on a statement by F. Hanssmann: "From the operations research viewpoint, the theory has been carried to a degree of mathematical sophistication in some areas which is not fruitful in light of the fact that the inventory problem is only one aspect of a complex system."[62]

In essence there is no unifying dimension in this model in terms of time or space. It is a single echelon, single location model, and order-cycle effects or delays are not considered. Stockouts are considered, but in terms of cost, not order-cycle considerations. Packer states that his is a static model. It has dynamic aspects, according to the definition presented in chapter 2. The current deficiency (surpluses) of the inventory affects future decisions via information feedback-control loops. The environmental inputs are established to implement the model for short-range planning by assuming that cost parameters are constant. For longer range Packer develops a set of curves relating cost parameters between items and over time. The model can therefore be classified as both short range and long range.

Packer's model includes only the inventory component, thus it cannot be considered as the basis for the general solution approach to the LREPS mathematical model. However, it provided the basis for development of the inventory component, which is treated in the Operations System of LREPS.

Ballou

A second model, developed by Ballou, is multicomponent with primary emphasis on the inventory component.[63] He describes the problem as one of a multiecheloned inventory situation involving three firms. The objective stated by Ballou is to test the effect of various inventory policies through a simulation period on cost and profit levels. Transportation costs are also altered to achieve sensitivity analysis. Decision rules are selected which yield the lowest total system cost under varying conditions.

The problem as stated includes elements of the inventory, transportation, and communications components. It is a multiecheloned inventory problem for a single, finished-goods inventory of several firms. The problem does not consider the location problem or distribution center operation. The planning horizon is primarily short term and the assumption is that the facility network does not change. The problem is sequential in that current decisions in the model influence future decisions. For example, when demand is in excess of inventory level, backorders are incurred. These backorders are eventually filled with reorders after a generated lead time.

The general solution approach is simulated with analytical subroutines such as computation of the EOQ incorporated as appropriate. The unifying dimension is time with a measure of service, backorder level, being partially dependent on the expected lead time, which is an element of the total order cycle. The system behavior is dynamic in the sense previously defined. Information feedback-control loops are developed for variables such as inventory level. Finally, the environmental inputs such as cost, lead times, product price, and so forth are modified via exogenous input to the model.

In summary, Ballou's inventory model does not consider all of the physical distribution components and thus cannot be used as a basis for the LREPS general solution approach. The model does provide important insight relative to the selection of the "best" inventory policy for stated assumptions and decision rules for managerial action.

The above literature review indicates that a long-range planning model for total physical distribution operations should consist of the following: a heuristic solution technique, dynamic time-varying interactions, time as the unifying dimension, and a procedure for changing environmental input factors.

The review also indicates that such a model has not been developed or at least has not been reported in the literature. The models surveyed did consider various combinations of the above attributes, but none of the models combined the two essential components: the location problem, and the evaluation of inventory policy into a dynamic long-range planning model that uses total order cycle as the key measure of service. These models, however, did provide the basis for formulating the transformations for the activities of the LREPS mathematical model.

SOLUTION APPROACH SPECIFICATIONS

The purpose of this section is to review the LREPS design criteria and to define the specifications of the simulation model required to achieve these criteria. The general nature of LREPS was previously defined in terms of independent variables. The design criteria for formulating the mathematical model were defined in terms of four general categories that would—

1. solve the specific physical distribution problem statement,
2. meet the general research requirements,
3. remain within the established model operating limits, and
4. achieve the desired model capabilities.

Each of the above categories is discussed in this section.

Physical Distribution Problem Statement

The problem statement required that the general solution approach be heuristic. Simulation, the heuristic technique selected, according to the literature, is essentially the only modeling technique practical for analysis and design of a problem as complex as a total physical distribution system. Since the problem considered the total physical distribution system, it was also essentially required that the unifying dimension be temporal rather than spatial. The fact that the problem included sequential or staged decisions suggested that the model be dynamic, incorporating feedback control loops and recursive relationships. The requirement that the problem consider a long-range planning period made it important that a second element of dynamics, the ability to modify over time the environmental factor inputs to the model over the planning horizon, be incorporated in the LREPS operating model.

Given the above problem statement design criterion, it was important to establish specifications for the LREPS simulation model. There are a number of classification schemes that could have been used to develop the specifications for the LREPS model. One such system classifies simulation models as: deterministic, stochastic, static, and dynamic.[64] The distinction of static and dynamic models was discussed previously in chapters 2 and 3. In summary, static models are those which do not explicitly take the variable time into account, whereas dynamic models deal with time-varying interactions. In deterministic models neither the exogenous or endogenous variables are allowed to be random variables, and exact mathematical relationships rather than probability density functions are used to define the operating characteristics. A model is usually considered to be stochastic if at least one of the operating characteristics is given by a probability function.

In terms of the above classification scheme, the LREPS model would be defined as being dynamic and stochastic. LREPS is dynamic in the sense that the model simulates the occurrence and action taken as the result of time-varying events (daily, weekly, monthly, and so forth) over a long-range planning horizon. In addition, first-order information feedback control loops are incorporated in the model for the inventory management, distribution center location, distribution center expansion, and sales modification subroutines. The LREPS model can be classified as stochastic because some of the units are subject to random variables. For example, order selection, customer selection, sales quota per customer, and the order-cycle time components are each random variables.

Simulation models can also be classified as continuous or discrete.[65, 66] A digital computer continuous-time simulator mimics the operations of an analog computer. Rather than acting according to a physical process, it acts according to mathematical equations that represent the physical processes. Time is advanced in small increments to approximate the continuous flow of time. Continuous time flow refers to the attempt to replicate time flow by a series of small, discrete, equally spaced steps. The measurements of time are taken at the discrete intervals to serve as approximation of the continuous function. A digital computer discrete-time simulator works differently. Time is divided into discrete intervals that represent the time between interactions among different elements of a system. Logical rather than mathematical equations move the replicated system from one interaction point to another in subprograms called events. Measures of system performance, taken at event times, are discrete and do not represent approximation of continuous flow.

Serious consideration was given to the question of whether LREPS should be developed as a continuous or discrete model. The decision was then made to develop LREPS as a discrete-simulation model. The primary reasons were: the physical distribution process for manufacturing firms is more realistically described as a discrete-event system; discrete-event simulation of manufacturing would be more readily understood by management of user companies; and because, at the time, the LREPS project research team was more experienced with discrete programming languages and model development.

Simulation models are also classified as being of fixed or variable time relative to the time-flow mechanism. Naylor states that "one of the most important considerations in formulating a computer model of an industrial system is the method used to move the system being simulated through time."[67] A fixed-time model increments the time indicated by a simulated clock in discrete intervals of time. For example, in LREPS the time unit is one day. The system thus is examined to determine if any events are due to occur that day. With a variable-time increment model, the clock time is advanced by the amount necessary to cause the next most imminent event to take place. The time between events is skipped. As pointed out by T. H. Naylor, "The final decision concerning whether to use fixed time increment methods or variable time increment methods on a particular system depends on the nature of the system."[68]

The computer language used to program LREPS, as discussed in more detail in chapter 5, is a variable-time increment method. However, as programmed, the LREPS model can be operated as either a fixed-time, or variable-time increment method. Currently, the model is operated as a hybrid incorporating aspects of both the fixed- and variable-time increment methods.

The final classification scheme to be considered is an open versus closed system. A system which does not allow for exogenous activity is referred to as a closed system, whereas an open system does have exogenous activities. In terms of this classification the LREPS model would be classified as an open system, which allows environmental inputs to change over time.

General Research Requirements

The second criterion is the general research goal or requirement that the model be modular and universal.

Modular Construction

Using a modular or "building block" approach means that formulation begins with a single module of the system of interest, and by adding modules the total system can be developed in terms of its separate components or as a total integrated system.[69] There are many benefits offered by the modular approach. It is appealing from a pedagogical point of view. Designing a model upward from identifiable and observable processes or from analogies is also a logical procedure with examples of success documented in the literature. Finally, the modular approach provides the model designer with the possibility of considerable flexibility. Additional benefits of modular construction are also discussed in the literature.[70]

An example of the modular construction in the LREPS model was the development of the inventory management module to operate with a heuristic inventory module with reorder quantity, reorder point, and safety stock set by management, or with a theoretical inventory module incorporating the standard reorder point policy, the optional replenishment policy, and/or a hybrid combination of both the reorder point and optional replenishment policies. These two modules were interchanged in the LREPS model without reprogramming.

Concept of Universality

A general criterion, which is not independent of modular construction, is the concept of universality. The concept of universality in the context of this monograph means that the model must be applicable, with little redesign, to a broad spectrum of industrial firms. This criterion requires that variables, components, parameters, and transformations (algorithms) be defined in general terms. For example, the variable defined as the demand unit must be flexible enough to refer to a county, an SMSA, an individual customer, a Zip sectional center, an individual household, and the like depending on which is selected in the supporting analysis for the particular application. A second example is the procedure for identifying the characteristics or attributes of the tracked products. The tracked products are identified by general characteristics that are common to all products, such as the density, cube, weight, case, individual unit, and freight class.

Model Operating Limits

The operating requirements, such as the design constraints for the formulation of the mathematical model and the computer model, are related to the elapsed computer time requirement for each full run of the model, the cost of running the model, and the computer core requirements. This aspect of the design criteria is discussed in chapter 5, "LREPS Computer Model."

Model Capabilities

The final category of design criteria is the requirement that the LREPS model have the capabilities to test the effect on, and/or the effect by, changes in the target variables, controllable variables, and environmental variables previously presented in figure 2-3.

In summary, the LREPS specifications are that the model be: (1) dynamic, (2) stochastic, (3) discrete-event, (4) a hybrid combination of fixed- and variable-time methods, (5) an open system, (6) modular, (7) universal, (8) operable within established hardware and software limits, and most important, (9) able to meet the desired model capabilities.

SUMMARY

This chapter, in its first section, presented a problem and model classification scheme that indicates the type of solution approach given the problem definition in terms of a set of independent variables. The second major section presented a review of selected physical distribution models which provided a basis for formulating the mathematical transformations for the LREPS model.

In the third section the LREPS model specifications were defined in terms of several classification schemes. Given the solution approach, the next task was to develop the LREPS model. The development of the mathematical model is presented in chapter 4.

4

LREPS MATHEMATICAL MODEL

The previous chapters presented the conceptual LREPS model and established the requirements for a general solution approach. This chapter first presents the design methodology for development of the mathematical model followed by an abbreviated description of the overall mathematical model.

DESIGN METHODOLOGY

The general solution approach adopted was dynamic simulation. In the development of a design methodology it was necessary to define a modeling philosophy; general and special design considerations were then developed.

Mathematical Model: Philosophy

The first step in developing the design methodology was to develop a modeling approach or philosophy. The next areas of discussion present this philosophy in terms of mathematical modeling terminology and process.

Mathematical Modeling Terminology

A mathematical model consists of four well-defined elements: components, variables, parameters, and functional relationships.[1] The primary components in the LREPS model are related to the entities or objects of the three primary systems. A mathematical model can also be defined as a set of equations whose solution explains or predicts changes in the state of the system.[2] The variables are used to relate one component or entity to another and may be conveniently classified as exogenous, status, and endogenous variables.

Exogenous variables are the independent or input variables of the model and are assumed to have been predetermined and given independently of the system being modeled. These variables may be regarded as acting upon the system but not being acted upon by the system. Exogenous variables can be classified as either controllable or noncontrollable. Controllable (or instrumental) variables are those variables or parameters that can be manipulated or controlled by the decision makers or policy makers of the system. Noncontrollable variables are generated by the environment of the system modeled and not by the system itself or its decision makers.

Status variables or entities describe the state of the system or one of its components at any point in time. The attributes, or characteristics of the entity, may change in value over time. The set of attribute values at any point in time defines the "state of the system." Thus the status variables are also referred to as state variables. Attributes are properties of entities and an entity is described by listing its attributes.[3]

Endogenous variables are the dependent or output variables of the system and are generated from the interaction of the system's exogenous and status variables according to the system's operating characteristics. The system state, status, and endogenous variables can be used interchangeably to define variables whose value is generated within the model.

The exogenous variables or parameters are classified as "factors." A simulation experiment consists of a series of computer runs in which tests are empirically made of the effects of alternative factor levels on the values of the endogenous levels. Parameters are considered to be those attribute values that do not change during simulation experiment(s).

Functional relationships or transformations describe the interaction of the variables and components. The terms *functional relationships, transformations,* and *algorithm* are used interchangeably. Each refers to the mathematical function, logical operation, or process operation that relates predictively an activity's output to its input.

An activity is a quantitative or logical relation of an input set of variables (or attributes) to an output set of variables (or attributes) by a mathematical function. Accomplishment of an activity usually results in a change of the system state. A general method of developing transformations is presented by Van Court Hare.[4]

Mathematical Modeling Process

W. T. Morris, in discussing the "art of modeling," states that the process of development of a model by a management scientist can best be described as intuitive.[5] The term *intuitive* as used by Morris refers to "thinking which the subject is unable or unwilling to verbalize."

According to Morris, three basic hypotheses exist relative to model building. First, the process of model building can be viewed as a process of "enrichment" or "elaboration." The model designer begins with a simple model and after obtaining a "tractable" model attempts to move in an evolutionary manner toward a more sophisticated one that more nearly reflects the complex management situation.

"Analogy," or association with previously well-developed logical structure, is the second major requirement for development of a successful model.

Third, and finally, the process of elaboration and enrichment involves several types of "looping" or "alteration" procedures. For example, as each version of the model is tested, a new version is developed, which leads in turn to subsequent tests. A second type of alteration is determining if a model version permits achievement of the designer's objectives. If it does, the designer may seek further enrichment or complication of assumptions. If, however, the model is not tractable (well behaved) or cannot be solved, the designer has to modify and/or simplify the assumptions.

Before a simulation model is designed, two important questions must be asked and answered: what use will be made of the model (what questions will be asked)? and what are the requirements of accuracy and precision? Answers to these questions determine the structure of a model.

The model's structure, as stated by P. J. Kiviat is affected by such factors as:

1. the purpose of the model;
2. the accuracy and precision required of the output;
3. the detail required in the model to achieve the required precision;

4. the assumptions required at the system boundaries;
5. the assumptions required within the system boundaries for
    status representation,
    decision parameters,
    decision rules; and
6. the availability of necessary data.[6]

The model design is thus complicated by a combination of theoretical and practical factors. The theoretical factors determine such things as the system boundary interactions and decision rules, whereas the practical factors modify the theoretical decision, such as the level of detail incorporated within the model. Kiviat states this as the reason for feedback loops in the modeling process itself.

The process is thus an iterative one which must take into consideration the criteria of the model designer and the constraints of the environment. The final model reflects in both structure and implementation the influences of the real-world system being studied, the questions that are of interest to the decision maker about the system, and the environment in which the model is to perform.

Modeling is therefore a continuous balancing of the costs of data collection and analysis against the costs (benefits) of precision, and program execution costs against the costs of model reprogramming. A five-stage iterative sequence describing the modeling process is presented in figure 4-1.[7]

Naylor states that "the formulation of mathematical models consists of three steps: (1) specification of components, (2) specification of variables and parameters, and (3) specification of functional relationships."[8] He states further that although a complete knowledge of the system being modeled as well as proficiency in mathematics are necessary prerequisites for the formulation of a valid model, they are in no sense sufficient conditions. A successful mathematical model depends also on: the experience of the model designer or analyst, trial-and-error procedures, and a considerable amount of luck.

Naylor discusses a number of suggestions relative to the development of mathematical models, which can be summarized below.

First, the question of how many variables to include in the model must be answered. Naylor indicates that the selection of endogenous or output variables is usually determined at the beginning of the study and thus does not cause much difficulty. The choice of exogenous variables is more difficult, since too few exogenous variables may lead

Figure 4–1
A Five-Stage Iterative Modeling Process

Iterative Modeling Process

Stage 1: Statement of a problem in general system terms.
Definition of gross system boundaries.
Statement of output(s) needed to solve the problem.

Stage 2: Statement of (initial) assumptions.
Definition of static and dynamic system structure.
Construction of minimal system model.
Assessment of assumptions in light of Stage 1 goals.

Stage 3: Determination of input data requirements and availability. If input data required are not available, modify assumptions and model structure by returning to Stage 2.

Stage 4: Determination of output possibilities. If output is insufficient, modify assumptions and model structure by returning to Stage 2.

Stage 5: Prepare precise specifications for final model. Select a modeling and programming language. Reassess the implications of all assumptions for the future. Prepare a detailed plan for use of the model.

SOURCE: P. J. Kiviat, *Digital Computer Simulation Modeling Concepts* (Santa Monica, California: The Rand Corporation, 1967).

to invalid models, whereas too many may render computer simulation impractical due to the computer and programming requirements.

The second major consideration is the complexity of the model. The number of variables in a model and its complexity are directly related to the programming time, computation time, and validity. A change in any one of these characteristics results in changes in all of the other characteristics.

A third area of consideration is the computational efficiency of the model. In this model, for example, the objective is to keep the total computer model processing time for a simulation run below a predetermined elapsed time. This objective has a direct influence on the development of the algorithms of the model.

Computer programming time represents a fourth area of consideration. Thus the amount of sophistication in the algorithms must be balanced against the increased programming efforts. The development of requirements such that one of the existing simulation languages can be used must also be evaluated.

The fifth area of interest is the validity of the model or the amount of realism incorporated in it. The model must adequately describe the real-world system and use of the model should give reasonably good predictions of the behavior of the system for future time periods.

The final consideration that Naylor presents is the compatibility of the model with the type of experiments that are going to be conducted with the model. Thus the basic experimental design must be formalized prior to development of the mathematical model.

At each level of model formulation, M. Asimow recommends the use of an activity analysis approach similar to that illustrated in figure 4-2 to specify the design problem. For each level, the procedure suggested by Asimow would be to—

1. derive the desired outputs of the system;
2. determine the undesired outputs of the system;
3. determine the inputs, which the system will transform into outputs;
4. determine the constraints for input and output variables;

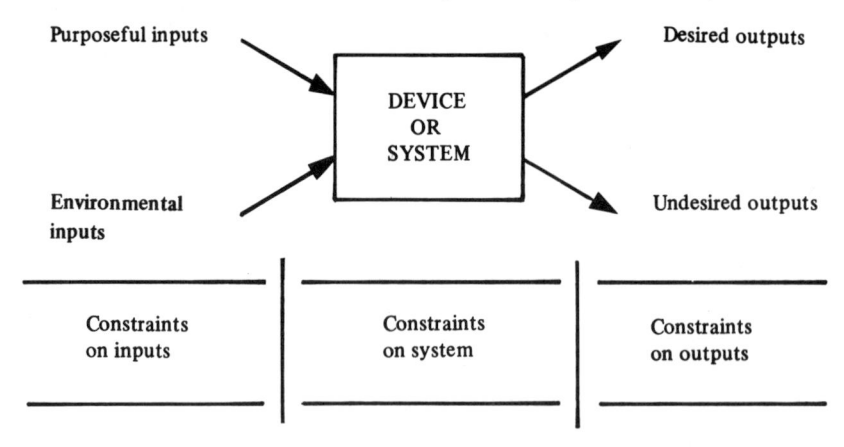

Units of measure of inputs, outputs, and constraints (independent and dependent variables) and associated measures of value where needed

Define overall objectives and the design criterion

SOURCE: M. Asimow, *Introduction to Design* (Englewood Cliffs, New Jersey: Prentice-Hall, Inc., 1962), p. 54.

Figure 4–2
Format for Activity Analysis—General Plan

5. consider the system constraints along with the design parameters;
6. establish the appropriate measures of value for the output and input variables and design parameters;
7. use the appropriate relationships among the variables to develop the criteria for measuring the goodness of the proposed systems.[9]

A few of the potential difficulties encountered in mathematical model building are also presented in the literature.[10, 11] These can be summarized as follows:

1. Variables may be present which affect the behavior of the system but are in a practical sense impossible to quantify or measure.
2. The number of required variables may exceed the capacity of the computer capabilities available.
3. All of the exogenous variables that affect the output variables may not be known.
4. Not all of the functional relationships between exogenous and endogenous variables may be known or possible to develop.
5. In many cases the relationships between variables may be too complex to express in a set of mathematical equations.

General Design Considerations

The definitions, description, and steps used in formulating the LREPS mathematical model are similar to those reported above. In this section the primary emphasis is placed on the procedure for developing the transformations for the lowest system level in the model, the activity. Activities are combined to form a component, such as the transportation component, inventory component, and demand component. Combinations of activities and components are formed and linked to develop the subsystems, which in turn make up the total LREPS model.

The initial design effort consisted of developing a comprehensive list of the activities required for each level of the model. The design approach at the activity level then consisted of the following procedures:

1. stating the objective of the activity,
2. developing a conceptual approach to a set of alternatives for the activity,

3. evaluating each of the alternatives,
4. selecting the alternative(s) for each activity,
5. developing the specifications for the selected alternative,
6. collecting, analyzing, and preparing data for selected alternative(s), and
7. programming the selected alternatives(s).

Multiple alternatives for each activity were developed to ensure that the full range of conceivable simplification to sophistication (or enrichment) of transformations would be covered. This approach also helped to ensure that the mathematical model would be modular and universal.

The decision was made to conceptualize four alternatives based on the fact that for many activities there appeared to be up to four methods, of varying levels of sophistication, that could be defined and that were both valid and practical. Each of the four alternatives was developed to the point that the outputs, inputs, and general nature of the transformation requirements were documented.

Evaluation of the alternatives for each activity was performed not only in regard to the requirements of the activity itself relative to availability of input data, validity, modularity, and universality, but also relative to the effect on the total model in terms of computer processing time and computer core requirements. In each case one alternative, referred to as Option 1, was selected as the primary alternative to be implemented in the initial version of the model. For a number of activities a second alternative, Option 2, was also selected either because the additional sophistication for Option 2 required very little marginal effort or both alternatives appeared to be equally desirable.

The next step required the development of detailed specifications for the outputs, inputs, and mathematical transformations for Option 1 and, if chosen, Option 2. Figure 4-3 illustrates the format used in recording the activity analysis. Flowcharts were also developed as needed to indicate the procedures for individual activities and the connecting links for combinations of activities which form the system's hierarchy.

Special Design Considerations

In formulating the mathematical model several additional concepts not previously reviewed were given consideration as they related to

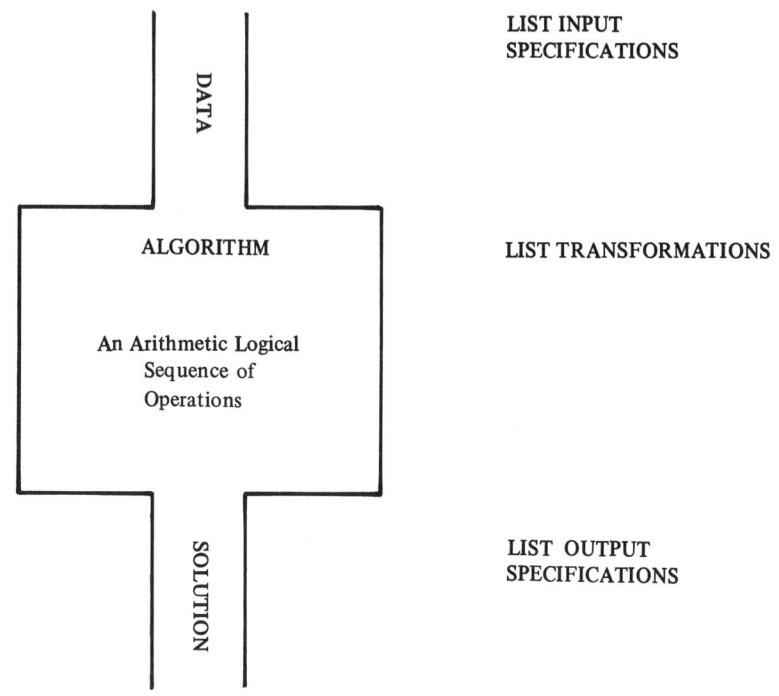

```
         |    |              LIST INPUT
         |    |              SPECIFICATIONS
       D |    |
       A |    |
       T |    |
       A |    |
         |    |
    _____|    |_____
   |                |
   |   ALGORITHM    |         LIST TRANSFORMATIONS
   |                |
   | An Arithmetic Logical |
   |   Sequence of  |
   |   Operations   |
   |                |
   |_____      _____|
         |    |
       S |    |              LIST OUTPUT
       O |    |              SPECIFICATIONS
       L |    |
       U |    |
       T |    |
       I |    |
       O |    |
       N |    |
```

Figure 4–3
Format for Activity Analysis in LREPS

the objectives of the LREPS model. These three concepts were: work flow structure, model simplification methods, and robustness or flexibility.

Work Flow Structure

Work flow structure is the first important special design consideration. W. K. Holstein and W. L. Berry define work flow structure as "the pattern of aggregate work flow through the production system . . . and . . . the relationship or pattern of functional processing sequences in the shop."[12] The work presented by these authors is specifically related to job-shop and manufacturing systems, but the general concept, nonetheless, appears to be applicable to the problem of formulating the system structure presented in chapter 2. Essentially, the authors develop a method for identifying the relative activity levels or importance of the links between individual work centers or nodes of the network.

The activity levels or work flow structure in a physical distribution network, for example, are partially dependent on the source of manufacture for each product, product demand, inventory stocking policy, and so on.

Holstein and Berry suggest the use of the important or strong links in job-shop simulations rather than assuming that all links are possible. The neglect of the "weak" links, in terms of frequency and amount of work flow, did not have a major effect on the results of simulations relative to the results achieved by previous authors who had considered all possible links of the job shops.

The above concept, which might be stated in terms similar to the ABC rule frequently used in inventory control—that 20 percent of the links account for over 80 percent of the activity—was used in the development of the LREPS model. For example, in the problem defined in this monograph, the assumption was made that the closest manufacturing center, the MCC, always supplies the product to a particular distribution center when more than one MCC manufactures the product. Thus the assumption was that the "weak" link, the small amount of volume or activity from the remaining MCCs for the product, would not have significant effect on the design alternatives. A second example where the above concept was incorporated was the situation in which a remote distribution center has a "stockout" for a particular product. Using the above "strong link" concept, the assumption was made that even though shipments of the product from a "second" best distribution center would actually be made occasionally, these shipments would not have a significant effect on the design alternatives.

Model Simplification

The second special design consideration is "model simplification" methods. Simplification methods can be divided into two main categories: first-order methods, which directly reduce complexity of the model; and higher-order methods, which simplify a system indirectly through a series of steps.

Direct attempts at system simplification usually involve the actions of "elimination" and "grouping." Either of these actions decreases the distinctions that need to be made in a system definition. Van Court Hare states that we simplify by elimination when the system objective requires optimization, isolation, and search of detailed action. We simplify by grouping, classification, and consolidation of detail when the system objective requires estimation, comparison, and test between blocks of detail.[13]

The approaches to elimination that were considered in this project were similar to the following three general methods: "(1) restricted ranges of measure, or interest; (2) logically or statistically restricted combinations, or patterns of acceptance; and (3) threshold and discrimination methods."[14]

Higher-order simplification is accomplished by working with the system's control structure hierarchy—the system goals, objectives, values, and measures of effectiveness.[15] The higher-order approach is concerned with the system's potential for improvement, growth, change, and optimization. It is a strategic approach. The higher-order approach stresses relevance rather than the completeness or precision as stressed in the direct simplification methods.

In this model design the hierarchy was LREPS model, system, subsystems, components, and activities. A primary design problem related to higher-order simplification was thus to coordinate the subsystems into a model that would enhance the overall purpose(s) of the total system. Van Court Hare states that

> the most likely trouble-spot in the design of a complex system, or the operation of an existing complex system, is not that the individual blocks do not operate "efficiently" or even effectively regarding their own stated goals, but that the goals guiding these operations do not, when combined, result in either efficient or effective operation of the entire system.[16]

Just as conflicting subsystem goals may restrict the achievement of the full overall system objective, it is possible that there are conflicting multiple goals at the total system level. Consideration of constraints, risks, and commitments are also important in the higher-level definition. Modification of these makes possible higher-order simplification.

Morris also discusses simplification of models.[17] He states that if a model in its current version is "tractable" (well behaved) it can be enriched or sophisticated, otherwise it may have to be simplified by making variables into constants, eliminating variables, using linear relations, adding stronger assumptions and restrictions, and/or suppressing randomness. Enrichment involves just the opposite type of modification.

Robustness or Flexibility

The third area of special consideration not previously discussed is "robustness." This term is defined by Morris to mean: "How sensitive is the model to changes in the assumptions which characterize it?"[18] Robustness also is defined by S. K. Gupta and J. Rosenhead as the measure of flexibility in a planned sequence of investment decisions.[19] The measure of robustness of a decision in the investment case is stated in terms of the numbers of "good" end-states for expected external conditions which remain as open options. An example of robustness reported by Gupta and Rosenhead is given for facility location in which the robustness score is the ratio of the number of occurrences of a given potential location, among the set of good systems, to the number of good systems.

This was a useful concept for the LREPS model. One problem in selecting the "best" set of staged decisions from among many good sets was the uncertainty of the environmental assumptions or inputs over time. An approach such as robustness aids in reducing the risk associated with decisions under uncertainty. For example, the location that appears most frequently in the final set of good systems facility network alternatives for various environmental and management inputs should be a lower risk (more flexible) decision than selecting a location that appears only in a few cases.

MATHEMATICAL MODEL

The purpose of this section is to describe the LREPS mathematical model.[20] The attempt is to present examples of the mathematical transformations developed for the LREPS model, since it is impractical and unnecessary to list all the equations to capture the essence of the model.

The transformations for a selected set of activities are presented for each of the three systems—Supporting Data System, Operating System, and Report Generator System. Primary emphasis, however, is placed on describing the mathematical model of the Operating System since it is the vehicle for testing alternative distribution plans. The activities and transformations of the three basic systems are discussed in this section.

Supporting Data System Activities

The Supporting Data System is the first of the three stages of the LREPS model, as previously depicted in figure 2-5. As the initial stage, the Supporting Data System serves three basic purposes. The first purpose is the analysis of basic data to determine their degree of completeness, reliability, and accuracy. Data can be gathered and grouped into various levels of detail with respect to many bases of dimensions. The first task therefore is to examine and test data to detect possible deficiencies or inconsistencies in the raw information. This off-line analysis simplifies and speeds up processing during later phases of model operation.

The second purpose of the Supporting Data System is to take the now complete set of data and prepare it to be inputted to the model's Operating System. Preparation includes checking to see that all data unique to the experiment have been specified, verifying that all data fields have been properly formatted, and identifying the exogenous data file with a specific and unique name. The final purpose of the Supporting Data System is to act as a filter through which all data that might be included in the data base must pass. The reason for this filtering process is obvious. A complex model such as LREPS should be as efficient as possible in order to minimize running time and expense. Inclusion of all data that could be collected would result in excess data reading time by the computer, not to mention wasted time in preparing and analyzing the data.

The analysis, preparation, and filtering processes are iterative in nature for a given set of data. In addition, for preparation of a particular exogenous data file, all three processes could be executed simultaneously for different data groupings.

As noted earlier, the Supporting Data System acts as a link between the firm's information system and the model Operating System's information base. Because of this relationship, the Supporting Data System can be described in terms of the four subsystems of the Operating System: (1) Demand and Environment, (2) Operations, (3) Measurement, and (4) Monitor and Control.

Demand and Environment

This subset of the Supporting Data System provides two basic types of data, an order file generator, which simulates demand, and the input data for the Demand and Environment Subsystem. The following activities were used to create these desired outputs:

1. invoice analysis
2. customer type analysis
3. product item analysis
4. regional analysis
5. customer demand generation analysis
6. basis for demand generation and processing analysis
7. demand unit analysis
8. order file generation analysis
9. demand allocation to customers analysis
10. customer sales quota analysis

The invoice analysis was performed to build a statistical profile, based on a sample of invoices, of the total invoice file. Customer analysis defined the type of customers to include in the model. The product item analysis was for the purpose of determining which products to incorporate into the simulation. Regional analysis was done to allow selection of the most appropriate of several possible regional breakdowns of the continental United States.

The remaining six activities all relate to the development of the demand function. The basis selected for demand generation and processing was a group of order blocks, as opposed to individual orders, in order to limit computer memory requirements and reduce input/output time. The demand unit selected for the initial version was based on ZIP codes. Other forms of customer groupings were also considered because it became evident that using individual customers as demand units would be just as prohibitive as processing individual invoices for many of the large U.S. corporations. The list of demand units that was evaluated includes individual customers, county, Standard Metropolitan Statistical Area (SMSA), groups of counties referred to as economic trading areas (ETA), ZIP codes, and REA modified grid. These alternatives are representative of the possible demand unit structures that various firms might wish to consider. The

LREPS model design has the flexibility to use any of these structures without major modification.

The demand unit attributes that were considered included size of unit, homogeneity, stability, flexibility, geographic continuity, and availability of periodically updated demographic data. The specific project considerations included:

1. availability of relevant data at the demand unit stage such as population and income,
2. appropriateness of demand unit for the markets served by the firm,
3. ability to determine distances from distribution center to demand unit, and
4. compatibility of demand structure with management information system.

Each of the alternative demand unit structures was evaluated in terms of the advantages and disadvantages for its universal application in general and the existing application in particular.

The order file generator creates the stream of daily orders that simulate the demand, which is allocated to the demand units and to the distribution centers. Allocation of demand to customers and distribution centers was based on a weighted relative index of independent variables, such as retail sales, population, personal income, and effective buying power. The general form of the transformation to calculate the weighted index for each demand unit is as follows:

$$\text{WTDINDX}(Y, DU) = \sum_{I}^{n} \left(\left(\frac{r^2(I)}{\sum_{J}^{n} r^2(J)} \right) * \left(\frac{x(I, DU, Y)}{\sum_{du} x(I, du, Y)} \right) \right) * 100,$$

where:

WTDINDX (Y, DU) = the weighted index, which is the percent sales for the period Y allocated to the demand unit DU;

r^2 (I)   = correlation analysis coefficient of the independent variable I against sales;

X (I, DU, Y)   = value of the independent variable I for demand unit DU for time period Y;

n   = number of independent variables.

The demand allocated to a demand unit is thus a function of the level of each of the Ith independent variables within the demand unit and the correlation coefficient of each of the Ith independent variables. The relative demand to a DC is determined by summing the weighted indices for all the DUs assigned to an in-solution DC. The number of independent variables that can be used to develop the weighted index can be set at any reasonable number. The limit with the current version is set at three.

Compound growth rates were applied to these independent variables to reflect their changing over time. Thus, the relative index for each demand unit is dynamic, dependent upon the relative weighting of the changing independent variables. Similarly, the demand handled by each distribution center changes as the sum of the weighted indexes of all demand units assigned to the distribution center changes. Finally, the customer sales quota for each distribution center was generated from a national sales forecast. Forecasted sales can be built into the simulation model via techniques such as exponential smoothing. Or sales forecasts of existing models can be used to generate the data outside the simulator. Also, sales can be forecast assuming no variation within days, weeks, or months. Thus, only yearly changes would be generated. Conversely, an activity to generate daily, weekly, and monthly variation can be handled with ease.

Operations

The Operations segment of the Supporting Data System provides the data for the basic physical distribution system components of transportation, materials handling, communications, inventory, and facility. Additional supporting analyses were performed to link manufacturing sites with distribution centers.

The inbound (to the distribution center from the manufacturing center) and outbound (from the distribution center to demand units) transportation components necessitated the development of transit times, shipping policies and statistics, and weight breaks. Included in the transit time analysis were consistency and availability of the various transport modes for all of the possible manufacturer-distributor and distributor-demand unit combinations. The shipping statistics relate to such data as average size of shipment in weight, cases, dollars, and orders. These data were needed to specify "typical" movements for each weight break interval. Several outbound shipping policies were examined, such as scheduled or pooled orders. The model was kept flexible so that the effect of alternate shipping policies could be examined. Reorders from the manufacturing site to the distribution centers were allowed on a combination: both or either of fixed shipment intervals or fixed shipment quantities.

The special analyses required to link distribution centers with manufacturing locations dealt with assignment priorities in the event that a product was manufactured in several locations. Also, the priorities among manufacturing sites for supplying the accumulated replenishment shipments to a particular distribution center had to be established. And the weight of the sample products had to be extrapolated to simulate shipping of the entire product line.

The materials handling component required, first, the establishment of the distribution center attributes of location, ownership, type, size, and level of automation. Then the partial-line distribution centers were distinguished from full-line centers by the number of inventory categories they handled. Next, the capacity limits, based on efficiency, were designed for the distribution centers. This limit was a function of both utilized and excess building space. The last materials handling component was the order processing and preparation time, a part of the total order cycle.

Development of the communications component centered on the specification of a communications network and the inherent time delays. The communications network consisted of three levels: (1) decentralized, from demand unit to remote distribution center with replenishment orders originating from the remote center; (2) regional, from demand unit to regional distribution centers with decision for replenishment of remote centers originating at the regional center; and (3) centralized, from demand unit to a central order processing facility which controls all replenishment orders. Time delays were simulated by analyzing the average delay and variability of transmission for alternative modes of communication, such as mail and telephone.

The inventory segment required an initial definition of the inventory nodes, which were described as remote, full-line, partial-line, and primary distribution centers and replenishment centers. The inventory control policy was essentially based on a sampling of the total product line, as developed in the product item analysis of the Demand and Environment Supporting Data System. Back orders were handled by allowing negative inventories until the next replenishment.

The last Operations component, facility, merely included the calculation of the initial sizes within one of five possible intervals and locations of existing and potential facilities.

Measurement

The Measurement Supporting Data System provides the analysis and preparation for the target variables of service and cost. Measures of service are related to both customers and distribution centers.

The first customer service criterion was the normal customer order cycle, comprised of customer order transmittal time, customer order processing and preparation time, and outbound transit time. An average was developed for each of the elements of normal order cycle, and a Monte Carlo function was utilized to develop a variance around the average. The total order-cycle time consisted of the normal order-cycle time plus a delay factor for possible stockouts. This element also was established with an average delay and a variance about this average.

The speed and consistency of customer service was measured by computing the percent of sales volume within various order-cycle times by distribution center. Distribution center service was measured in terms of the reorder-cycle time, stockout delay, and percentage of case units backordered. The elements of the total reorder-cycle time were the reorder-transmittal time, reorder-processing and preparation time, inbound transit time, and the shipment dispatch. These elements were computed in the same manner as were their corresponding elements in the total customer order-cycle time. Other measures of distribution center service were percentage of case units backordered, number of reorders, number of stockouts, and average inventory-on-hand.

Supporting analysis and preparation were needed to develop rates for the inbound and outbound transportation components discussed in the Operations Supporting Data System. Outbound transportation rates were computed using weighted average freight and weight classes. Because of the large number of linkages possible among over 400 demand units and more than 50 distribution centers, similar links were combined to develop regression equations with distance as the independent variable and the weighted average freight rates as the dependent variables. Point-to-point rates were computed for inbound transportation cost because of the relatively few distribution center-manufacturing center links. These rates were based on different weight breaks, assuming mixed goods shipments.

Throughput costs (cost of moving goods through the distribution centers) required evaluation of standard costs, selection of cost element of fixed and variable cost factors for each size and type of of fixed and variable cost for each size and type of distribution center.

The communications network in LREPS was developed to simulate either decentralized, regional, or central order processing. The cost structure therefore was developed to include the flexibility to change from one type of network to another. The supporting analyses required to develop the communications cost component included: evaluation of standard costs, definition of cost elements for the three networks, selection of possible cost modification factors, and establishment of fixed and variable cost factors for each size and type of communication network.

Inventory costs included the development of both carrying costs and reordering costs. An interest rate level and a measure of the value of inventory-on-hand had to be generated to compute the carrying cost. Reorder costs were based on the number of single and multiple product reorders placed by the distribution centers.

The investment of facilities was composed of several elements: land, facilities, and equipment for each size interval. This value was then converted to a per square foot basis. An investment value in terms of equivalent annual cost was derived using the straight-line depreciation computation.

Monitor and Control

The two primary functions of the Monitor and Control Subsystem are to supervise and control the activities of LREPS. Within the supervisory and control functions, supporting analyses and data preparation were required for the following subfunctions: executive, gateway, review, and update.

The executive subfunction required the selection of a time flow mechanism and the programming language. A combination of fixed time (compressed real time) and variable time (event oriented) was selected. The language chosen was GASP IIA, a FORTRAN compatible simulation language.

The gateway subfunction is related to the input/output activities. Analysis revealed that the exogenous variables should be capable of being varied each quarter of a simulated year.

System changes during the simulation cycle were the responsibility of the review subfunction. It was decided to implement changes in the physical distribution system components of location, materials handling, and inventory via information feedback control loops. Communications and transportation would be modified through exogenous input changes.

The three basic location algorithm approaches evaluated were: linear programming, a heuristic algorithm, and a dynamic programming algorithm.[21, 22, 23] These approaches were considered because they have been previously implemented for facility location problems. The heuristic algorithm approach was selected as Option 1, however, even though sufficient data appeared to be available within the model to use either of the other two alternatives. The dynamic programming approach was not selected because of the complexity of implementation. A linear programming algorithm was not selected for initial implementation but is currently available as an option for the LOCATE algorithm.

Analysis of the various relevant factors such as adequate transportation networks, carrier availability, labor availability, general acceptability to management, and so on, suggested that a fixed list of N potential sites or cities be used from which the location algorithm would select the new distribution centers.

The materials handling algorithm, which in the current version expands existing distribution centers, essentially is based on a comparison of existing capacity with current throughput. The most critical distribution centers are the ones which approach or exceed the throughput capacity by the greatest percentage.

Inventory analysis in the Monitor and Control Supporting Data System consisted of evaluating the alternatives of a reorder point system, a replenishment system, a heuristic policy, or hybrid combination of the reorder point and the replenishment systems.[24] All of these options were developed for the LREPS model.

The update subfunction was required to evaluate demand unit to distribution center assignments as distribution centers were added to or deleted from solution. Thus, a priority list was developed. The criteria used were a hybrid of minimum distance and minimum transportation cost between demand unit and distribution center.

The above discussion serves to describe the functions of the Supporting Data System. Next, the Operating System activities for each of the four basic subsystems are presented.

Operating System Activities

Earlier the four subsystems of the Operating System were enumerated and described. The overall purpose of the Operating System is to simulate the operation of the physical distribution system using input from the Supporting Data System and to produce output data for the Report Generator System. The activities of each of the four subsystems are discussed below under separate headings.

Demand and Environment Subsystem

The primary function of the Demand and Environment Subsystem (D&E) is to generate information for the Operations Subsystem related to forecasting of sales, customer order generation, and the assignment of these orders to demand units.

The daily domestic sales quota is derived from the annual domestic sales forecast. The number of simulated workdays in a year and a modifier function which adjusts for any assumed variability by day, week, or month are utilized in the transformation.

The second major event of the D&E processes the daily sales of the demand units assigned to a distribution center, the DC-DU link. In this activity, the simulated daily sales for each in-solution distribution center is determined. This is based on the percent of the sum of the weighted indices of the demand units assigned to the distribution center for the current operating period.

The demand units consists of the 560 ZIP sectional centers in the United States, although as noted earlier, other demand units such as counties, SMSAs, or individual customers can be used. These demand units are assigned to a distribution center based on a criterion such as minimum distance, minimum transit time, minimum transportation cost, or a heuristic combination of these criteria.

The sum of weighted indices for the assigned demand units, the daily domestic sales quota, and the exponentially smoothed value of the ratio of the actual to desired service are used to generate the daily sales quota for a distribution center.

The transformation for each customer type is of the form:

$$\text{DCSALS (ID, IDC)} = \text{DSQ (ID)} * \Sigma\text{WI (IQ)} * \text{NWSMF (IQ)} * \text{CSPLTP (ICT)},$$

where:

DCSALS (ID, IDC) = the simulated actual daily sales dollars for the DC for the day ID;

DSQ (ID) = the daily sales quota (forecast) for the day ID;

ΣWI (IQ) = the sum of the weighted indices for all DUs assigned to the DC for the quarter IQ;

NWSMF (IQ) = the current exponentially smoothed value of the ratio of actual to desired service;

CSPLTP (ICT) = the customer type ICT dollar split percentage.

Sufficient order blocks are generated, "pulled," from the order matrix to meet the daily sales forecast for each demand unit for each customer type. At this point it is possible to introduce pseudo orders with different order characteristics from the order matrix to test the effect of changes such as variations among existing customer buying patterns, introduction of new customer type, new product introduction, and so on.

The output of the Demand and Environment Subsystem, the daily sales dollars (orders) allocated to each demand unit and assigned by demand unit to a distribution center, provides input to the Operations Subsystem.

Operations Subsystem

The Operations Subsystem (OPS) deals with the flow of products and information through the physical distribution system. The orders allocated by the D&E must be processed at the remote distribution centers. Thus, for each remote facility in the physical distribution network, orders will arrive each day from the customer demand units. The batch of orders from each demand unit is then assigned a communications delay referred to as the customer order-transmittal time. This time delay is the first element of the total order cycle, CT1. The order-transmittal times are selected from a discrete probability distribution based on the expected variation around the average time delay.

The orders are then processed to determine if sufficient inventory for each of the tracked products in the orders is available. If sufficient product units are in stock, the order is prepared and a shipment dispatched to the demand unit. The order processing and preparation are assigned a combined time delay which is also based on a discrete probability distribution, CT2.

The transit time from shipment dispatch until shipment arrival at the demand unit is based on the reliability of achieving the average service time stated for the distance from the distribution center to demand unit, CT4. A discrete probability distribution formed the basis for developing the reliability function.

If the inventory for a particular product is insufficient, back orders are created. As inventory reorder points or periods are triggered, replenishment orders are dispatched to the firm's replenishment centers. The shipment (replenishment) is then scheduled to arrive at the distribution center after a time delay due to order transmittal to, order processing and preparation at, shipping schedules at, and transit time from, the replenishment center. The information from these time delays determines the replenishment reorder-cycle statistics which are used to generate the mean and standard deviation of reorder-cycle time. The average customer order-cycle time is thus a function of the customer order-transmittal time, the customer order-processing and preparation time, the average stockout-delay time, and the customer-transit time.

The effect of information flow for various communications networks can be tested using different values of, and functions for, the various order-transmittal and order-processing time delays in the OPS.

The OPS performed the above function via a series of fixed and variable events. The fixed-time activities included the following four areas:

1. the processing of individual orders, which included the allocation of and accounting for sales information at the demand unit plus the generation of and accounting for customer service statistics at the distribution center level (INDIVIDUAL ORDER);
2. the processing of the tracked-product multiorder summaries, the order blocks, both sales and product, detail information at the distribution center level (ORDSUM);
3. the distribution center End-of-Day Activities by which the distribution center's tracked-product inventory levels are checked with the appropriate inventory management policy variables to determine if reorder for product replenishment should be dispatched from the distribution center to the supplying manufacturing control centers (DC-EODAY);
4. the End-of-Day Activities at the distribution center to determine if any shipments are ready to be dispatched to the distribution center from the supplying manufacturing control centers (DC-EODAY).

The variable-time events, which do not occur within every basic time unit, in this model the day, for the DC-MCC links were grouped under two major categories:

1. the arrival of a multiple-product reorder at a MCC which was placed by a DC (MCORAR);
2. the arrival of a replenishment shipment at a DC for a supplying MCC (DCSHPAR).

The output of OPS is the volume of activity for each simulated operating period, each facility, and each distribution path in the system in terms of the orders processed and products moved.

The fixed event—individual order—allocates the sales information to the demand units and generates some of the customer service statistics at the distribution center. The activities of this event include generation of the elements of the customer order-cycle time:

1. order-transmittal time from customer to DC, CT1,
2. order-processing and preparation time at the DC, CT2,
3. outbound-transit time for the DC-DU link, CT4.

Each of these elements includes a constant time for a given path and a random variance function to simulate variability of service.

The fixed event—order summary—processes the order blocks at the DC level. This allocates the appropriate order split depending on whether the DC is a partial- or full-line distribution center. The event also accumulates the number of orders processed and the weight shipped to each DC-DU link. This event also processes the order block detail for the tracked products to update inventory-on-hand as follows:

$$IOH\ (ITP, ID) = IOH(ITP,(ID-1)) - ORDBLKTP\ (ITP, ID),$$

where:

$IOH\ (ITP, ID)$ = inventory-on-hand end-of-day ID for tracked product ITP at the DC being processed;

$IOH\ (ITP,(ID-1))$ = inventory-on-hand end-of-day (ID-1) for tracked product ITP at DC being processed;

$ORDBLKTP\ (ITP, ID)$ = order block demand on day ID for tracked product ITP at the DC being processed.

Activities of the fixed event—end-of-day—are primarily related to the review and update of the inventory levels and the shipment of product replenishments from the MCCs to the DC.

The initial activity of this routine updates the inventory status variables under the following conditions: normal updating of time-integrated inventory-on-hand, and stockout of the product.

The normal updating at the end of quarter divided by the number of workdays in the quarter provides the average inventory at the DC for the product. The transformation for this activity is:

$$\text{TINTIOH (ITP, ID)} = \text{TINTIOH (ITP(ID-1))} \\ + \text{IOH (ITP, ID)},$$

where:

TINTIOH (ITP, ID) = time-integrated (QTD) inventory-on-hand for end-of-day ID for tracked product ITP;

TINTIOH (ITP, (ID-1)) = time-integrated (QTD) inventory-on-hand for end-of-day ID-1 for tracked product ITP;

IOH (ITP, ID) = inventory-on-hand for end-of-day ID for tracked product ITP;

and:

$$\text{AVGINV (ITP)} = \text{TINTIOH (ITP)/NWKDYS},$$

where:

AVGINV (ITP) = the average inventory-on-hand for tracked product ITP quarter-to-date (QTD);

TINTIOH (ITP) = time-integrated inventory-on-hand for tracked product ITP quarter-to-date;

NWKDYS = number of workdays, quarter-to-date.

The stocked-out situation requires update of two variables. A time-integrated stocked-out cases variable is updated by adding the number of case units that were stocked out for the current day. The transformation for the second condition is:

$$\text{TINTSOCU (ITP, ID)} = \text{TINTSOCU (ITP, (ID-1))} \\ + |{-}\text{IOH}| \text{ (ITP, ID)},$$

where:

TINTSOCU (ITP, ID) = time-integrated (QTD) stocked-out cases for end-of-day ID for tracked product ITP;

TINTSOCU (ITP, (ID-1)) = time-integrated (QTD) stocked-out cases for end-of-day ID-1 for tracked product ITP;

|−IOH| (ITP, ID) = absolute value of negative inventory-on-hand for end-of-day ID for tracked product ITP.

This variable provides the Measurement Subsystem (MEAS) with the information to determine the customer-service penalty time, CT3, for inventory stockouts. As previously stated in the Supporting Data System-Measurement, the normal customer order cycle, NOCT plus CT3, equals the total customer order cycle, TOCT.

The second variable calculated for measures of stockout is the stockout days for the product. This variable, updated each day that a product is stocked out, enables the calculation of the average and standard deviation of the product stockout days given that a stockout had occurred. The transformations to calculate the stockout days are:

$$\text{NDASO (ITP, ID)} = \text{NDASO (ITP, (ID-1))} + 1,$$

where:

NDASO (ITP, ID) = number of days (QTD) a stockout occurred for tracked product ITP for end-of-day ID;

NDASO (ITP, (ID-1)) = number of days (QTD) a stockout occurred through day ID-1 for product ITP.

If there were any DC product reorders outstanding the reorder quantity ROQ is added to the time-integrated inventory-on-hand to approximate the total average inventory for this product at the DC. The transformation is stated as follows:

TOTINTIOH (ITP, ID) = TINTIOH (ITP, ID)
$$+ \text{ROQ (ITP, ID)},$$

where:

TOTINTIOH (ITP, ID) = total time-integrated (QTD) inventory-on-hand for the end-of-day ID for tracked product ITP;

TINTIOH (ITP, ID) = time-integrated (QTD) inventory-on-hand for end-of-day ID for tracked product ITP;

ROQ (ITP, ID) = reorder order quantity outstanding for tracked product ITP at end-of-day ID.

Looping through all of the tracked products within an inventory category is necessary since an inventory policy is assigned to categories rather than individual products and certain summary data are accumulated only by inventory category.

Selection of the inventory policy is the next major activity of the routine. As previously discussed in the Supporting Data System for the Operations and Monitor and Control Subsystems, three basic inventory management policies were developed: optional replenishment system, reorder point system, and hybrid of the reorder point system and the optional replenishment system. The details of these three policies are presented as a Monitor and Control Subsystem Routine-Inventory Management Module. In this section the emphasis is on the operation of inventory management policy. The assumptions were made that all tracked products in an inventory category would be managed by the same inventory policy.

If the policy selected for a category is an optional replenishment policy with periodic review, the routine checks to determine if the current day corresponds to the time for inventory review for the inventory category. If it is time for a review the reorder transformation is as follows:

ROQ (ITP) $= $ S (ITP) $-$ IOH (ITP),

if IOH (ITP) $<$ ROP2 (ITP),

where:

ROQ (ITP) = reorder quantity of tracked product ITP;

S (ITP) = the replenishment level set by M&C Subsystem for tracked product ITP;

IOH (ITP) = inventory-on-hand tracked product ITP;

ROP2 (ITP) = reorder point set for optional replenishment system set by M&C for tracked product ITP

If the policy established for the inventory category was the daily reorder point system, the reorders are established by the following transformations:

ROQ (ITP) $=$ S (ITP) $-$ IOH (ITP),

if IOH (ITP) $<$ ROP1 (ITP),

where:

ROQ (ITP) = reorder quantity of tracked product ITP;

S (ITP) = EOQ (ITP) $+$ ROP1 (ITP);

EOQ (ITP) = economic order quantity, set by M&C Subsystem for tracked product ITP;

ROP1 (ITP) = reorder point set by M&C Subsystem for tracked product ITP;

IOH (ITP) = inventory-on-hand of tracked product ITP.

The hybrid system combines the above policies to develop the following reorder transformations:

ROQ (ITP) $=$ S (ITP) $-$ IOH (ITP),

if either

1. IOH (ITP) $\leq$ROP1 (ITP) for the daily reorder point, or

2. IOH (ITP) $\leq$ROP2 (ITP) for the inventory check at the review period for the optional replenishment system.

In each of the above situations if no reorder was necessary the next tracked product for the inventory category is processed. After each product within each category has been processed a check is made to determine if any single product reorders are required. If single product reorders have been generated, the next step requires dispatching of these reorders from the DC to the MCC, the DC-MCC communications link, RT1. If no reorders are required for any products within all inventory categories for the DC, the routine checks for shipment dispatches from MCC to DC, the MCC-DC link, RT4.

The prior activities generated the single-product reorders for each product that required replenishment at the DC. The reorder dispatch routine develops the multiple-product reorders that are dispatched to the MCC supply points for the DC. The transformations for calculating the amount of weight moved from the MCC-DC link is determined as follows:

WTMCC (IMC, IDC) = PCMCC (IMC, IDC)
* TRKWT (IDC) * EXRT,

where:

WTMCC (IMC, IDC) = weight moved from MCC (IMC) to DC (IDC) for the replenishment order;

PCMCC (IMC, IDC) = percent of total weight assigned to MCC (IMC) for shipment to DC (IDC) as part of replenishment order;

TRKWT (IDC) = tracked product weight for the replenishment shipment;

EXRT = extrapolation ratio of tracked products relative to total products.

The shipment of outstanding reorders is the final routine of the DC end-of-day event. This routine, the MCC-to-DC shipment dispatch, processes any reorder shipments ready to be shipped to the DC.

The two variable events are the MCC order arrival and DC shipment arrival. The primary activity of the MCC order arrival is to add the product detail on the reorder from the DC to the list of tracked products for future shipment dispatch to the DC. The DC shipment arrival updates the inventory status variables at the DC when a shipment dispatched at an MCC arrives with a reorder at the DC. The inventory-on-hand is updated using a linear, first-order difference equation as follows:

$$IOH\ (ITP, (ID+1)) = IOH\ (ITP, ID) + ROQ\ (ITP, ID),$$

where:

$IOH\ (ITP, (ID+1))$ = inventory-on-hand for beginning of day $ID+1$ for tracked product ITP;

$IOH\ (ITP, ID)$ = inventory-on-hand for beginning of day ID for tracked product ITP;

$ROQ\ (ITP, ID)$ = reorder quantity received on end-of-day ID for tracked product ITP.

The Operations Subsystem events, the three fixed-time events—individual order, order summary, and DC end-of-day—and the two variable events—MCC order arrival and DC shipment arrival—provide the activities and sequencing necessary to simulate the operation of the total physical system structured for the LREPS model. The next section of the Operating System presents the Measurement Subsystem, which develops the measures of cost, service, and flexibility.

Measurement Subsystem

The function of the Measurement Subsystem (MEAS) is to process the results of the previous operating period to develop values of the target variables cost, service, and flexibility (robustness). These variables provide the basis for evaluation and selection from among the various sets of sequential decision outcomes of the LREPS model. The design criteria for MEAS required that it provide service, cost, and flexibility information suitable for strategic decision making. Extrapolation of inventory characteristics was also required.

The output included a measure of total physical distribution costs, which required consideration of fixed investment costs of the physical distribution centers, inventory costs, distribution center operations (throughput) costs, transportation costs, and communications costs. Basic measures of customer service included the total order cycle, percent customers served within a set of designated service times, percent sales volume served within a set of designated service times, stockouts and order-cycle delays due to inventory policy, service to major customers, and finally, a measure of service relative to competition. The final criterion was that the subsystem develop the necessary output to develop measures of flexibility (robustness) or, as previously defined, the degree of "non" risk associated with a particular decision.

Service Measures

The first set of activities calculates the measures of service, which are:

1. customer-service penalty time, CT3
2. mean and standard deviation of customer order-cycle time, NOCT
3. mean and standard deviation of customer outbound-transportation time, CT4
4. total customer order-cycle time, TOCT
5. percentage of case units backordered
6. mean and standard deviation of product-stockout delays
7. normal order-cycle time proportions
8. domestic average service time
9. average lead time for each DC-MCC link

The customer-service penalty time, CT3, results from DC stockouts of tracked products during a past period's operations. The calculation of the CT3 penalty time is performed for each inventory category and then a weighted average, based on total tracked-product sales, is developed for the DC.

The calculation of the mean and standard deviation of the previously defined customer order-cycle time (NOCT) and outbound transit time are calculated for the previous operating period.

The sum of the normal customer order-cycle time (CT1 + CT2 + CT4 = NOCT) and the customer-penalty time, CT3, is added to produce the total customer-order cycle, TOCT.

The percent of tracked-product case units backordered due to inventory stockout is developed relative to the total tracked-product case units sold for all inventory categories at a DC. The mean and standard deviation of tracked-product delivery delays due to all product stockouts is based on the accumulated days' delay and the stockouts for all the products.

The proportions of DC sales dollars and orders delivered to its customer-demand unit within a set of specified normal customer order-cycle time intervals is calculated by taking the ratio of sales dollars and orders within a set time interval against the total sales dollars and orders for the DC.

The domestic (national) average total customer order-cycle time is calculated as a weighted average of total customer order-cycle time for all of the DCs combined.

The average total reorder lead times for each DC-MCC link are calculated as the ratio of total accumulated reorder-cycle time for the link divided by the number of multiple-product reorders.

The next major set of activities, EXTRAP, developed additional measures of inventory characteristics. This routine was necessary to extrapolate or generalize the average inventory characteristics developed from the results of activities of the tracked products to the total product line.

The first activity of the inventory extrapolation routine calculated the category modifier, CM, which was used to extrapolate the inventory characteristics for a particular inventory category. CM was calculated by the following transformation:

$$CM\ (IC) = TNCTPD\ (IC)/TKPDCT\ (IC),$$

where:

$CM\ (IC)$ = inventory category modifier to extrapolate inventory characteristics to all products in the category IC;

104   DYNAMIC SIMULATION

TNCTPD (IC) = total number of products in the inventory category IC;

TKPDCT (IC) = tracked products in the inventory category IC.

Thus, if all products were tracked, the CM (IC) would equal one and no extrapolation would occur. However, in the initial version of LREPS, the extrapolation ratio was of the order of from four to twenty depending on the inventory category, since the percent of products tracked varied from approximately 25 percent in the A category to 5 percent in the C category.

The extrapolation of stockout and single-product reorders was calculated next based on the following transformations:

$$\text{EXSKOTDC (IC)} = \text{CM (IC)} * \text{TKSKOTDC (IC)},$$

where:

EXSKOTDC (IC) = extrapolated stockouts for inventory category IC;

CM (IC) = category modifier for inventory category IC;

TKSKOTDC (IC) = tracked product stockouts for inventory category IC;

and:

$$\text{EXRORDC (IC)} = \text{CM (IC)} * \text{TKSPRORD (IC)},$$

where:

EXRORDC (IC) = extrapolated reorders for inventory category IC;

CM (IC) = category modifier for inventory category IC;

TKSPRORD (IC) = tracked single-product reorders IC.

The next activity extrapolated the average cubic inventory-on-hand as follows:

$$\text{EXTKCUB (IC)} = \text{TINTIOH (ITP, IC)} * \text{CUBCS (ITP)} * \text{CM (IC)},$$

where:

EXTKCUB (IC) = extrapolated average inventory cube for each inventory category IC;

TINTIOH (ITP, IC) = time-integrated inventory-on-hand for each tracked product ITP in inventory category IC;

CUBCS (ITP) = cube per unit for tracked product ITP;

CM (IC) = category multiplier for inventory category IC.

The extrapolated investment of the tracked products was next calculated as follows:

$$\text{EXTKINVST (IC)} = \sum_{\text{ITP}=1}^{\text{ITNPC}} \text{TINTIOH (ITP, IC)} * \text{CGCU (ITP, IC)} * \text{CM (IC)},$$

where:

EXTKINVST (IC) = extrapolated average inventory investment for each inventory category IC;

TINTIOH (ITP, IC) = time-integrated inventory-on-hand for each tracked product ITP in inventory category IC;

CGCU (ITP, IC) = cost of goods sold per case unit for tracked product ITP;

CM (IC) = category modifier for inventory category IC.

The above extrapolations were processed at the end of each quarter for all tracked products in an inventory category and all inventory categories. After both these loops were completed control returned to the measurement service routine.

Physical Distribution Cost Components

The final section of MEAS presents the transformations that developed the costs of each of the components of the physical distribution system as follows:

1. outbound transportation cost for the DC-DU links
2. inbound transportation costs for the MCC-DC links
3. throughput cost for movement of goods through the DC
4. communications cost for order transmittal and order processing
5. facility investment costs for the equivalent annual cost resulting from capital expenditures (rent or lease) on DCs
6. inventory carrying cost

Outbound transportation is defined as the transportation cost developed for shipments made from a DC to an assigned DU, the DC-DU link. The general approach used to develop the outbound costs, regression equations based on regional weighted average freight rates, was discussed in the Supporting Data System—Measurement.

The first set of activities processes the DUs assigned to the DC to develop the outbound transportation cost. The transformation uses outbound freight rates developed as follows:

$$OR(IDC, IDU) = ((1.0+R1)^{IY} * a) * R3 + ((1.0+R2)^{IY} * b) * R4 * XDIS,$$

where:

OR (IDC, IDU) = freight rate in dollars per pound for DC (IDC)-DU (IDU) link;

R1, R2 = regional annual compound rates at which cost structure as defined by the "a" and "b" coefficients is assumed to be changing;

R3, R4 = regional adjustment factors to reflect the use of negotiated rates at the RDCs instead of class rates;

a, b = coefficients of regression equation;

IY = the simulated year, 1 . . . . . 10, where base is 1969;

XDIS = distance in spherical miles adjusted to highway miles for the DC (IDC)-DU (IDU) link.

The R1, R2 factors were included to automatically adjust the freight rates based on the expected rate of change-over time. The R3 and R4 adjustment factors allowed the adjustment of the rates to reflect negotiated freight rates for the DC-DU links. These factors were developed by region.

For example, if the volume through a DC is greater than a set level for the quarter, the R3 and R4 factors are set at values less than one to reflect the use of negotiated rates. If the volume is below the set amount, R3 and R4 are set equal to one.

The distance is obtained from the distance routine that converts latitude-longitude of the DC and DU to a highway distance for the DC-DU link.

The above outbound rate is further modified for the partial-line distribution centers to reflect the higher costs of the smaller average-size shipments from a partial-line DC:

ORC (IDC, IDU) = OR (IDC, IDU) * RCF,

where:

ORC (IDC, IDU) = corrected outbound transportation rate for DC (IDC)-DU (IDU) link where DC (IDC) is an RDC-P;

OR (IDC, IDU) = outbound transportation rate for DC (IDC)-DU (IDU) link where DC (IDC) is an RDC-F;

RCF = rate correction factor to reflect higher cost of small shipments from partial-line DC.

The outbound freight rate, OR, is also modified for PDCs because it was assumed that the larger volumes being shipped from the PDCs warrant pooled or consolidated shipments to the DUs. These pooled shipments are shipped via a scheduled distribution policy. The transformation for this modification is:

$$\text{ORC (IDC, IDU)} = \text{OR (IDC, IDU)} * \text{POOLCF (IDC)},$$

where:

ORC (IDC, IDU) = corrected outbound transportation rate for the DC (IDC)-DU (IDU) link where DC (IDC) is a PDC;

OR (IDC, IDU) = RDC-F outbound transportation rate for DC (IDC)-DU (IDU) link;

POOLCF (IDC) = rate correction factor to reflect pooled rates for large, mixed TL or CL shipments.

For each PDC, if the distance and accumulated weight for the PDC-DU links is above set minimums, the POOLCF is set at a value less than one to reflect pooled rates. The outbound transportation cost transformation is then of the form:

$$\text{OTBD (IDC)} = \sum_{\text{IDU}} \text{ORC (IDC, IDU)} * \text{WT (IDC, IDU)},$$

where:

OTBD (IDC) = outbound transportation costs for DC (IDC) for the quarter for all DUs assigned to the DC;

ORC (IDC, IDU) = corrected (or OR (IDC, IDU)) freight rate for outbound transportation DC (IDC)-DU (IDU) link;

WT (IDC, IDU) = total accumulated weight shipped for DC (IDC)-DU (IDU) link for the quarter.

Inbound transportation costs are developed for shipments from the manufacturing control centers, MCCs to the DC, the MCC-DC link. The inbound costs for each DC is calculated using transformations of the form:

$$\text{INBD (IDC)} = \sum_{\text{IMC}} \sum_{\text{IC}} (\text{IR (IWC, IMC, IDC)} * \text{WTCAT (IWC, IMC, IDC)}),$$

where:

INBD (IDC) = inbound transportation costs for DC (IDC) for the quarter;

IR (IWC, IMC, IDC) = freight rate for inbound transportation MCC (IMC)-DC (IDC) link for weight category IWC;

WTCAT (IWC, IMC, IDC) = weight shipped MCC (IMC)-DC (IDC) for category IWC for the quarter.

The freight rates were obtained via rate tables for each of the MCC-DC links and three weight categories. The weight for each MCC-DC link is accumulated in the Operations Subsystem. The calculation of inbound transportation cost for the MCC-PDC uses the identical transformation, but the freight rate for the largest weight interval is applied to all weight accumulated for the PDC links to represent rail car shipments.

The throughput cost activity calculates the cost of preparing the customer orders for shipment. The transformation is of the form:

THRUPC (IDC) = THRUCF (IS, IT) * WTSL (IDC),

where:

THRUPC (IDC) = throughput cost for DC (IDC) for the quarter;

THRUCF (IS, IT) = throughput average cost factor by DC size interval IS and type IT;

WTSL (IDC) = throughput average cost factor by DC (IDC) for the quarter.

The total weight moved through the DC is accumulated via an Operations Subsystem activity.

The cost of order transmittal and preparation up to the point of the physical preparation of the order is defined as communication cost. The transformations which develop the fixed cost and variable cost for the DC are of the form:

COMFCDC (IDC) = CMFCDC (IS, IT),

where:

COMFCDC (IDC) = communications fixed cost for DC (IDC) for the quarter;

CMFCDC (IS, IT) = communications fixed cost for DC size interval IS and type IT;

and:

COMVCODC (IDC) = CMVCODC (IS, IT) * NMORDS (IDC);

where:

COMVCODC (IDC) = communications variable cost for orders processed for DC (IDC) for the quarter;

LREPS Mathematical Model

CMVCODC (IS, IT) = communications variable cost factor for orders for size IS type IT;

NMORDS (IDC) = number of orders processed for DC (IDC) for the quarter;

and:

COMVCLDC (IDC) = CMVCLDC (IS, IT) * NMLNS (IDC),

where:

COMVCLDC (IDC) = communications variable cost for lines processed for DC (IDC) for the quarter;

CMVCLDC (IS, IT) = communications variable cost factor for lines for size IS type IT;

NMLNS (IDC) = number of lines processed for DC (IDC) for the quarter.

The fixed and variable cost factors were developed for the five size intervals IS and three types IT (PDC, RDC-F, and RDC-P) in the Supporting Data System—Measurement.

Communications costs are also included for regional and national levels to allow the flexibility of simulating regional or centralized order-processing systems costs. The transformations for the regional and national costs are of the same general form as for the DC level.

The facility investment cost activity developed the fixed cost per quarter for capital investment in equipment, building, and land. The transformations developed for this activity are:

FINV (IDC) = INVEST (IS, IT),

where:

FINV (IDC) = total investment in dollars for equipment, building, and land for DC (IDC);

INVEST (IS, IT) = fixed total capital investment for a DC size interval IS and type IT for the quarter;

and:

$$\text{FINVC (IDC)} = \text{CLF (IDC)} * ((\text{FINV) IDC)} \\ * \text{PCSD (IS, IT)/DPE} \\ + \text{FINV (IDC)} * \text{PCLD (IS, IT)/DPB})),$$

where:

FINVC (IDC) = facilities cost allocated for the quarter for DC (IDC);

CLF (IDC) = cost of living factor by DC (IDC);

PCSD (IS, IT) = percentage of investment dollars assumed with short depreciation period (equipment) by DC size interval IS type IT;

DPE = depreciation period, for equipment;

PCLD (IS, IT) = percentage of investment dollars assumed with long depreciation period (building) by DC size interval IS type IT;

DPB = depreciation period for building

The calculation of the cost of carrying and handling product inventories by DC for the quarter requires the following transformations:

$$\text{INCCST (IDC)} = \text{AVDCINV (IDC)} * \text{DICC},$$

where:

INCCST (IDC) = inventory carrying and handling cost for DC (IDC) for the quarter;

AVDCINV (IDC) = average inventory investment for the DC for the quarter;

DICC = daily carrying charge.

LREPS Mathematical Model

The cost of preparing multiple-product reorders for shipment dispatch at each of the supplying MCCs for the DC being processed required the following transformation:

$$\text{DCMCRCST (IDC)} = \sum_{\text{IMC}}^{\text{NMCCS}} \text{NOMPRDS (IDC, IMC)} * \text{MCROCST (IMC)},$$

where:

DCMCRCST (IDC) = reorder cost for all of the MCCs supplying the DC (IDC);

NOMPRDS (IDC, IMC) = number of multiple-product reorders for all MCCs supplying the DC;

MCRCOST (IMC) = reorder cost for each MCC (IMC) supplying the DC.

The cost of processing the reorder for the DC-MCC link is not included in the inventory cost routine because it had already been included in the DC communications cost. After calculation of the inventory costs, control is transferred to the Monitor and Control quarterly routine.

The Measurement Subsystem as presented provides the capability for measuring each of the target variables of service, cost, and flexibility. In addition, a special routine to explode the tracked-product statistics is required. The next and final section in the Operating System, the Monitor and Control Subsystem, presents the information feedback control loops, algorithms, routines, and activities required to develop the dynamic aspects of the control function.

Monitor and Control Subsystem

The tasks of the Monitor and Control Subsystem are to supervise the activities of the Operating System and to control the information feedback loops within the model. The supervisory function can be further subdivided into executive, gateway, and scheduler subfunctions.

Supervisory Function

The executive program controls the sequence of activity execution for the Operating System. The executive selects events to be processed from an event file constructed on a (FIFO) first-in-first-out basis with the smallest time unit being a day. The LREPS model fixed-time events relate to beginning-of-cycle, beginning-of-year, beginning-of-half-year, beginning-of-quarter, beginning-of-month, beginning-of-day, and end-of-cycle activities. In addition, variable-time events which initiate the Operations Subsystem processing of a manufacturing center order arrival from a distribution center and processing of a distribution shipment arrival are included in the model.

Duties of the gateway subfunction are to input and output data. The input subfunction is that of reading in the exogenous input data required for the Operating System. The first output subfunction is that of computing and preparing data to be used by the Report Generator System to develop the special and standard management reports. These reports are currently prepared at the end of each quarter year, but could also be prepared at the end of each week, month, half-year, and so on. The remaining output subfunction is to initialize the endogenous variables for the next quarter's activities.

The fixed-time schedules use current clock time generated within the model to schedule the next imminent event. As mentioned earlier, the smallest time interval is one day. The clock is incremental by one day, and the current clock time is compared with the fixed-event times to select the appropriate event for the workday. This event is then scheduled for the day by being placed in the event file. The executive program takes over and processes all scheduled events, variable-time events first and then fixed-time events. Next, the clock is advanced by one day and the entire process is repeated until the end-of-cycle event is processed.

Control Function

The second major task of the Monitor and Control Subsystem is to generate the information feedback responses for sequential decision making. This task is a two-fold one. One set of equations reviews and develops the endogenous feedback responses, and the second set implements (updates) the system changes at the appropriate clock time.

The first set of routines, each of which will be briefly described, includes:

1. calculation of the distribution center and regional sales forecast modification factors—which modify sales forecasts for deviation from the desired level of physical distribution system performance;
2. calculation of a new regional total to tracked-product weight ratio for manufacturing center shipment weight extrapolation;
3. calculation of new inventory-control variables and selection of new inventory-management policies—reorder point and optional replenishment policies and a hybrid of the two;
4. determination of the requirement for and scheduling of any distribution center facility systems additions or deletions— the facility location algorithms;
5. determination of the requirement for and scheduling of a distribution center expansion—the facility expansion algorithms.

The sales modification factors, SMF, are used to modify sales forecast for deviations of service from the desired level. The actual service in terms of the percentage of sales dollars within the established order-cycle intervals, i.e., (IOT = 3, 5, 6, 9, >9 days) and the desired service percentage within a specified interval are used to develop the new exponentially smoothed SMF for each in-solution DC. The transformation is of the form:

$$\text{EDCSMF (IDC, IQ)} = \text{Alpha} * \text{ACDCSMF (IDC, IOT, IQ)} + (1\text{-Alpha}) * \text{EDCSMF (IDC, (IQ-1))},$$

and:

$$\text{ACDCSMF (IDC, IOT, IQ)} = \text{PCD (IDC, IOT, IQ)} / \text{DSDSV (IR, IOT, IQ)},$$

where:

EDCSMF (IDC, IQ) = new exponentially smoothed sales modification factor for DC (IDC) for quarter IQ;

Alpha = smoothing constant;

ACDCSMF (IDC, IOT, IQ) = actual sales modification factor for DC (IDC) order-cycle interval IOT for quarter IQ;

PCD (IDC, IOT, IQ) = percent sales dollars within interval IOT for quarter IQ;

DSDSV (IR, IOT, IQ) = desired service stated for initial LREPS as percent sales dollars (orders) within interval IOT for region IR for quarter IQ;

EDCSMF (IDC, (IQ-1)) = previous exponentially smoothed sales modification factor for DC (IDC) for quarter IQ-1.

The new exponentially smoothed sales modification factor is calculated for each in-solution DC.

A sales modification factor is also calculated for each region using the accumulated sales by region to develop the percentage by order-cycle interval, IOT. The transformations are of the same general form as those presented above for the DC sales modification factors.

The regional weight ratio routine calculates a new regional total to tracked-product weight ratio for MCC shipment weight extrapolation each quarter. This ratio is used to extrapolate up the weight of the tracked products for each MCC shipment in the region to the total weight representative of all products.

The inventory-management routine provides the capability for testing the effect of the (1) reorder point policy, (2) optional replenishment policy, and (3) a hybrid of the reorder point and replenishment policies.[25, 26] This routine provides the inventory-management decision rules and develops the inventory parameters used in inventory control in the Operations Subsystem. Inventory management and control in the LREPS model was established by inventory-product category rather than by individual tracked product. The basic policies and transformations for the inventory categories provided the LREPS model with the capability for implementing a dynamic inventory-management algorithm. The activities within the routine include:

1. calculating initial average reorder lead time for new DCs
2. calculating exponential average product demand
3. averaging daily demand for each tracked product for DC being measured
4. determining standard deviations of reorder lead time, review period, and average daily demand for DC being measured
5. calculating buffer stock and EOQ for each tracked product being measured
6. selecting appropriate inventory policy
7. calculating ROP1 level-1 reorder point
8. calculating ROP2 level-2 reorder point
9. calculating initial inventory level for new DCs coming in-solution
10. calculating S-level for existing in-solution DCs after processing all tracked products and in-solution DCs
11. returning control to Monitor and Control Subsystem

The routine was called at the beginning-of-cycle to set the initial values of inventory and quarterly to update the inventory-control parameters based on the past querter sales volume and inventory condition. The inventory-management system as designed therefore included the time interactions or recursive relationships necessary to be classified as a dynamic model.

Initially, a check is made to determine if the DC being processed is a new DC just coming into solution. If yes, the initial activity of the inventory management is to calculate the initial average reorder lead time between the new DC and each of its supplying MCCs.

For each tracked product the expected level of quarterly sales for the next quarter is calculated using the exponentially averaged total-product demand for the tracked product. The transformation is:

$$\text{PTPDEM (IQ, ITP)} = (1\text{-Alpha}) * \text{PTPDEM ((IQ-1), ITP)} \\ + \text{Alpha} * \text{ATPDEM ((IQ-1), ITP)},$$

where:

PTPDEM (IQ, ITP) = predicted sales for tracked product ITP for quarter IQ;

Alpha = exponential smoothing constant;

PTPDEM ((IQ-1), ITP) = predicted sales for tracked product ITP for quarter IQ-1;

ATPDEM ((IQ-1), ITP) = actual sales for tracked product ITP for quarter IQ-1.

The next series of activities calculates the tracked-product inventory-control variables for each in-solution DC. For each DC-MCC link, first the average daily demand for each of the tracked products is developed, followed by an activity that determines the standard deviations of the average reorder lead time, review period, and average daily demand. The assumption was made that each of the above has a Poisson distribution. Thus the standard deviations are calculated as the square cost of the average of each of these variables.

The next activity calculated the buffer stock and economic order quantity, EOQ, for each of the tracked products. The transformation for the buffer stock is:

$$\text{BUF (ITP)} = \text{NSD (ITP)} * \text{SDLT (ITP)} * \text{SDEM (ITP)} + \text{ADEM (ITP)} * \text{SDRP (ITP)},$$

where:

BUF (ITP) = buffer or safety stock for tracked product ITP;

NSD (ITP) = factor for the number of standard deviations or level of safety desired for the tracked product ITP;

SDLT (ITP) = the standard deviation of lead time for tracked product ITP;

SDEM (ITP) = the standard deviation of the daily demand for tracked product ITP;

ADEM (ITP) = average daily demand for tracked product ITP;

SDRP (ITP) = the standard deviation of the review period for tracked product ITP.

The EOQ was calculated using the standard EOQ formula as follows:

$$\text{EOQ (ITP, IQ)} = ((2 * \text{PTPDEM (ITP, IQ)} * \text{DCWI} * \text{ORDCST (IDC, IQ)})/(\text{DICC} * 63 * \text{CGCU (ITP)}))^{1/2},$$

where:

EOQ (ITP, IQ)   = economic order quantity for tracked product ITP for quarter IQ;

PTPDEM (ITP, IQ) = predicted total demand for tracked product ITP for quarter IQ;

DCWI (IDC)   = sum of weighted index for DC (IDC);

ORDCST (IDC, IQ) = order cost for DC (IDC) for quarter IQ;

DICC   = daily inventory carrying charge;

CGCU (ITP)   = cost of goods sold per case unit for tracked product ITP.

After calculating the buffer stock and the EOQ, the next activity selected appropriate inventory policy for the tracked product being processed. If the product category was assigned a reorder-point policy or a hybrid system, the transformations for the reorder point, ROP1 were:

$$\text{BUF (ITP, IQ)} = \text{NSD (ITP)} * \text{SDLT (ITP)} * \text{SDEM (ITP)},$$

and:

$$\text{ROP1 (ITP, IQ)} = \text{BUF (ITP, IQ)} + \text{AVGLT (ITP)} * \text{ADEM (ITP, IQ)},$$

where:

BUF (ITP, IQ)   = buffer or safety stock for tracked product ITP for quarter IQ;

NSD (ITP) = factor for the number of standard deviations for tracked product ITP;

SDLT (ITP) = the standard deviation of lead time for tracked product ITP;

SDEM (ITP) = the standard deviation of daily demand for tracked product ITP;

ROP1 (ITP, IQ) = reorder-point level-1, used for reorder-point policy and hybrid policy;

AVGLT (ITP) = average reorder lead time for the tracked product ITP;

ADEM (ITP, IQ) = average daily demand for tracked product ITP for quarter IQ.

At this time the value of ROP2 was set equal to ROP1 if the product-category policy was the reorder-point system. If the product used the replenishment policy or hybrid system the transformation was:

ROP2 (ITP, IQ) = BUF (ITP, IQ) + ADEM (ITP, IQ)
* (AVGLT (ITP) + AVGRP (ITP)/2),

where:

ROP2 (ITP, IQ) = reorder-point level-2, used for the optional replenishment system and hybrid system;

BUF (ITP, IQ) = buffer or safety stock for tracked product ITP for quarter IQ;

ADEM (ITP, IQ) = average daily demand for tracked product ITP for quarter IQ;

AVGLT (ITP) = average reorder lead time for the tracked product ITP;

AVGRP (ITP) = average review period length for tracked product ITP.

If the DC was new the initial inventory was calculated as follows:

INIV (ITP) = EOQ (ITP) + BUF (ITP),

where:

INIV (ITP) = initial inventory for tracked product ITP;

EOQ (ITP) = economic order quantity for tracked product ITP;

BUF (ITP) = buffer for safety stock for tracked product ITP.

The standard S-level was calculated for each inventory policy as follows:

SLINV (ITP) = EOQ (ITP) + ROP2 (ITP),

where:

SLINV (ITP) = S-level inventory for tracked product ITP;

EOQ (ITP) = economic order quantity for tracked product ITP;

ROP2 (ITP) = reorder-point level-2.

These activities were performed for each tracked product for each in-solution DC. After completion of these activities control was returned to the executive routine-review. The inventory-management routine demonstrates an example of the modular and universal aspects of the LREPS model, since this routine can simulate the policies of a large variety of multiproduct companies. The theoretical inventory-management module can also be replaced by a specific heuristic inventory-policy module for a particular company. This was accomplished during initial runs of the LREPS model.

The facility LOCATE algorithm reviewed the need, selected the location(s), and scheduled the addition and/or deletion of DCs in the physical distribution (PD) system configuration. The LOCATE algorithm included the following routines:

1. review of national constraints
2. review of regional decision rules for feasibility and priority for PD system changes
3. process list of regions to select region for PD system change
4. process list of DCs to select location for addition or deletion
5. implement DC addition
6. implement DC deletion

The first routine of the LOCATE algorithm checks the constraints established as management parameters. Any reasonable number of constraints could have been implemented via this activity. For the initial LREPS model the constraints are:

1. total PD system in-solution constraints
    a. maximum number of DCs in-solution
    b. maximum dollar investment in DCs in-solution
2. total PD system in-process constraints
    a. maximum number of DCs in-process of addition
    b. maximum number of DCs in-process of deletion
    c. maximum dollar investment in DCs in-process

The possibility to add and/or delete a new DC location in a given quarter is feasible if, and only if, the appropriate constraints are not reached. If at least one constraint was reached, control is returned to the Monitor and Control Subsystem and LOCATE is not processed for the quarter since no action can be taken. If the constraints are not reached, the next step checks to determine if exogenous changes, add and/or delete, were programmed for this quarter. The introduction of DC locations via LREPS exogenous input for addition and/or deletion takes precedence over the "free" run of the LOCATE algorithm. This allows the decision maker to introduce new DCs or delete DCs if desired at any given quarter. However, in any one quarter DC changes are allowed only via one method, either endogenously through LOCATE or exogenously through EXOG, not both.

If the change in the PD system was set to be endogenous via LOCATE rather than exogenous, the next LOCATE routine reviewed the regional decision rules in terms of: reviewing the regional constraints, and determining the priority by region for PD system change.

The regional constraints for the initial version of LREPS are similar to the national constraints. Thus, addition and/or deletion are possible if, and only if, the in-solution or in-process constraints are not reached. Any region where the constraints are reached is bypassed and thus is not considered as potential for modification of the current distribution center network during this quarter.

For the regions not eliminated from further consideration, the next set of activities within the routine develops the regional priority for implementing PD system change. The LOCATE algorithm can be set to select that region of the country for addition (deletion) of a distribution center which has (1) the greatest deficiency (surplus) in service relative to a desired level, (2) the greatest need in terms of cost relative to desired cost standards, or (3) a combination of cost and service. In this monograph only Option 1, which bases addition of DCs on service and deletion on cost, is presented.

This priority is calculated in terms of the Regional LOCATE Sales Modification Factor, RLCSMF. The RLCSMF was similar to the SMF used to modify forecasted sales at the DC level, which is based on the ratio of actual to desired service. However, the RLCSMF is calculated to reflect not only actual service of in-solution DCs but also an assumed level of service for the in-process DCs, which come on-line after a four-quarter delay time. The RLCSMF for the quarter is developed using the following transformations:

$$\text{RLCSMF (IR)} = [\ \frac{\text{NDCREG(IR)}}{\text{NDCREG(IR)} + \text{NMIPSREG(IR)}} * \text{EXPSMF(IR)} + \frac{\text{NMIPSREG(IR)}}{\text{NDCREG(IR)} + \text{NMIPSREG(IR)}} * \text{SMFNDC(IR)} - \text{SMFBASE(IR)}\ ] / \text{SMFBASE(IR)},$$

where:

RLCSMF (IR) = locate sales modification factor for region IR;

NDCREG (IR) = number of DCs in-solution for region IR;

NMIPSREG (IR) = number of DCs in-process of addition for region IR;

EXPSMF (IR) = exponential smoothed sales modification factor for region IR;

SMFBASE (IR) = reference or base sales modification factor; initially set equal to 1.0 for the region IR;

SMFNDC (IR) = sales modification factor set for each in-process DC, and used as initial value for first quarter DC in-solution for the region IR.

A DC in-process by definition does not contribute to the regional service. However, a value was assumed for each in-process DC to acknowledge the fact that the in-process DC, by being selected for implementation in one year, reduced the need for further addition of DCs via LOCATE in the same region during each of the next four quarters. This concept is similar to the use of inventory position to indicate the inventory-on-hand plus on order. In the case of facilities the facility position equaled the DCs in-solution plus the DCs in-process. The recognition that a DC was in-process by taking credit for the service it will provide when it comes on-line reduced the chances of adding a second unnecessary DC in the same region in the immediate quarters following a previous quarter addition of a DC.

The RLCSMF for each region was compared against the "upper" and "lower" limits for the SMFBASE set as management parameters. The upper limit established the level above which the region was considered to have a surplus of service. Each such region, thus being a candidate for deletion of a DC, was entered in the list for possible deletion, RLISTDL.

The lower limit established the level below which the region was considered to have a deficiency of service. Each such region, thus being a candidate for addition of a DC, was entered in the list for possible addition, RLISTAD.

After all regions were reviewed, if no regions were placed in the RLISTDL or RLISTAD list, the control was returned to the Monitor and Control Quarterly event. Given, however, that at least one region was placed in RLISTDL or RLISTAD, the next routine processed the list of regions to select the region for physical distribution system change.

The first activity determined the region with the highest priority for the physical distribution system change. In the initial version of LREPS addition is given priority over deletion. Therefore, if the RLISTAD list includes at least one region, the region with the greatest deviation from the LWLMTSMF is selected as the region to which to attempt to add a DC. The next set of activities determines if a DC can be added to this region using an iterative process which selected the DC that, if added, would contribute the greatest increase in service.

Once a DC is selected from among the potential list for the region, the DC is scheduled for addition if, and only if, the volume is at or above the minimum established as a management parameter. The final routine required to add a facility is to set the time for the new DC to come into solution. The delay time is a variable, but in the initial version one year was assumed as the time required to implement the facility after the decision to locate. The in-process constraint variables were then updated and if the limits were not reached and service is still deficient, the add routine is repeated.

After processing the add routine using RLISTAD, the delete list RLISTDL is checked to determine the greatest deviation from the upper limit to attempt deletion of a DC. If no region was above the upper limit, RLISTDL was empty and control was returned to the Monitor and Control Quarterly activity.

Given that the region was above the upper limit of the base or desired SMF, the control, after processing the add routine in RLISTAD, was transferred to the delete routine. The first activity of the delete routine reviewed the possibility of endogenous deletion of a DC. This was accomplished by reviewing the list of in-solution DCs in the region. A DC could only be a candidate for deletion if the following conditions were present: the DC was currently in-solution, and the DC was not currently being deleted.

The above process developed the preliminary list of eligible DCs from which the DC with the maximum cost per unit of throughput was selected as the primary candidate for deletion. The transformation for developing the cost per unit was:

DCSTLB (IDC, (IQ-1)) = DCTOTCST (IDC, (IQ-1))
/DCWT (IDC, (IQ-1)),

where:

DCSTLB (IDC, (IQ-1)) = cost per unit of sales for DC (IDC) for the previous quarter IQ-1;

DCTOTCST (IDC, (IQ-1)) = total cost for DC (IDC) for the previous quarter IQ-1;

DCWT (IDC, (IQ-1)) = total units moved through the DC (IDC) for the previous quarter IQ-1.

The DC with the highest cost per unit for the region is then selected for possible deletion. The next activity in the delete routine checks to determine if the DC has been in-solution at least the required period of time, which is a variable that can be set to zero or any finite number of quarters. If not, the DC is not eligible for deletion, and the region is eliminated from further consideration.

If the DC has been in-solution long enough, the deletion is scheduled allowing a delay time required to take the facility out of service. The in-process constraint variables are then updated, and if the limits are not reached and service is still higher than desired the delete routine is repeated.

Once the add and delete routines are processed, control is returned to the Monitor and Control Subsystem to process additional quarterly activities.

The last algorithm included in the review section uses an information feedback control loop to expand in-solution DCs. The algorithm EXPAND, developed similarly in logic to the LOCATE algorithm, consists of the following routines:

1. review of domestic constraints
2. review of regional decision rules
3. process of list of regions to select region for PD system change
4. process list of DCs to select the DC(s) to be expanded
5. implement DC expansion

The first routine reviews the domestic constraints to determine if any expansion can take place. If not, the EXPAND algorithm is bypassed and control is returned to the Monitor and Control to continue quarterly activities. The domestic and regional constraints for expansion are essentially the same in-process and in-solution variables as previously presented for the add and delete routines.

The need for expansion of each DC is based on the ratio of current sales processed to capacity relative to a specified base ratio, LMTRATIO, which is set as a management parameter in the exogenous input. A DC is defined as requiring expansion if, and only if, the actual ratio is greater than or equal to the limit ratio, LMTRATIO. Each DC at or above the limit ratio is then entered in a list RLISTEX as a DC designated for expansion. The DC with the largest sales to capacity ratio above the limit ratio is then selected and scheduled for expansion after a delay time for the implementation.

The domestic and regional in-process and in-solution constraint variables are then updated. If other DCs require expansion, and if the constraint levels are not reached, additional DCs are selected and scheduled for expansion. After processing of the EXPAND algorithm, control is returned to process additional quarterly activities.

An additional set of control routines is required to implement any exogenously or endogenously scheduled activities for changing the physical distribution systems. These routines implement the distribution center additions, deletions, and expansions in the appropriate quarter after the delay time has elapsed.

The Monitor and Control Subsystem performs the supervisory and controller functions. In reporting the Monitor and Control Subsystem, the controller function received the primary emphasis because the controller provides, via information feedback control loops, the dynamic aspects of the model which enable the consideration of the sequential decision problem.

The four subsystems presented above represent the Operating System of the LREPS simulation model. At this point the reader has been introduced to the input data and analyses requirements via the Supporting Data System, and the transformations via the Operating System. Next, the Report Generator System is described with emphasis on the desired output information content and format for the initial LREPS model.

Report Generator System

The third and final stage of the LREPS model is the Report Generator System. The Report Generator System (RPG) has the task of preparing meaningful managerial reports using the output data from the LREPS simulation runs. Three essential tasks were associated with the development of this system. These tasks were:

1. the development of the data base of information from which the reports can be prepared;
2. the determination of the level of analytical sophistication at which this system will analyze, prepare, and present model results;
3. the determination of the format, content, and frequency of the reports which present the desired information.

These three related tasks were important considering the possibly large amount of information that can be required for and generated by a model spanning a ten-year planning horizon.

RPG Development Tasks

In relation to task number one, the development of the data base of information includes the specification of information that is both essential to the running of the system model, such as the number and location of active distribution centers, and information that is descriptive in nature and not essential to the running of the model. Such items of information as product names or distribution center names are needed only in the preparation of reports. These items can be inputted directly from the model's Supporting Data System and need not be processed in the model's Operating System.

Also related to the first task was the determination of the level of aggregation of the information that is outputted from the model's Operating System. The problem of determining the level of aggregation can be viewed from at least two perspectives. From a spatial perspective, one must be concerned with the stage of the distribution system at which information is agglomerated and retained. For instance, in a model of this nature is it necessary to retain all measures of sales information at control units of demand or only at the distribution center or regional levels of demand?

Related to the temporal perspective is the timing or frequency with which information is outputted from the model's Operating System, status variables reinitialized, and further accumulations of information over the planning horizon continued. The essential question is concerned with the level of detail that is deemed necessary to answer the strategical questions posed for distribution analysis.

One last activity related to the first task was determining the medium for storing the output of the model's operating and supporting data systems. To do further analysis of the model output without having to execute the complete LREPS system model from the beginning can provide significant savings in computer processing times and costs plus possibly speeding up the process of developing managerial reports. This last activity required that the data be retained on magnetic tape or some other such storage medium at the lowest practical level of spatial and temporal detail without putting undue requirements upon storage space and costs.

The second task involved the level of analytical sophistication at which the results of the system model are analyzed in the Report Generator System. A. Amstutz discusses eight levels of sophistication beginning with the mere retrieval and display of a specified record of information from one tested, alternative distribution plan, and progressing to highly sophisticated systems that include algorithms for evaluating alternative parameter settings or model structures in relation to the assumed or actual base environment data. A brief description of his eight levels of analytical sophistication follows:

1. Retrieval—retrieving a specified record of information and displaying it
2. Aggregation—gathering numbers from one or more records to produce a total or subtotal
3. Arithmetic Operations—arithmetic averaging or computation of differences
4. Logical Analysis—use of classification schemes through which data are aggregated within subsets or conditionally segmented
5. Statistical Estimation—use of statistical techniques to develop extrapolations from historic data, statistical best estimates, analyses of variance, or trend estimates
6. Macro-Process Models—use of models to relate multiple factors in the decision environment to current or expected future conditions
7. Behavioral Simulation—use of simulation to produce an artificial environment paralleling the real-world environment monitored by the information system
8. Adaptive Heuristics—use of highly sophisticated information systems designed to evaluate alternative parameter settings or model structures against data from the monitored environment.[27]

These last levels of sophistication would begin to analyze the results of many alternative distribution plans, or what could be classified as multicycle or multidistribution plan analyses.

The approach utilized in the development of LREPS managerial reports has been evolutionary in nature. Reports concerning single cycles or distribution plans that include the first three or four levels of analytical sophistication listed by Amstutz were initially developed. At first, the most automated type of analysis will possibly include the use of discounting or present-value techniques. Further analysis of many single-cycle reports will be done manually.

Later with experience or analyzing the outputs of several distribution plans, more sophisticated systems for multicycle analysis will be developed. Analytic behavioral models that will allow distribution managers the flexibility of direct interaction with the LREPS system model will also be developed.

The last task in the development of the Report Generator System was the determination of the content of the desired managerial reports, the frequency with which the output of the system model is aggregated and presented, and the format of the reports.

Report content is related to and limited by the level of analytical sophistication developed in the second task. Report content should essentially, however, include operational information, similar to the information presented in profit and loss statements, based upon spatial and temporal aggregations of model output. Reports should also contain status-oriented information that identifies the levels of status variables, such as the levels of inventories and the number of remote distribution centers at certain points in time. The purpose of status-oriented information is to aid in the evaluation of the distribution system configuration that was in effect over a certain period of time. This information is very similar to balance sheet information.

Related to status-oriented information is information recording the specifications of management-decision parameters. In order to be able to identify the particular distribution system that was being tested, this last type of information can be very important when comparing the results of several distribution plans. Flexibility in distribution planning is closely related to an analysis of this last type of recorded information.

Included in task three is the activity of preparing reports for different levels of temporal aggregation. Daily, weekly, monthly, quarterly, annual, or cyclic reports could be prepared dependent upon the problems to be solved. Reports for strategic purposes would generally cover long periods of output information. For aiding in the solution of tactical or operational problems, reports covering smaller intervals of time would most likely be more useful than longer reporting periods. The data for shorter periods of time would generally contain more detail and variability, which is needed to solve short-range tactical problems.

One additional consideration involved in the determination of the level of temporal aggregation is the level of management or supervision that will be examining the results of the system model. Top management would generally be more interested in higher levels of aggregation—only going to more detailed spatial and temporal reports on an exception basis. Thus, highly aggregated reports could be initially prepared and then more detailed reports prepared on a request basis.

The last consideration involved in the actual preparation of model reports is the format of the data. Model output should be presented in a form that does not overload the analyst or manager examining the reports. Instead of designing reports that include thirty pieces of information on one page, reports can be designed that group similar types of information on one page. For instance, instead of having all measures of cost, sales, and customer service by distribution center on one page, each of these categories of information could be put on separate pages. Thus, the analyst can focus his attention on one type of information without confusion.

Another factor involved in report design was the presentation of a smaller number of measures of certain types of information for more highly aggregated levels of reports. Annual reports could, for example, contain only one measure of sales information, while monthly or quarterly reports could contain many measures of sales.

This concludes the discussion of the approach used to develop the Report Generator System. The next section presents the report design requirements.

Management Report Design Requirements

In this section the requirements of the managerial reports are presented in terms of output information content, output information frequency, and output information formats.

Output Information Content

The content includes the following types of information: operational, status, sensitivity analysis and validation, and flexibility-robustness. The operating reports, similar to the profit and loss statement, are required to provide information related to the activity level of the model entities over the reporting period(s). Examples of the LREPS operating information required for management decision making and researcher experimentation include:

1. DU level
   a. sales dollars for the period
   b. sales weight for the period
2. DC level
   a. cost—total and PD component costs for transportation, throughput, communications, facility investment, and inventory
   b. sales—dollars, weight, cube, cases, lines, and orders
   c. service—customer order cycle, backorder time, outbound transportation time
   d. inventory- average inventory-on-hand, number of stockouts, number of reorders, backorders, and stockout delay
3. total PD system
   a. costs—discounted and end-of-planning horizon totals
   b. sales—discounted and end-of-planning horizon totals
   c. service time—averages and variances for planning horizon both regional and national
   d. status data—average investment
   e. flexibility—investment and robustness

The status reports, similar to balance sheets, were required to provide information related to the system state or status of the physical distribution network profile, market profile, product profile, and competitive profile at the end of the reporting period. Examples of the LREPS status information required for management decision making and researcher experimentation included:

1. DU level
   a. weighted index
   b. DC assignment
2. DC level
   a. number of DUs served
   b. list of DUs served
   c. inventory-on-hand
   d. accumulated weighted index
   e. dollar size capacity
   f. sales modification factor

3. total system
    a. number and list of DUs per region
    b. number and list in-solution in each region
    c. number and list of DCs in-process of addition in each region
    d. number and list of PDCs in each region
    e. number and list of DCs in-process of deletion in each region
    f. number of tracked products and their characteristics

The LREPS information requirements for validation and sensitivity analysis are presented in more detail in chapters 6 and 7. Validation analysis requires information output that enables the determination of the stability of the model and reasonableness of the model results. In general, sensitivity analysis requires information output that provides the capability for determining the effect on the target variables of sales, cost, service, and flexibility for various levels of the factors presented in chapter 2, figure 2-3.

The concept of flexibility or robustness developed for the LREPS model relates to the robustness score, which, for example, can be defined as the ratio of the number of occurrences of a given potential DC location, among the set of good systems, to the number of good systems. The robustness measures developed for the initial LREPS version include:

1. ratio of quarters a DC was in-solution to the total quarters simulated for one planning horizon, assuming most probable factor levels;
2. ratio of quarters a DC was in-solution to the total quarters simulated for a set of planning horizon cycles assuming most probable factor levels;
3. the ratios of number 1 and 2 above combining the three factor levels for sales: pessimistic, most probable, and optimistic.

The primary use of the Flexibility-Robustness Ratios is to improve decision making under uncertainty. For example, a DC location or subset of locations that has a relatively high ratio for Flexibility-Robustness measure number 3, which combines three factor levels, should result in a more flexible physical distribution system than a DC location which has a high ratio for only one level.

Output Information Frequency

The definition of the reporting period(s) was an important factor in the development of the Report Generator System. The smallest unit of time and thus the most frequent reporting period possible in the LREPS model is the day. The largest unit of time and thus the longest reporting period is the total planning horizon. In designing the LREPS model, especially the Measurement Subsystem and the Monitor and Control Subsystem, primary emphasis was placed on the management information requirements for decision making. The primary objective of the LREPS model is for strategic planning rather than operating or tactical decision making. The reporting of daily, weekly, or monthly totals was therefore not considered to be of primary importance. The quarterly and longer operating periods were believed to be the most useful in terms of relevant information for strategic planning and decision making. As the full capabilities of the LREPS model are explored, generation of information for additional operating periods such as for the day and/or week for given intervals of time within a simulation cycle could prove useful for analysis of the dynamics of inventory management.

Output Information Formats

There were an infinite number of report formats that could have been designed for the initial version of LREPS. The basic types of managerial reports developed were: Summary Reports and Distribution Center Detail Reports. The format and information content of each of the individual types of reports are presented as Appendix 3.[28]

SUMMARY

The tasks described in the above section—Report Generator System—were required to develop the data base and the initial report formats for the LREPS model. Chapter 4 in total has attempted to present an abbreviated version of the mathematical model with discussions of the three major systems: Supporting Data, Operating, and Report Generator. The next step reported in the design process is the development of the operational computer model, chapter 5.

5

LREPS: COMPUTER MODEL

Following development of the mathematical model, the next general step in LREPS design was computer operationalization.[1] The process of computerizing a model as encompassing as LREPS is a major undertaking. In a sense, achieving an operational computer model is a critical point in project development since many models have been developed from a conceptual and mathematical perspective only never to be computerized and practically utilized. In this chapter, the overall philosophy and procedure that guided successful computerization of seven versions of the LREPS mathematical model is reported. The chapter consists of three major sections: the design approach, the computer model, and operationalizing LREPS. The first section presents the design criteria and methodology, followed by a discussion of the procedure used to select the computer language for LREPS. The second section presents an overview of the computer model flowcharts and system linkages. The final section discusses the procedure of operationalizing LREPS by implementing seven versions of LREPS. In this section the resultant computer model is evaluated in terms of the design criteria and preliminary validation is presented.

DESIGN APPROACH: COMPUTER MODEL

The mathematical model served as basic input for the computerization process. Mathematical model results emphasized the definition related to: (1) system boundaries and assumptions, (2) model general inputs and outputs, (3) mathematical transformations or operating characteristics among inputs and outputs, (4) constraints on inputs, outputs, and system configuration, (5) measurement bases for evaluating alternative distribution systems, (6) management decision parameters that serve as the basis for calibrating the initial LREPS model, (7) estimation of parameter values via initial data collection and analysis, and (8) preliminary evaluation of model validity.

The general computerization problem with respect to the mathematical model was to develop a model that: satisfied the needs and specifications of the abstract model, was valid, specified data-base requirements, and functioned within the constraints of the overall computerization process.

Design Requirements

In planning the computerization of LREPS, design criteria were established to provide constraints as well as general guidelines for the computerization process. These design requirements included:

1. the selection of the appropriate programming language
2. the use of subprograms or modules
3. the use of hardware and software features to facilitate generation of new versions of LREPS
4. the use of hardware and software features to produce efficient processing of the great amount of information required for a ten-year planning horizon
5. the development of efficient report generator programs
6. the compatibility of the model among different computer operating systems
7. the feasibility of running the model on medium-size computer operating systems
8. the feasibility of a computer program of the main operating system of LREPS that will:
    a. cycle through a ten-year planning horizon within a total elapsed computer time of thirty minutes
    b. fit within a computer memory limitation of 36K decimal words
    c. require no more than three input/output files

Each of these design considerations contributed to the development of the design methodology as presented in the following section. In the final section of this chapter the LREPS computer model is evaluated with respect to each of these design requirements.

Design Methodology

Based on the above design considerations, the following five-step methodology was established to guide computerization:

1. specify the data base
2. select the programming language
3. segregate and program the activities
4. combine the subprograms
5. test and debug the combined subsystems

In the following paragraphs brief comments are presented concerning each step of the design methodology. The remainder of this section is concerned with the evaluation and selection of a program language.

Specification of the computer system model's data base is based on the mathematical model specifications and the broad system flow charts. The selection of the predominant computer programming language for the simulator was made from general compiler languages such as FORTRAN, ALGOL, and from simulation languages such as GASP, FORDYN, and SIMSCRIPT. A set of criteria for selecting the predominant language was developed to make this decision.

The activities and their respective data-base requirements were segregated and programmed according to the three main sections of the model: (1) the Supporting Data System, which was primarily developed for collection, preparation, and reduction of data inputs to the LREPS Operating System, (2) the Operating System programs, which were those programs and activities directly involved in the LREPS simulator, and (3) the Report Generator System programs for the development of the reports containing the model's results.

The procedure followed for each LREPS subprogram was as follows:

1. Identify the respective system model activities within the program.
2. Identify the information flowing in and out of the subprogram plus any key endogenous variables.

3. Block diagram the basic, logical steps for generating the program's outputs after considering alternative computer systems and programming techniques.
4. Code the program using the most appropriate computer programming language(s).
5. Test and debug the program using a test case that had been developed.
6. Present any computerization problems, and any peculiar or unique programming techniques.

The next step of the methodology consisted of combining the subprograms and their respective inputs, outputs, and data-base requirements and making any necessary revisions. The final step was to test and debug the combined subsystem models to operationalize and calibrate the LREPS model. The Operating System was operationalized and calibrated by subsystem versions.

The above methodology required feedback at each level of development as more detailed and concrete system characteristics were formulated. Since the selection of an appropriate computer language is a critical factor, the remainder of this section reviews selection criteria, evaluation of alternatives, and the basis for selection of GASP IIA as the programming language for LREPS.

LREPS Programming Language

The purpose of this section is to discuss the selection of GASP IIA as the predominant language used in programming LREPS. Predominance is stressed because supplemental programming languages in addition to GASP IIA were utilized in the total computer model.

The literature is abundant with articles comparing and evaluating alternative programming languages. Naylor et al. state:

> Clearly one way to approach programming simulation experiments is to write a special program for simulating each system to be studied in one of the well-known, general-purpose languages such as FORTRAN, ALGOL, COBOL, or IBM's PL/I. To be sure, this alternative offers the programmer maximum flexibility in (1) the design and formulation of the mathematical model of the system being studied, (2) the type and format of output reports generated, and (3) the kinds of simulation experiments performed with the model.[2]

In models similar to LREPS, difficulty is often encountered in trying to write routines to step the model through simulated time. To assist in overcoming such difficulties, simulation programming languages have been developed. These simulation languages serve essentially three vital purposes: to reduce the programming task, to provide conceptual guidance, and to allow flexibility for change. Essentially a simulation package consists of a programming language and "runtime" routines.

After reviewing significant literature concerning available programming languages and their applicability to simulation, criteria for selecting the most appropriate language for LREPS was developed.

Language Selection Criteria

The criteria used to evaluate and compare languages are listed in figure 5-1. These ten criteria were used to reduce the potential predominant programming languages to a choice between four. The alternatives evaluated were the general purpose language FORTRAN and simulation languages GPSS, SIMSCRIPT, and GASP II.

The first criterion in figure 5-1 refers to the structure of the programming language and how it lends assistance in getting the system model computerized. Specifically, the language must be compatible with the type of system model. For example, system models can be

Figure 5–1
Criteria for Selecting Predominant
Computer Programming Language

1. Programming language structure
2. Level of required programming skill
3. Ease of converting logical block diagrams to computer program
4. Simulation procedures associated with
    A. Initial values
    B. Data generation and manipulation
    C. Time flow mechanisms
    D. Output assistance
    E. Stacking of a series of cycles
5. Debugging and error assistance offered by language
6. Computer costs of compilation and execution
7. Compatibility of language among different computer operating systems
8. Availability of computer hardware
9. Ease of changing system modules
10. Applications of language to date

developed as either continuous-change or discrete-change models. The computer language selected must be compatible with this selection.[3, 4] In regard to selecting the language, the available conceptual guidance provided for computerizing and development of the system model must be considered. This concept is stressed by several authors who emphasize the overlap in mathematical modeling and formulation of the computer model.[5, 6] Associated with conceptual guidance, several authors have commented on the assistance provided in getting a simulation model computerized via written subroutines to produce the model's activities.[7, 8, 9] A final point is the flexibility and ease of use of the language. H. S. Krasnow and R. A. Merikallio mention the flexibility and range of using simulation languages considering simulator-defined concepts, user-defined concepts, and concepts and values defined at the start of the simulation and during the simulation.[10]

The second criterion concerns the level of programming skill required. This criterion is essentially concerned with: the availability of experienced programming skill, the cost, and the ease of learning the language.[11, 12] In addition, one of the biggest problems with using many simulation languages is the lack of adequate documentation and instructional material.[13]

The third criterion cuts across the mathematical modeling and computerization tasks. It is concerned with the ease of converting logical block diagrams to computer programs. Some of the languages offer special flowcharting symbols that help in systemizing the model plus leading directly to model computerization.[14, 15] One problem that frequently arises is that the flowcharting symbols are not consistent among languages. Thus, this aspect promotes inflexibility in the use of different languages.

The fourth criterion is concerned with some of the special features of the language in accomplishing more or less menial tasks in programming. Given the system model and desired outputs, simulation languages offer assistance in initializing values and arrays,[16] data-generation routines,[17, 18] data-manipulation operations,[19] output assistance,[20, 21, 22, 23] and stacking of a series of cycles through a simulation computer model.[24, 25] Krasnow has a good discussion of these simulation procedures in his article.[26] Krasnow and Merikallio even talk of the man-machine interaction during simulation that some languages are beginning to offer.[27]

The next criterion deals with the debugging and error assistance offered by the language. In getting the model to execute, many of the languages have tracing routines to help one know where he is in a simulation either at the time of errors or change in simulated time.[28, 29, 30] They can be very helpful given that the supporting instructional material clearly states just how to use these features. All the languages provide the normal diagnostics for errors associated with programming rules.

The sixth criterion concerns the computer cost for compilation and execution. The efficiency of a computer run is concerned not only with execution time but also the time that it takes to get the program compiled into a machine language program. Also involved in the programming of the model are the size and the type of data structures that are available with the use of a programming language. Data structure types include simple variables, arrays, and packed variables.[31, 32] If a simulation model is input/output bound, the capability of multiprogramming execution can also be very important in reducing computer costs.

The seventh criterion is concerned with the compatibility of the language among different computer operating systems. A computer operating system is defined as that combination of computer hardware and software that approaches the optimum use of a particular computer. Given the operating systems that are available on different sizes and makes of computers, one can be restricted by not only the available computer systems but also the compiler requirements on the system.[33] In addition, the reliability of the compiler must be considered. A compiler may be available but never effectively tested and utilized.

The eighth criterion concerns the availability and cost of computer hardware itself. Some languages are just not available on certain machines.[34, 35] This criterion is also concerned with the availability and use of auxiliary equipment such as disk or tape files.[36] Massive amounts of information may require disk or tape files.

The ninth criterion concerns ease of changing the model system.[37] Although general-purpose languages allow one to model a system in more detail, they cut down on the flexibility and ease of system changes. Simulation languages promote this type of system flexibility.

The final and very important criterion for evaluating alternatives is the past record of language applications.[38]

The LREPS system model was designed to be universal in nature with a high degree of flexibility in processing system entities or objects. Primary emphasis in model design was the easy adaptation of the model to a large class of multiproduct, multiechelon, consumer, and industrial firms. In serving these classes of potential users, the purposes of the system model were conceptualized as both lending direction in the strategic design and testing tactical or detailed procedures for day-to-day operations of alternative physical distribution system configurations.

Given the desire for universal applicability and for serving the general purposes specified above, the ability to process alternative combinations of system entities and dynamically change system state over simulated time was necessary. An example list of system entities includes: (1) demand units for potential agglomerated customer demand, (2) customer classes of trade, (3) tracked-product items, (4) customer orders, (5) dispatched customer orders from demand units to distribution centers, (6) full- or partial-line distribution centers for processing customer orders, (7) dispatched customer shipments from distribution centers to demand units, (8) customer backorders resulting from product stockouts at distribution centers, (9) multiproduct reorders from distribution centers to supplying replenishment centers, (10) multireorder, dispatched shipments from replenishment centers to distribution centers, (11) potential distribution center locations, (12) manufacturing control centers for replenishing product inventories of replenishment centers, (13) inventory categories for grouping similar tracked products, and (14) market regions to allow for variations in regional customer demand and service requirements.

Procedures for processing system entities, either singularly or in combination, were conceptualized on a discrete-change, event basis. Preliminary analysis indicated that detailed modeling procedures were necessary to: (1) randomly allocate daily customer orders to a subset of all demand units; (2) dispatch customer shipments either on a daily basis or in consolidated shipments on greater than a daily basis; (3) process reorders dispatched from distribution centers to replenishment centers, triggered by varying inventory control values and occurring on an intermittent basis; and (4) dispatch shipments from manufacturing control centers to distribution centers on an intermittent basis which varied with the accumulated amount of product on reorder plus other time-oriented, shipment-dispatch policies. The use of discrete-change, event-processing programming languages was considered most appropriate for the task confronted.

The discrete-change events were conceptualized as occurring at a fixed time or randomly as conditions in the model dictated. Events were also conceptualized as being processed chronologically and on a first-in, first-out (FIFO) basis. The designed events could then be processed on a detailed day-to-day or week-to-week basis dependent upon the conditions specified in the event subprograms and model input.

Since system entities were conceptualized as being processed in discrete-event activities, programming systems for processing continuous-change, simulation models were excluded from serious consideration. The excluded computer systems included analog systems that treat the processing of system entities on a continuous-flow basis, and digital systems that process system entities as continuous-flow rates on a discrete-change basis. The use of such programming systems requires that system entities be treated on a macro or aggregative basis rather than on an individual basis as conceptualized in the LREPS system model. If system processing procedures had been conceptualized on a macro basis, then continuous-change simulation languages would have been seriously considered.

Considering the above factors and programming languages that were reasonably available to Michigan State University, and which could process discrete events on both a fixed- and/or variable-time basis, FORTRAN, GPSS, SIMSCRIPT, and GASP were evaluated in terms of the selection criteria in figure 5-1.

Selection of Language: GASP IIA

In consideration of the alternatives, GASP IIA was selected. The IIA level of GASP incorporates integer attributes for data filing and also floating point or real attributes.[39] Given that the system model is discrete oriented, any of the alternative languages could have been used. FORTRAN alone was ruled out because of the greater assistance available from SIMSCRIPT and GASP. GPSS was eliminated on the basis of execution speed. Considering the higher-level languages, SIMSCRIPT received the edge over GASP IIA because of its variable-time orientation toward the execution of the model's activities. SIMSCRIPT was also appealing from the standpoint of its efficient utilization of core memory considering the large amounts of information that were to be handled.

All three languages offered assistance in simulation procedures associated with initial values, data generation and manipulation, time-flow mechanisms, output assistance, and stacking of a series of cycles. The languages also assisted in debugging and error tracing. These attractive aspects of simulation languages again supported the decision not to program the model in FORTRAN alone.[1]

There were tradeoffs back and forth between the languages concerning computer costs of compilation and execution. All of the languages have facilitating features for changing the system model, although GPSS and SIMSCRIPT have the advantage over GASP. SIMSCRIPT has a very important advantage over both GASP and GPSS in report generation because of its flexible report generator.

Three main factors concerning the use of SIMSCRIPT were questionable. The first factor was the lack of an available reliable compiler and good instructional material for SIMSCRIPT 1.5. The second factor, related to the first, was the lack of an available compiler for SIMSCRIPT II, the latest and most sophisticated version.[40] The last, and perhaps most important factor, was the very limited supply of personnel knowledgeable in the use of SIMSCRIPT.

The final decision to use GASP IIA was based on six factors:

1. the high compatibility of the FORTRAN-based, simulation language among computer operating systems. The latest, most powerful versions of GPSS and SIMSCRIPT only have compilers for International Business Machines (IBM) computers;
2. the minimization of the cost of using the model in different geographic locations if the model could be designed to be compatible among different computer operating systems;
3. the good familiarity of the LREPS project team with the general-purpose programming language FORTRAN;
4. the ready availability of sophisticated FORTRAN programming personnel;
5. the ready availability of MSU's research computer center to operationalize LREPS;
6. GASP was the only discrete-event simulation language operational on MSU's CDC 6500. If SIMSCRIPT II had been operational at MSU, then it would have received major consideration as the predominant computer programming language.

COMPUTER MODEL

After the system was mathematically modeled, the computerization required a general overview of how to interrelate all the described activities. The essential goal in programming the model was to process data with the least possible redundant operations. This goal was especially critical when considering the large amounts of information that would be manipulated. In line with these desires, figure 5-2 was developed to conceptually direct the overall computerization of LREPS.

As viewed in figure 5-2, much of the data needed within the operating system of LREPS was prepared off-line in the Supporting Data System. These off-line data were read into the Operating System as exogenous inputs at specified periods of time. Also supplementary or identifying information not needed in the Operating System was sent directly to the Report Generator System.

In developing this manipulation concept, a total-system data base had to be defined. The total data base included all the information that was needed in the system in order to develop and analyze the results of simulation cycles. This data base was further segregated into two classes. The first class of data was the common data base required within the operating system of LREPS that was to be shared among, between, or used individually by the major subsystems of the model Operating System. This first class of information, the data base, is listed in appendix 1. The other class of information was the supplementary data needed by the Report Generator System to prepare the managerial reports.

By examining the Operating System's common data base in appendix 1, it is noted that the data were classified as to type of data, how often they were changed, whether it was an endogenous or exogenous change, what subsystem altered or set the data, what subsystem used the data and the mode of the data. The mode was used to classify the data as integer, real, or packed information.

After the Operating System's common data base was developed, a control problem concerning the inflow of exogenous inputs at specified time intervals was confronted. It was desirable not to have each major subsystem of the Operating System inputting its own information. Therefore, interface nodes between the Operating System and the two other computer systems were identified. An interface is defined as the nodal point in data flow where two major computer sys-

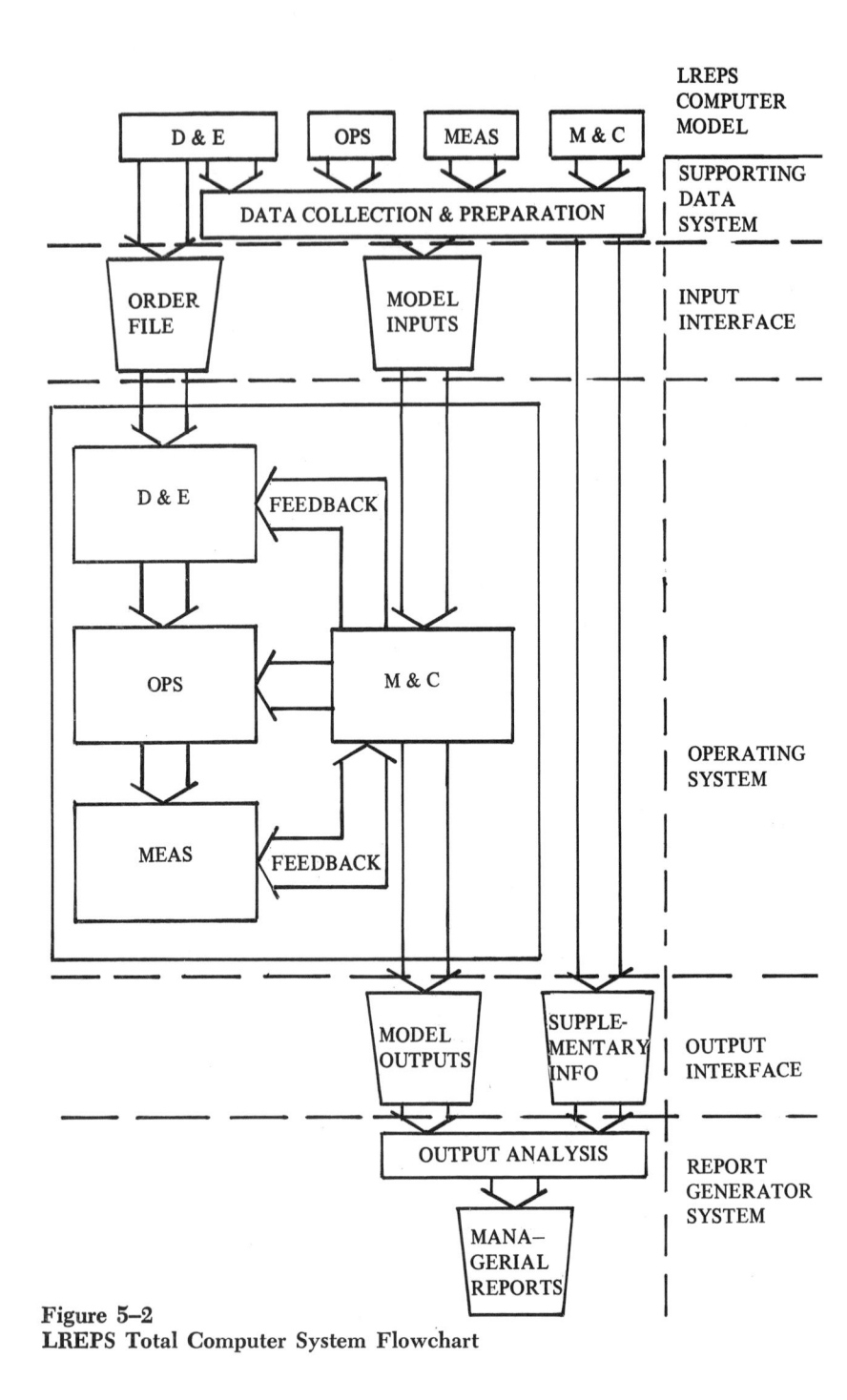

Figure 5-2
LREPS Total Computer System Flowchart

tems interact. The input interface consists of two parts. The first part is the order file. Because of the large amounts of information related to individual customer orders, orders were generated off-line in the Demand and Environment Supporting Data System and read in as a separate file. The other part of the Operating System's inputs is a file containing the remaining exogenous inputs.

The file of exogenous inputs was designed to agglomerate all of the model's subsystem inputs into one file that would be inputted into the Monitor and Control Subsystem. The Monitor and Control Subsystem was structured as the gatekeeper responsible for controlling the flow of exogenous inputs into the Operating System's common data base.

Figure 5-3 illustrates in more detail the Supporting Data System program to collect and prepare the exogenous inputs for each specified time period. This program is directly related to a catalogued or segmented data base and provides a convenient method for preparing and controlling the inputs into the Operating System. Figure 5-4 illustrates the Operating System's interaction not only with the input interface but also the output interface.

As figures 5-2 and 5-4 illustrate, the Monitor and Control Subsystem was conceptualized as the gatekeeper controlling the outflow of information from the Operating System. The Monitor and Control Subsystem basically wrote an output interface containing run control information, specific distribution center information, and the common data base for processing by the Report Generator System.

Figure 5-5 illustrates the activities of the Report Generator System in processing not only the Operating System's output but also the supplementary information sent, provided direct by the Supporting Data System. Both cyclic and multicyclic reports are conceptualized as being prepared in this computer system.

System Linkages

Figure 5-6 illustrates the linkages between the major subprograms of the LREPS Operating System and the model's major subsystems. The subprograms are divided into GASP and non-GASP routines. The non-GASP routines represent the user-written routines that were developed by the LREPS project team. These non-GASP routines are further subdivided on the basis of event activity. For each event activity, the lines below the event subprogram block indicate the

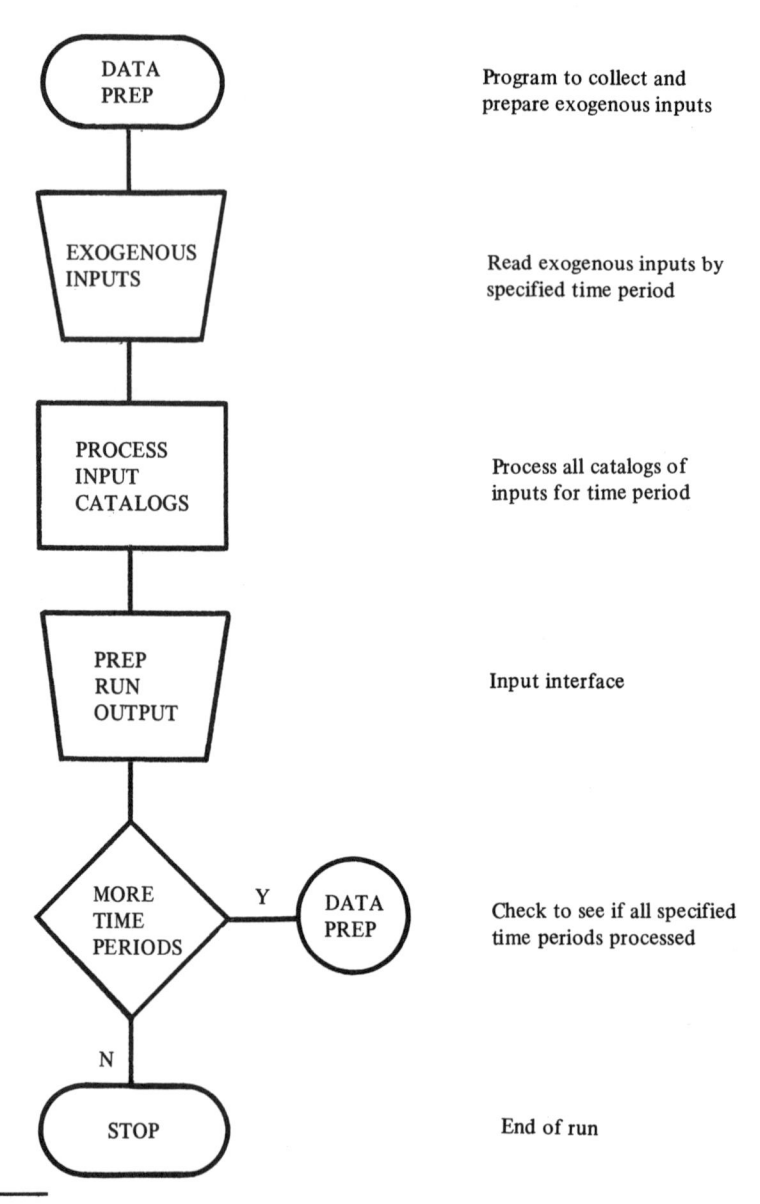

```
   ┌─────────┐
   │  DATA   │        Program to collect and
   │  PREP   │        prepare exogenous inputs
   └────┬────┘
        │
   ╱─────────╲
  ╱ EXOGENOUS ╲       Read exogenous inputs by
  ╲  INPUTS   ╱       specified time period
   ╲─────────╱
        │
   ┌─────────┐
   │ PROCESS │        Process all catalogs of
   │  INPUT  │        inputs for time period
   │CATALOGS │
   └────┬────┘
        │
   ╱─────────╲
  ╱   PREP    ╲       Input interface
  ╲   RUN     ╱
   ╲ OUTPUT  ╱
        │
     ╱MORE╲    Y   ┌──────┐
    ╱ TIME ╲──────▶│ DATA │  Check to see if all specified
    ╲PERIODS╱      │ PREP │  time periods processed
     ╲    ╱       └──────┘
        │ N
   ┌─────────┐
   │  STOP   │        End of run
   └─────────┘
```

SOURCE: E. J. Marien, "Development of a Dynamic Simulation Model for Planning Physical Distribution Systems: Formulation of the Computer Model" (Ph.D. dissertation, Michigan State University, 1970).

Figure 5–3
Exogenous Input Preparation

```
LREPS ─────────────── LREPS Operating system

TIME PERIOD ───────── Process each specified
                      time period

PROCESS INPUTS ────── Process exogenous inputs
                      for time period

END OF PERIOD ─────── End of time period activity

OUTPUT RESULTS ────── Output results from last
                      period's operation

MORE PERIODS? ─Y─ TIME PERIOD     Process all simulated
     │                            time periods
     N

STOP ──────────────── End of run
```

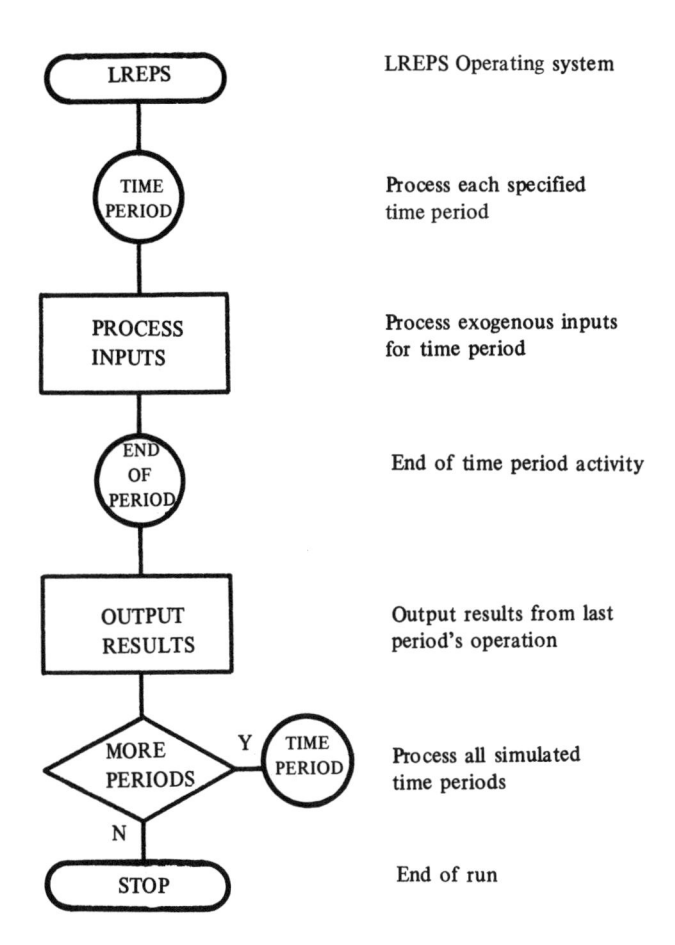

SOURCE: E. J. Marien, "Development of a Dynamic Simulation Model for Planning Physical Distribution Systems: Formulation of the Computer Model" (Ph.D. dissertation, Michigan State University, 1970).

Figure 5–4
Operating System's Interface with Input/Output

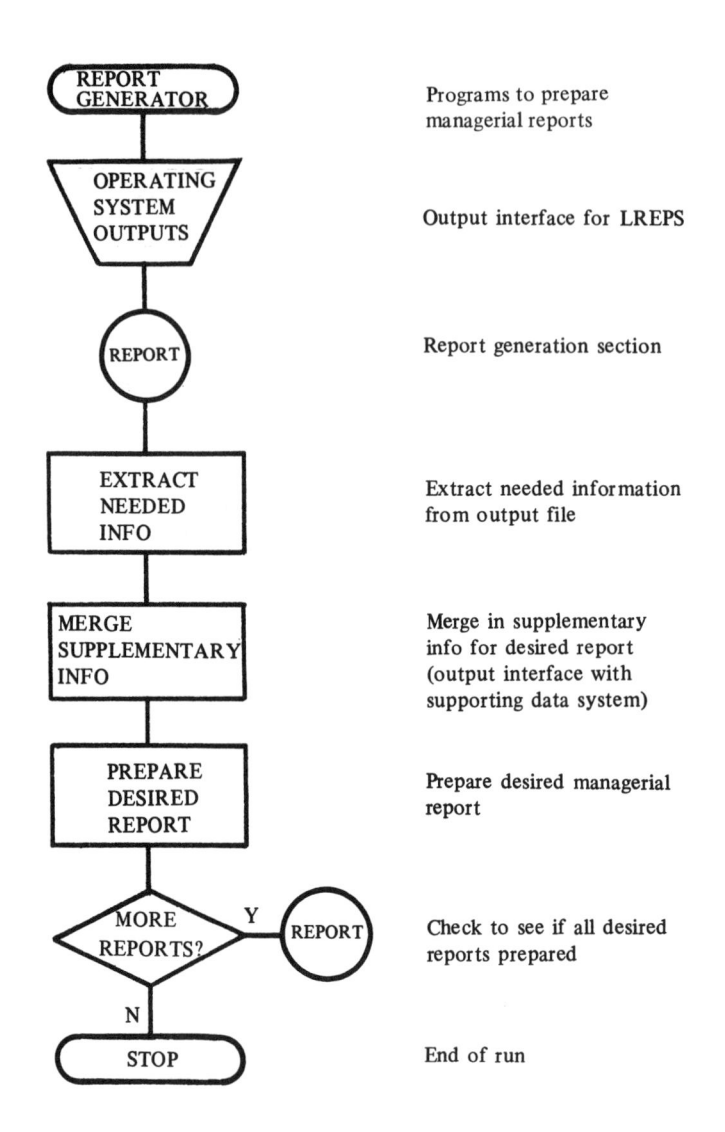

REPORT GENERATOR	Programs to prepare managerial reports
OPERATING SYSTEM OUTPUTS	Output interface for LREPS
REPORT	Report generation section
EXTRACT NEEDED INFO	Extract needed information from output file
MERGE SUPPLEMENTARY INFO	Merge in supplementary info for desired report (output interface with supporting data system)
PREPARE DESIRED REPORT	Prepare desired managerial report
MORE REPORTS? — Y → REPORT	Check to see if all desired reports prepared
N ↓ STOP	End of run

SOURCE: E. J. Marien, "Development of a Dynamic Simulation Model for Planning Physical Distribution Systems: Formulation of the Computer Model" (Ph.D. dissertation, Michigan State University, 1970).

Figure 5-5
Report Generator System

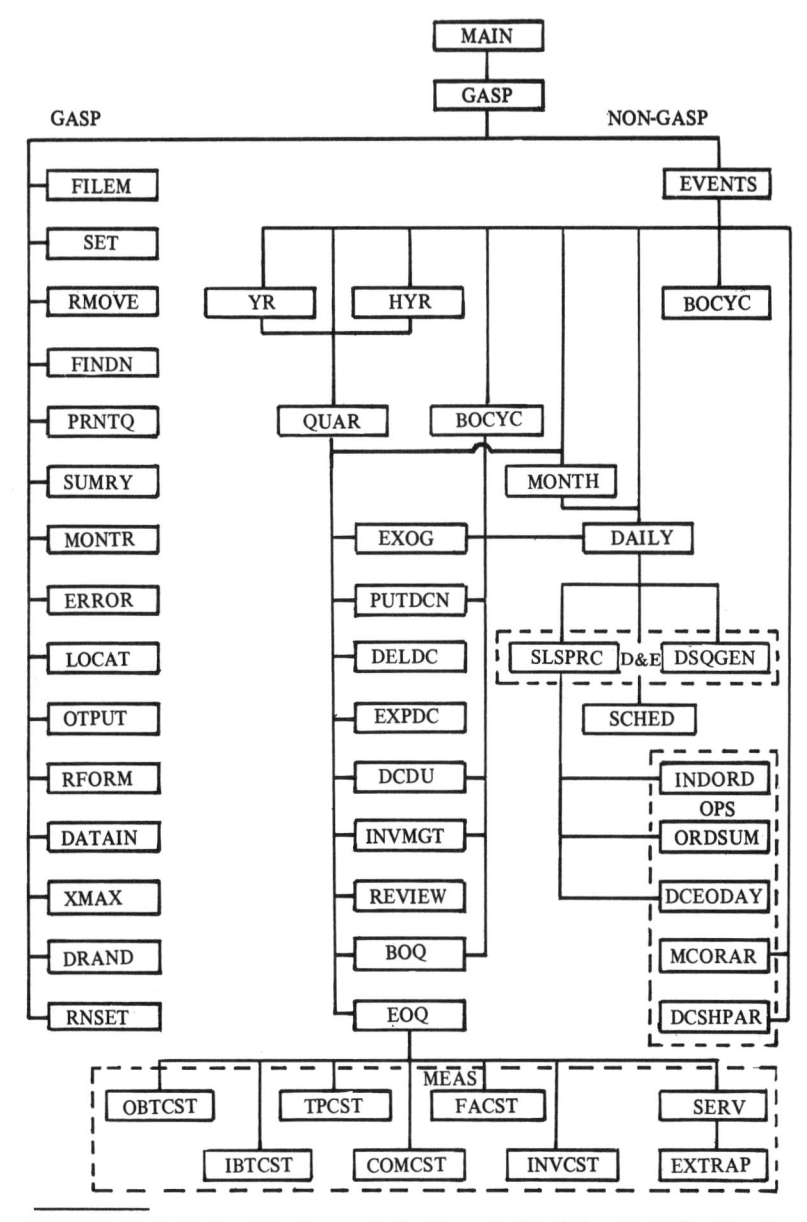

SOURCE: E. J. Marien, "Development of a Dynamic Simulation Model for Planning Physical Distribution Systems: Formulation of the Computer Model" (Ph.D. dissertation, Michigan State University, 1970).

Figure 5–6
LREPS Operating System Linkages

routines to which it is linked. The linkages between the subprogram blocks flow downward, to the right and to the left. The downward orientation signifies that a routine or routines below a certain subprogram block to which they are connected are called by the upper routine during program execution.

Figure 5-6 also serves as an illustration of the connection of the major subsystems in the Operating System. The two subprograms of the Demand and Environment Subsystem are identified in the box outlined with bold dashed lines and labeled "D&E." Below the Demand and Environment subprograms are the Operations Subsystem routines, some of which were called on a fixed-time basis from the Demand and Environment Subprogram SLSPRC and the other two routines called on a variable-time basis from the Monitor and Control EXECUTIVE. At the bottom of figure 5-6 the Measurement Subsystem routines are identified, plus their linkages to the Monitor and Control end-of-quarter subprogram. The remaining subprograms in figure 5-6 are associated with the major sections of the Monitor and Control Subsystem.

Figure 5-6 does not entirely identify all linkages among the Operating System's subprograms. The linkages between some of the user-written subprograms and the GASP subprograms FILEM, which was called by several user-written routines, and FINDN and RMOVE, which were called by the Monitor and Control subprogram DELDC, have not been shown. Also the linkages among the GASP subprograms themselves are not illustrated. The main purpose of figure 5-6 is to identify the entire set of Operating System subprograms, the GASP and non-GASP routines, the linkages among the user-written subprograms, plus the linkages among the Operating Subsystems. A general flowchart of the overall LREPS model is contained in appendix 2.

OPERATIONALIZING LREPS

In developing a computerized model of LREPS, the approach was to serially introduce the operating subsystems. As these subsystems were operationalized, they were merged to form the alternative versions of LREPS. After the four subsystems were operationalized and merged to form the first total LREPS computer model, new versions of LREPS included sophisticated versions of existent subprograms.

LREPS Computer Model

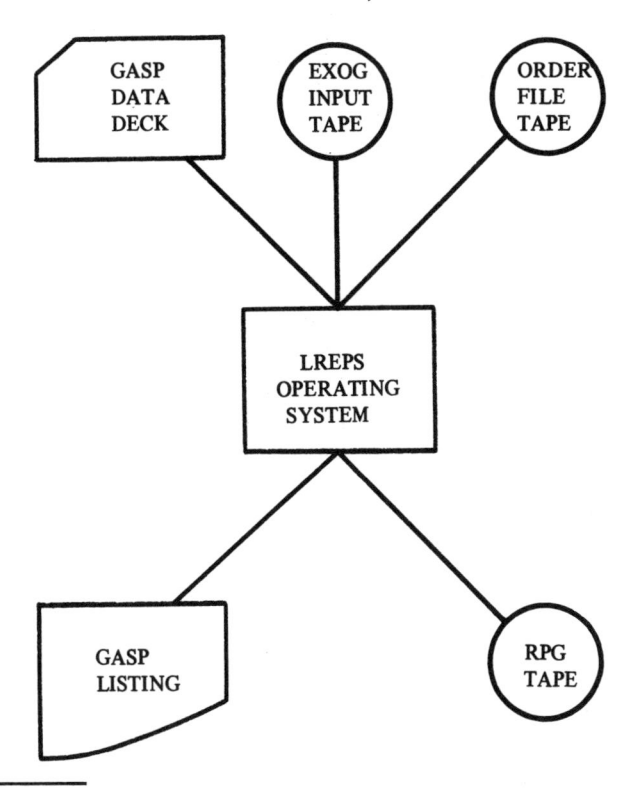

```
    GASP          EXOG          ORDER
    DATA          INPUT         FILE
    DECK          TAPE          TAPE
              \     |      /
               \    |     /
                LREPS
                OPERATING
                SYSTEM
               /         \
              /           \
         GASP              RPG
         LISTING           TAPE
```

SOURCE: E. J. Marien, "Development of a Dynamic Simulation Model for Planning Physical Distribution Systems: Formulation of the Computer Model" (Ph.D. dissertation, Michigan State University, 1970).

Figure 5–7
LREPS Operating System Input/Output Flowchart

In order to operationalize a specific version or level of LREPS, an input-output computer system flowchart of the LREPS operating system was needed. Figure 5-7 shows the flow of information into and out of the LREPS Operating System. The inputs included the GASP card deck of GASP run-control cards and the exogenously set BOCYC and EOCYC events for the GASP filing arrays NSET and QSET. The remaining inputs were the order file and the exogenous input magnetic tapes. The outputs of the program included the GASP run-control listings plus the RPG magnetic tape.

LREPS Versions

Using the approach for computerizing the model plus the input-output system flowchart illustrated in figure 5-7, the objective of the first version of LREPS, LREPS-1, was to operationalize primarily the D&E subsystem. All D&E subsystem Supporting Data and Operating System program routines were programmed. Besides the D&E program routines, the GASP subprograms, plus the user-written routines MAIN, EVENTS, BOCYC, EOCYC, YR, HYR, QUAR, MONTH, DAILY, SCHED; a simple PUTDCN routine to initialize the starting DC configuration; a basic DCDU routine to link the DUs to the starting DCs and to generate their cumulative weighted indices; a basic EOQ routine to output the LREPS data base, EXOG and BOQ, used to initialize the DU and DC data-base variables were developed. Besides operationalizing the Demand and Environment Supporting Data System programs, the Monitor and Control Supporting Data System programs for preparing the exogenous input tape plus the program that packed the feasible DCs per DU were developed.

The primary reason for operationalizing LREPS-1 was to begin experimenting with alternative techniques for processing the customer order file. Use of a tape file would have reduced the Operating System to an input-bound program resulting in excessively long computer execution time to process a simulation cycle. Therefore, LREPS-1 was a critical step in the overall research, since reducing the input time was fundamental to the operationalization of the mathematical model.

The output of LREPS-1 was sales information at the DC and DU stages of the physical distribution network. Sales information was also accumulated at the regional and national levels. This output was printed using the RPG "Variables List" routine.

The purpose of the second version of LREPS, LREPS-2, was to operationalize the merged Demand and Environment and Operations Subsystems. The system flowchart contained in figure 5-7 applied, although more inputs were now added to the EXOG input tape.

The Operations Subsystem computer program subroutines were programmed and added to those routines tested in LREPS-1. At this point several of the routines used to operationalize LREPS-1 were sophisticated. In particular, DCDU was sophisticated to calculate distances and customer-service times. The Monitor and Control Operating System subprograms RWRC, used to calculate the ratio of total to tracked-product weight sales, and a basic INVMGT, used to calculate the inventory control variables, were also added to the LREPS operating system.

LREPS-2 had the capacity to process customer orders through the DCs, generate customer-service times, and effect MCC to DC interactions as a result of customer sales. The outputs were printed using the RPG "Variables List" program. Besides the sales information listed for LREPS-1, LREPS-2 outputted DC inventory information, MCC to DC reorder information, basic customer-service times data, and domestic tracked-product sales information. In addition to the Operations Subsystem Supporting Data System program, the Monitor and Control routine to calculate the DC X and Y rectangular coordinates was operationalized.

The third version of LREPS merged the Measurement Subsystem program routines with LREPS-2. In addition, the Monitor and Control Operating System subprogram EOQ was revised to output not only the LREPS data base but also the quarterly control and DC files of information. The Measurement Supporting Data System cost information was also added to the exogenous input tape in order to determine the measures of cost for the physical distribution system configuration that was initialized at the beginning of cycle and simulated in the LREPS Operating System over the planning horizon. The LREPS-3 computer model could not, however, add or delete DCs or modify the sizes of DCs.

In LREPS-4, the remaining Monitor and Control subprograms were merged with LREPS-3 to develop the first complete version of LREPS. LREPS-4 did not, however, include the LOCATE, EXPAND, and INVMGT routines. Rather, LREPS-4 included a basic LOCATE routine that only allowed the addition of DCs and a modified INVMGT routine that calculated inventory control variables according to the policies being used by the industrial research supporter. The output of this version was the same class of output as developed in LREPS-3. The Supporting Data System inputs were expanded to include the management control parameters and the constraints on allowable physical distribution system changes. All RPG programs were at this point operationalized.

The substitution of the sophisticated LOCATE routine plus the addition of the EXPAND routine were implemented in LREPS-5. LREPS was now capable of adding, deleting, or modifying the DC facility configuration either exogenously on a fixed basis or endogenously on a free basis. With this more sophisticated version of LREPS was the requirement of setting additional constraints on the allowable changes to the physical distribution system configuration.

In LREPS-6 the use of partial-line distribution centers was operationalized. LREPS-7 introduced the theoretical INVMGT routine.

COMPUTER MODEL EVALUATION

This final section focuses on an overall evaluation of the computer model based on the eight design requirements presented at the outset of this chapter.

Evaluation of GASP IIA

In reference to the Operating System, the GASP IIA simulation package satisfied and expedited computerization. The user-defined and simulation-defined concepts provided by this language assisted in the conceptualization of the computer model. The GASP EXECUTIVE routine alleviated the need to design routines to direct the model through simulated time.

In implementing the GASP IIA simulation package on Michigan State University's CDC 6500, a small delay was experienced because some subprograms required minor modifications. Any subprogram that used the pseudo-random number generator DRAND had to be changed to use the pseudo-random number generator, RANF, for the CDC 6500 computer operating system. In addition, the GASP IIA subprograms TMST, COLCT, and OTPUT had not been completely modified for the floating point array, QSET. Although these three GASP IIA subprograms were not used in the LREPS Operating System, they were used in implementing and debugging the GASP IIA simulation package and, therefore, required modification. One other subprogram had to be modified. The GASP IIA subprogram DATAN had to be renamed as DATAIN since the previous name was already used by CDC as the name of the double precision, arc tangent function. In summary, the GASP IIA simulation package was sound even though it required a few minor modifications.

In reference to the Supporting Data and Report Generator Systems, the use of the general compiler language FORTRAN was generally the most appropriate programming language. The primary exception to the use of FORTRAN was the use of the CDC 6500 assembly language, COMPASS, for tape handling. The use of COMPASS for tape handling was necessary since FORTRAN is generally an inefficient language where considerable tape handling is required. The FORTRAN tape handling routines are usually slow; also their use of magnetic tape storage space is inefficient.

In summary, the use of a simulation language, a general compiler language, and an assembly language was necessary to computerize LREPS. The complexities of the system model, the desire for efficiency in program execution and core memory utilization, plus the use of magnetic tapes required the use of all three programming languages.

Model Building Procedures

The use of building blocks as the common basis for many activities facilitated the development of the computer model. In particular, the basic building blocks programmed in the LREPS Operating System served four major purposes:

1. The use of these blocks allowed the project team to efficiently allocate their time among the specific activities of the mathematical model.
2. The blocks facilitated the changing of the computer program when a better approach to the computer modeling of an activity was developed.
3. Basic building blocks forced the examination of common elements of system activities. Instead of developing a subprogram for each potential DC location, the general or universal aspects of the functions of a DC were modeled and computerized. Thus, the same computer subprograms could be used for the functions of many DCs.
4. Basic building blocks saved computer memory while execution time increased slightly because of the additional subprogram linkages.

In general, the use of basic building block subprograms facilitated the overall development of the computer model and especially the LREPS Operating System. Changes in a major activity of the mathematical model were easily made by changing the subprogram associated with that activity. Initially, the direction was to have a proliferation of subprograms with its accompanying set of program linkages' problems. Later, however, the subprograms were redefined in respect to the major components of the mathematical model. This redefinition partially alleviated the problem of many, little subprograms.

The future use of computer subprograms for model sophistication would seem to be easily and practically achieved. Their use of broadening the computer model's Operating System to encompass additional horizontal and vertical aspects of the total business system is limited only by the remaining amount of computer memory and the applicability of the present building blocks to the possible activities that would be added to LREPS.

The universal implications of the present building blocks for different firms are limited by their compatibility with the activities defined in the model framework of a physical distribution system. The overall design of the model would not have to be modified, although some of the model's activity subprograms may require slight modifications.

Software and Hardware Features:
Minimize Reprogramming

With the use of both the special hardware features and the sophisticated software features of the CDC 6500, the required reprogramming for alternative versions of LREPS was minimized. The hardware features centered on the effective use of magnetic tapes, disks, and punched cards where speed and controls were needed in programming and debugging LREPS. The software features centered on the definition of the LREPS common data base plus the effective use of the program and information, and storage and retrieval systems. Although the use of many of these storage and retrieval systems is somewhat difficult to learn, MSU's systems were easily learned, which expedited the computerization process of alternative versions of LREPS.

Software and Hardware:
Efficient Processing

Research considering alternative methods for storing, retrieving, and processing the computer model's data base of information resulted in the use and disuse of certain computer hardware and software features. The more important features that were investigated are discussed below.

Sequential, magnetic tape files received major use for the inflow and outflow of information manipulated in the LREPS Operating System. Initial tests using random-access, disk files for banks of information related to the order file showed this method of information processing to be much slower and more expensive than the tape-handling procedure. The remaining information in the data base that could effectively be random-accessed was so small that this information was kept in high-access, core memory. The use of low-access, extended core storage (ECS) for this information was not possible since ECS was unavailable.

The periodic input and output of information into the LREPS Operating System via the Monitor and Control gatekeeper proved to be efficient and effective. Magnetic tape was also used as the medium for this input and output. The only exception was the limited use of punched cards and printer listings.

The use of computer program overlays for those portions of the LREPS Operating System that were only referenced quarterly or less frequently was also investigated. Program overlays were not used because the present overlay procedure for FORTRAN programs on the CDC 6500 is not easily implemented and quite complicated.

The procedure of packing more than one piece of information in a computer word of memory was used. Much of the information in the model was based upon a zero-one, binary representation.

Model Output

The periodic output of simulation results via magnetic tape has proved to be very efficient and effective. The reports described in appendix 3 were easily prepared, and also the basic simulation data are retained for further analysis. By establishing the DAILY and MONTH fixed-time events in the LREPS Operating System, the use of these routines to print any additional data was easily effected. In summary, the periodic orientation to model results was satisfactory.

Compatibility among Computer Systems:
FORTRAN Version

LREPS in FORTRAN is at present machine dependent and has low compatibility among other computer operating systems. Low compatibility among computer operating systems is stressed because it would be fairly difficult to implement the present computer model on even another CDC 6500. Large computer operating systems for machines such as the CDC 6500 generally have peculiarities that have been developed by university personnel and which cause conversion problems.

Considering other computer manufacturers' operating systems, LREPS' implementation would be very difficult on their systems. Because more than one piece of information was packed into many computer words, the availability of EXTENDED FORTRAN routines to unpack the information would be required. Associated with the packing of information are the differences in the physical sizes of the computer memory words among different computers. The CDC 6500 has sixty bits per word while the IBM 360 series has thirty-two bits per word. Since some of the LREPS data-base variables have more than thirty-two bits of information packed into one computer word, the LREPS data base would have to be redesigned for two words of IBM memory.

The level of the FORTRAN compiler itself would prohibit some computer operating systems from being used for LREPS. MSU's FORTRAN compiler is an advanced version that includes such features as "logical" storage and instructions, tape buffering routines, plus NAMELIST and variable formatting procedures.[41] The use of such features requires a large, sophisticated FORTRAN compiler.

Computer Size Requirements:
FORTRAN Version

The results concerning requirement seven are closely related to requirement six. The present design of the LREPS computer model requires a large-scale system with significant amounts of high-access computer memory. To retain the universal aspects of LREPS, a sophisticated computer operating system that allows one to retrieve and compile quickly the LREPS program routines is also needed. With these requirements on the size and speed of the computer operating system, a medium-size system would generally not be capable of processing effectively and efficiently the LREPS simulator.

Operating System Requirements:
FORTRAN Version

In reference to the computer memory utilized in the execution of the LREPS Operating System, the most sophisticated version requires at present a little less than 32,000 decimal, computer words of memory. Without the capability of packed computer words, the restriction of fitting the LREPS Operating System within 36K decimal words of computer memory would not have been satisfied.

In order to restrict the amount of information that was inputted and outputted from the LREPS Operating System, it was desired that the computer program utilize only three input/output files. This restricted use promoted efficient computer utilization. Figure 5-7 illustrates the use of five input/output files. Originally, it was planned that no cards be read from the card reader or no output be printed during program execution of the LREPS Operating System. The fact that GASP required card input and outputted control listings on the printer was initially overlooked.

In order to minimize the cost of executing the LREPS Operating System, the desire was to develop a computer program that would process a ten-year cycle of information in thirty minutes. This execution time includes both computer central processing and peripheral processing time. Examining the computer times of several test runs, the length of time for running a ten-year cycle was primarily a function of two factors.

The first factor was the total sales dollar forecast for the market regions being processed. If all the regions were being processed, then it was the national total sales dollar forecast. The running time had a high, direct correlation to this factor when considering the method for processing customer sales from the order file. With the buffering of the order file into the LREPS Operating System, the central processing time of program execution was just slightly greater than the peripheral processing time associated with input and output. Given a larger or smaller sales forecast, then the model took respectively more or less time to process the sales.

The second major factor affecting execution time was the average sales dollar amount per customer order. This factor had an inverse relationship to the amount of time required to execute a simulation cycle. If the average dollar amount per customer order was large, then the sales dollar quotas per day were filled much faster, which caused the Operating System to execute faster. Other factors were considered in the timing investigation. One such factor was the number of tracked products. After running the program with twelve tracked products and then fifty tracked products, there was no appreciable difference in running time.

In order to obtain some idea as to how fast the program would run given various levels of the two major factors, the execution times of several LREPS tests were analyzed in detail to derive a formula that could be used to approximate the running time of the LREPS Operating System. The formula which gives the computer time in minutes of computer central processing unit (CPU) time is:

$$T = \sum_{i=1}^{NYRS} \frac{45 * TDSF_i}{ADPCO_i}$$

where:

T is the total amount of CPU time per simulation cycle,

NYRS is the total number of simulated years to be run,

$TDSF_i$ is the total sales dollar forecast (in millions of dollars) for the ith year and the market region(s) under analysis,

and

$ADPCO_i$ is the average sales dollars per customer order in year i.

Computer Compatibility and Size Requirements:
COBOL Version

As discussed above, LREPS was originally written in FORTRAN for the Michigan State University CDC 6500. Due to differences among various manufacturers' operating systems, LREPS implementation was generally incompatible with systems other than the CDC 6500 series. This incompatibility problem, however, has been to a great extent eliminated by converting the LREPS model to COBOL on a Bur-

Figure 5-8
One-Year Validation Results

Information Category	Data Base Variables	Simulated Versus Actual	PD Stages
Cust Sales	DU(13-14)	Within Limits	DU, DC and
	DCIS(16-21)	Within Limits	Domestic
Cust Dollar Sales/Order	DCIS(16)/ DCIS(21)	Within Limits	DC and Domestic
Cust Wt Sales/Order	DCIS(17)/ DCIS(21)	Within Limits	DC and Domestic
Line Items per Order	DCIS(20)/ DCIS(21)	Within Limits	DC and Domestic
Cust Serv—			
NOCT-Avg	DCIS(9)	Within Limits	DC and Domestic
NOCT-Std Dev	DCIS(10)	No Data Avail	DC and Domestic
T4-Avg	DCIS(11)	Within Limits	DC and Domestic
T4-Std Dev	DCIS(12)	No Data Avail	DC and Domestic
Dollar Props	OCTDIS(1)	No Data Avail	DC only
Order Props	OCTDIS(2)	Within Limits	DC only
DC-MCC	DCMCC(1)	Within Limits	DC only
Reorder	DCMCC(2)	Within Limits	DC only
	PRDC(6)	Within Limits	DC only
	PRCTDC(2)	Within Limits	DC only
DC Stockouts	PRCTDC(1)	No Data Avail	DC only
	DCIS(13-15)	No Data Avail	DC only
DC Avg IOH	PRDC(3)	Within Limits	DC only
Cust Ship Accums	WTACUM	Difficult to Compare Because of Small Sample Avgs in Cust Order Blocks	DC and Domestic
MCC Ship Accums	DCMCC1	Within Limits	MCC only
Total Prod Demand	TPDEM(2)	Within Limits	Domestic only
PD Cost	DCCOST(1-6)	Within Limits	DC and Domestic
	DCIS(6)	Within Limits	
	PDTCST	Within Limits	
Cum Wt Indices	DU(7)	Sales Allocation	DU, DC
	DCIS(5)	Basis	and Regional
	REG(8)	Within Limits	

roughs 2500. The LREPS model, in COBOL, now operates, with segmentation, in 35K bytes of core storage.

The LREPS programs can now be readily converted to any byte-oriented decimal machine, such as the IBM 360 series.

The only drawback as the result of the conversion of LREPS to COBOL on the Burroughs 2500 has been an increase in running time. The increase has not, however, been significant enough to limit the practical use of the model.

Preliminary Model Validation Results

The preliminary validation of the simulation model centered on activities involved in the calibration of the model's output to a specified base year's data. The model was initially set to simulate a four-year period. The first year was the year with which the model was calibrated. The following three years were used to check the model for steady-state implications including no fluctuations in the model's output.

Figure 5-8 lists the categories of variables checked for reasonableness, the specific data-base variables checked, an indication as to whether the variables were within a reasonable percentage of the base year data plus the physical distribution stage for which the information was checked. This basic validation of the model results was static in nature. One full year's actual results were compared to the simulated results. No sophisticated techniques for simulation validation were used for preliminary validation.

SUMMARY

Chapter 5 presented in three major sections the design approach, the computer model, and operationalization of LREPS. In this chapter preliminary validation (face validity) was also reported. The next chapter considers in-depth validation of computer models in general and LREPS in particular.

6

VALIDATION

The previous chapters of this monograph presented the first three major steps of the LREPS design procedure: problem definition, mathematical model development, and computer model formulations.

This chapter presents the fourth step in the design procedure—validation. The chapter initially develops a general philosophy and process of validation for computer simulation models. The second section presents a literature review for a few of the more documented computer simulation models. The third major section presents the general design procedure for LREPS validation. The next section describes the techniques used in validation. The fifth and final section presents a discussion of the validation results for LREPS in terms of long-term stability of the model, comparison of simulated data streams with actual historical data, and the sensitivity of model assumptions.

PHILOSOPHY AND PROCESS OF VALIDATION OF COMPUTER SIMULATION MODELS

Validation of the operation of a simulation model is as necessary as the validation of the operation of any other scientific experiment. While the basic problem of validation is no different for a simulation experiment, the complexity of the model is such that the processes by which its validity is established are quite different. With most scientific experiments it is rather easy and inexpensive to carry out several independent replications. Due to the complexity of most simulation models, the expense of performing more than one experiment is often prohibitive, while longitudinal observations during this one experiment are autocorrelated.

The amount of time and effort needed to develop and make operational a computer simulation model is at present so great that the problem of its validation has generally been neglected. A common attitude seems to be that crude judgmental and graphic methods[1] are preferable to completely ignoring validation.

To validate a model in a strict sense means to prove that the model is true. Fortunately, most simulations are seldom concerned with proving the "truth" of the model (an exception might be G. P. E. Clarkson's model to simulate the behavior of a bank's trust investment officer[2]), since criteria for what is "true" and what is "not true" are obviously hard to develop. K. R. Popper, therefore, suggests that efforts should be concentrated on determining the degree of confirmation rather than verification.[3] Models should be subjected to tests capable of showing them to be false. Each such test passed will add confidence to our assumption that the model behavior confirms the behavior of the real system. "Thus, instead of verification, we may speak of gradually increasing confirmation of the law."[4]

R. Van Horn describes validation as the "process of building an acceptable level of confidence that an inference about a simulated process is a correct or valid inference for the actual process."[5] The focus for validation should be to understand the input/output relationships in the model and to be able to translate "learning" from the simulation to "learning" about the actual process. T. H. Naylor and J. M. Finger[6] basically agree and provide some insight as to how this focus can be operationalized. The computer simulation model and its output are based on inductive inferences about behavior of the real system in the form of behavioral assumptions or operating characteristics. Therefore:

> The validity of the model is made probable, not certain by the assumptions underlying the model . . . the rules for validating computer simulation models and the data generated by these models are sampling rules resting entirely on the theory of probability.[7]

Three major methodological positions on validation are summarized by Naylor and Finger: rationalism, empiricism, and positive economics.

> *Rationalism.* A model or theory is a system of logical deductions from a series of synthetic premises of unquestionable truth.

Validation is the search for the basic assumptions underlying the behavior of the system.

Empiricism. The opposite view to rationalism is that empirical science is the ideal form of knowledge. The model should be constructed with facts, not assumptions. So any postulates or assumptions which cannot be independently verified should not be considered.

Positive Economics. This view championed by M. Friedman is that the validity of a model depends upon its ability to predict the behavior of the dependent variables and *not* on the validity of the assumptions on which the model rests.

These three positions are combined into a multistage verification procedure, each stage of which is necessary but not sufficient. Stage one is the formulation of a set of postulates or hypotheses describing the behavior of the system. This involves specification of components, selection of variables, and formulation of functional relationships using observation, general knowledge, relevant theory, and intuition. Stage two is the attempt to verify the assumptions of the model by statistical analysis, and the final stage is to test the model's ability to predict the behavior of the system under study. The multistage verification procedure attempts to include all major ways in which to build confidence in a model.

A final view on validation is that of G. S. Fishman and P. J. Kiviat,[8] which is a narrower concept because they divide simulation testing into three parts:

> (1) Verification ensures that a simulation model behaves as an experimenter intends. (2) Validation tests the agreement between the behavior of the simulation model and a real system. (3) Problem analysis embraces statistical problems relating to (the analysis) of data generated by computer simulation.[9]

Given the nature of the validation process on a theoretical level, the actual validation procedures used in some of the more recent and well-documented computer simulation models is of interest. Therefore, a brief review of the literature is presented as the next major area.

LITERATURE REVIEW

Six computer simulation models are briefly reviewed in this section. The general nature of the problem situations modeled is:

1. aggregate behavior of the shoe and leather industry
2. behavioral theory of the firm
3. selection of an investment portfolio
4. West Coast lumber industry
5. a firm's production-distribution system
6. competitive market response

Cohen

K. J. Cohen (1960) constructed two simulation models to describe the aggregate behavior of shoe retailers, shoe manufacturers, and cattlehide leather tanners between 1930 and 1940. This aggregate behavior was described in terms of selling price, production or sales, and receipts. While the first model (Model II) was a "one-period-change" model determining values for these endogenous variables only one time period in advance, the second model (Model IIE) was a "process" model which determines endogenous variable values for an arbitrarily large number of future time periods. Cohen's model is discrete and dynamic with a time increment of one month.

Visual comparison of the time paths of the model predictions of selling price, production, and receipts to the actual historical time paths of these variables comprised the only validation of the model.

> The simulation runs for both Models II and IIE generate time paths for the endogenous variables which, although not in complete agreement with observed time paths, indicate that our models may incorporate some of the mechanisms which determine behavior in the shoe, leather, hide sequence.[10]
>
> Both models produce time paths which fluctuate around the observed time paths. For most variables, the amplitude of the oscillations is greater for Model IIE than for the actuals, with Model II having the largest amplitude. However, none of the time paths for either Model seem to be either explosive or overly damped.[11]
>
> The findings are also similar for the average price. The time paths of both Models II and IIE are reasonably on course with observed values,

although Model II shows even wider fluctuations about the actuals than for the preceding prices.[12]

Bonini

Continuing a research effort started principally by R. M. Cyert and J. G. March,[13] C. P. Bonini (1963) constructed a computer model of the behavioral theory of the firm. In order to show the effects of organizational, informational, and environmental factors upon the firm's decision-making process, Bonini decided that price, level of inventory, cost, sales, profit, and amount of pressure would be an adequate endogenous variable set to represent the behavior pattern of the organization. The model was used as an exploratory device to describe the relationship between various informational flow patterns and the firm's decision process. From these relationships design changes for the firm could be recommended.

Bonini was not concerned with modeling an actual firm. He was concerned with a comparison of the behavior of his theoretical firm, after a proposed change, with the original behavior. This comparison involved analyzing two sets of six time series (one time series for each of the variables: price, level of inventory, cost, sales, profit, and amount of pressure before and after the proposed change). Because these time series did not exhibit any tendency to obtain steady-state or equilibrium values over time, Bonini settled for a measure of central tendency (the arithmetical mean), a measure of dispersion (the standard deviation), and a measure of trend (the least-squares regression coefficient) to describe the output time series of his model. Bonini determined the requirements for the length of these time series in the following fashion:

> On the one hand, the run should extend over sufficient simulated periods so that extreme values in the time series can be averaged out (that is, so there will be relatively small sampling error associated with the above three measures. On the other hand, limitations of computation time would argue for keeping a reasonably short number of periods. In addition, if we are going to apply our results to real organization, we would be more interested in the immediate and short-run effects (of particular changes) than in what might be the average level over, say 20 or 30 years. In view of these considerations, I have chosen 108 time periods . . . as the length for the simulation runs [14]

Clarkson

G. P. E. Clarkson (1962) developed a simulation model to duplicate the procedure by which a trust officer in a bank selected stock for any particular client's portfolio. The model combines a set of decision rules which are selected on the basis of information available about the client's financial situation and requirements.

The output of the model is not a data stream but a selection of a variable number of shares of a variable number of stocks, given the client's position. Clarkson applies two types of testing procedures to his model: those pertaining to the output of the model alone and those pertaining to the decision processes incorporated in the model.

For testing output Clarkson notes:

> Since the problem of determining the type of error when comparing generated to actual output has not yet been solved, statistical tests on the goodness of fit of the generated output are not very meaningful. The only statistical test that has much meaning is to test whether the generated data give a significantly "better fit" than that which would be produced by some random or naive mechanisms.[15]

Clarkson tested the model against a "random selector" from the total population. He rejected the hypothesis that the probability of randomly selecting the same portfolio as the trust officer was equal to the percentage of matching or "correct" responses generated by the model. The size of the list was reduced to include only those issues which displayed the characteristics desired by the client, and the hypothesis was still rejected.

Naive decision rules replaced the random selection procedure, and the hypothesis was still rejected. The decision rules considered were:

1. rank growth stocks on the basis of growth in price over the last 10 years
2. rank growth stocks on the basis of growth in earnings over the last 10 years
3. rank growth stocks on the basis of growth in sales over the last 10 years
4. rank growth stocks on the basis of growth low yield over the last 10 years
5. rank yield stocks on the basis of growth high yield over the last 10 years

His objective, Clarkson contends, is to simulate investment behavior; to select the correct portfolios with the same processes and for the same reasons as the investment officer. Therefore, the need to test the decision processes exists. A. M. Turing's test[16] was used: Can an impartial observer discriminate between the output of the model of human behavior and the output of the actual human behavior?

Balderston

F. E. Balderston and A. C. Hoggatt (1962) constructed a computer simulation model of the West Coast lumber industry. The emphasis of the model is not to describe the real firms making up this industry, but to study the dynamic behavior of firms in a two-stage market from the viewpoint of an economic theorist. The model simulates wholesalers to whom suppliers provide and from whom customers purchase. While flows of information, material, and money move vertically through the market, no horizontal movement is allowed. At the end of each market period decisions about output and price, and entry and exit to the industry are made.

Concern for the validity of the model centered on the question of viability. Viability, as used by Balderston and Hoggatt, does not require equilibrium of the endogenous time paths, but only requires that "behavior should persist over a significant time interval."[17] Persistent behavior means that the time path is stable. Stable in the sense that it settles into a state which exhibits properties of convergence, or stable in the sense that change over time is steady with proportional (or acceptable) changes in the other endogenous variables.

This is the extent to which the original study considered the model's validity. Hoggatt in a later article[18] applied G. E. P. Box's[19] method of system analysis to the model. At this time more sophisticated validation techniques were introduced. Hoggatt states that he would consider the model valid if it "duplicated (the) trends and frequency response of (the) real system"[20] rather than aiming to have the model duplicate the time paths of the real system. In order to measure the frequency response of the model, he used the autocorrelation function.

Forrester

Industrial Dynamics was developed by J. W. Forrester (1962) from his original dynamic simulation model of a firm's production-distribution system. Forrester has tried with limited success to convert his model building techniques into a general management philosophy. He describes Industrial Dynamics as

> the study of the information-feedback characteristics of industrial activity to show how organizational structure, amplification (in policies), and time delays (in decisions and actions) interact to influence the success of the enterprise. It treats the interactions between flows of information, money, orders, materials, personnel, and capital equipment in a company, an industry, or a national economy.
> Industrial Dynamics provides a single framework for integrating the functional areas of management—marketing, production, accounting, research and development, and capital investment. It is a quantitative and experimental approach for relating organizational structure and corporate policy to industrial growth and stability.[21]

The greatest contribution of the Industrial Dynamics models was to point out the extraordinarily large fluctuations that can occur in the inventory held at the retail level when a change in customer demand is reflected through the lagged order delivery sequence: retailers—distributors—factory-warehouse—factory—factory-warehouse — distributors—retailers. From this basic production-distribution model many possible changes can be tested: limit factory capacity, eliminate the distributors, add additional sectors such as a market sector, include advertising.

How well the model serves its purpose is Forrester's test of its validity. The purpose of Industrial Dynamics is to design better management systems; therefore, validity can only be tested after an Industrial Dynamics approach has been applied to a situation and the results measured in concrete terms, such as increased profits. Defense of the model prior to use can only be given in terms of an individual defense of each detail of structure and policy, so that in sum the total behavior of the model shows performance characteristics associated with the real system. The validity of the model at this stage as a description of a specific system can only be examined relative to the system boundaries (are the boundaries suitable relative to the objectives of the experiment?), to the interacting variables, and to the values of the parameters. If the similarity of the model output to the actual characteristics of the system is not sufficient, these three factors must be examined and changed. These views on validity can be summarized in the following quotations:

Validity as an abstract concept divorced from purpose, has no useful meaning.[22]

The ability of a model to predict the state of the real system at some specific future time is not a sound test of model usefulness.[23]

Data may serve to reject a grossly wrong decision-making hypothesis, but they can scarcely prove a correct one.[24]

Forrester believes the final test of validity is whether the actual system is being controlled to agree with the model.

Amstutz

In order to define and analyze management problems involving the environment of the firm, A. Amstutz (1967) developed a simulation model of competitive market response.

The objective of the study was to model the firm and the environment external to the firm so that the total effect of changes in variables which can be controlled by management could be measured. Amstutz set up his system structure in terms of three sets of elements. Active elements are human. They can originate and react to signals. The eight active elements involved in the model are the producer, his competitors, distributors and wholesalers, salesmen, retailers, consumers, government officials, and research workers. "Elements of flow are the vehicles of interaction between active elements."[25] These are the elements management can manipulate in order to try and achieve its objectives. The elements of flow are product, information, and capital. The last set of elements are the passive elements (time delays, dissipators, and storage) which describe the channels through which the flow elements move between the active elements. By means of this formulation the dynamic effects of the origination of a signal by management can be examined.

The tests Amstutz carried out in an attempt to analyze the worth of his model were of two types—reliability testing and validity testing.

The purpose of reliability testing is to determine if the results of the model are reproducible. Are the results obtained on sequential runs sufficiently alike to justify the assumption that they are two samples drawn from the same population of data?

Validity testing is concerned with "truth." As there is no objective measure of truth, Amstutz argues that a subjective evaluation of the consistency of the model's performance with theory and prior knowledge must be made: "Validity of a model can be established only by examining the realism of the assumptions on which it is based."[26]

Evaluation of the model's performance is possible using the Turing Test. If a person knowledgeable in the area to be modeled cannot distinguish the model from the real system when provided with responses from both, then the model is realistic. Other tests for validity can be performed once the validity of the assumptions on which the model is based has been established. *Tests for viability:* This is a very gross test which is usually satisfied without explicit consideration. Does the model generate behavior which persists over a significant time interval? *Tests for stability:* Variables and processes which are stable in the real work must also exhibit stability when modeled. *Tests for consistency:* Is there consistency between model behavior and behavior observed in the real world? The extent to which the assumptions of the model agree with known facts must be tested as must the internal consistency or "deductive veracity" of the model —does the model "make sense." This testing may be done subjectively as "face validity" testing (does the model appear to be satisfactory) or analytically with sensitivity analysis. *Duplication of historical conditions* is the fourth set of tests, and the last set is *prediction of future conditions*. The ability of the model to predict cannot be tested until after the passage of time over which the predictions were made unless "pseudo predictions" are made of past results.

Amstutz carried out these tests in the following manner. Reliability was tested by calculating "interrun deviations" when changing the seed in the random number generator. Subjectivity and "eyeball" testing confirmed viability, stability, and consistency requirements, to determine the extent to which the simulated exogenous time paths matched historical data, and absolute error between simulated and actual was summed and averaged. The predictive ability of the model was not examined.

Two conclusions can be drawn from this examination of these six computer models. The first conclusion is that a more extensive effort should be made in attempting to establish the validity of an operational simulation model. The second is that regardless of the type of simulation used or the aims of the analyst, much of the activity that has to be carried out in order to validate the model is the same. The next section, based on the sections on the process of validation and literature review, discusses the development of the LREPS validation procedure.

DESIGN OF LREPS VALIDATION PROCEDURE

When large amounts of money and manpower have been applied to a project over an extended period of time, there is a natural reluctance (maybe not explicitly stated or felt) to subject the finished model to scrutiny, the result of which may indicate the worthlessness of the expenditures. Because the industrial sponsor in this research project had the foresight to encourage critical examination of the completed model, the question of the validity of the model was examined formally.

From the rather diverse views of validation examined earlier, a procedure was developed. After examining the six simulation models, it was concluded that it is possible to develop validation procedures suitable for application to any simulation model. These validation procedures were developed into three categories. The validity of the LREPS computer simulation model was measured with respect to the model's ability to satisfy the three distinct validation procedures. These three validation procedures are to:

1. determine if the time series of the endogenous variables is statistically under control,
2. compare the model output to actual historical data, and
3. examine the sensitivity of model assumptions.

If the values of the key endogenous variables are sensitive to the nature of the assumption, then managerial knowledge and intuition must be applied to confirm the assumption, or else the model must be restructured to eliminate or replace the assumption.

Validation Procedures

For the *first* procedure, data streams for several endogenous variables need to be generated by the model over an extended time period to establish the stability or viability of the model over the long run. Do the data streams examined show persistent behavior over this time interval?

The *second* validation procedure requires a measure of the extent to which the model is an accurate representation of the real system. Time paths of selected endogenous variables, which are representative of the physical distribution system's behavior, are generated by the model over a past time period. Statistical analysis of these data with actual historical data over the same time period will provide the required measure.

Two critical building blocks in the LREPS model are the use of a stratified sample of fifty products to represent the total product line and the method of generating demand unit orders. The model should be constructed so that reasonable changes in these two procedures do not have a significant effect on the model output. To carry out this *third* validation procedure, analysis of selected endogenous data streams before and after the change will be required. An example of such a change is the alteration of the composition or size of the stratified sample.

The methods proposed for these three types of analysis are examined in the section "Validation Techniques."

Types of Validation

Concern is directed in varying degrees to two distinct types of validation—validation of the basic underlying processes of the model and validation of the data stream output of the model. Because the basic design and assumptions used in any model are certain to differ from those used in any other model, validation of design procedures must of necessity be tailored to the particular model under consideration. This type of validation is probably best carried out by interactions between the model builders and those who are familiar with the real system being modeled both during and after construction of the model. After completion of the model, the Turing Test can be used to increase confidence in the validity of the basic design. This type of model validity is design validity; validity of the output data stream is output validity.

Design validity will not be considered to any great extent for two reasons. First, as indicated, design validity is a concept specific to the particular model at hand; and second, if the model satisfies the requirements of output validity, it is not unreasonable to assume that the basic processes of the real system must have been modeled reasonably accurately. Friedman adds weight to the decision not to consider design validity. He believes that the validity of a theory is not based on the realism of its assumptions (complete "realism" is unattainable) but on the accuracy of its predictions.

Design validity is the point at which many normative model builders (in particular, Forrester) stop. They argue that a normative model is not built to represent the actual system, but to represent the system the way it should be. Missing from this argument is a rational method of moving from the actual state to the desired state. A functional normative model might well be one which first models the actual system (at which point output validity testing can be performed) and then the desired corrections are made from this basis.

But it must be recognized that the testing for design validity is important during the process of constructing the model and as an initial procedure on its completion. This testing involves checking the functioning of the model and its components for reasonableness. Do the values of the endogenous variables examined fall within acceptable limits? This procedure is sometimes known as determining the model's face validity. That is, determining the extent to which the assumptions of the model agree with known facts and also the internal consistency or "seductive veracity" of the model. In other words, the model must "make sense." The results of this type of validity checking were reported in chapter 5. Figure 5-1, previously presented, contains a partial list of the LREPS variables tested for face validity. A comparison of simulated versus actual data for an information category is designated "within limits" if the variance is less than 5 percent.

The third general validation procedure previously proposed was to examine the sensitivity of the major assumption employed by the model. To the extent of the analysis of the data streams generated before and after a change in these assumptions, this is output validity. But the determination of the particular assumptions to be examined is a problem of design validity.

Gross malfunctions of a particular model can be discovered by analysis for face or design validity. Once the model has satisfied these criteria, the more general and sophisticated procedures for establishing output validity can be applied. Emphasis will be placed on this second aspect of computer simulation validation.

The general validation procedure and its application to the LREPS model have been outlined. Remaining is the consideration of statistical and graphical techniques to be used to implement the procedure.

VALIDATION TECHNIQUES

Many statistical and graphical techniques have been proposed and used in attempting to validate the output of computer simulation models. In order to determine which of these techniques is most suitable for each of the three types of analysis, the nature of the techniques should be examined.

The Chi-Square Test

The chi-square statistic can be used to measure the discrepancy between observed and expected frequencies. If the value of chi-square is zero, perfect agreement between observed and expected frequencies exists, while the larger the value of chi-square, the greater the discrepancy between the two. When using the chi-square test, expected frequencies are developed from a hypothesis. It is reasonable to expect the calculated chi-square value to be less than a critical value at a selected level of confidence. If this turns out to be the case, the hypothesis is accepted; otherwise, it is rejected.

Theil's Inequality Coefficient

When comparing predicted results against actual outcomes, it is desirable to be able to establish the quality of the prediction. One way to do this is to calculate H. Thiel's inequality coefficient.[27] The coefficient is equal to the square root of the sum of the differences between predicted and actual outcomes squared, divided by the sum of the actual outcomes squared. If the coefficient is zero then the forecasts are perfect. While it should be observed that if the coefficient has a value of one it indicates a prediction error equal to that obtained by the naive method of no-change extrapolation, it should also be noted that the coefficient has no finite upper bound. Worse methods of forecasting than simple extrapolation are therefore possible. Comparison of the technique being used and extrapolation provides valuable information. Decomposition of the square of the numerator of the coefficient into three terms shows the relative importance of errors of central tendency, errors of unequal variation, and errors due to incomplete covariation.

Spectral Analysis

Because all data generated by time series are autocorrelated to some degree, a method of analysis which will account for this autocorrelation is desirable. After transforming the data from the time domain to the frequency domain, spectral analysis[28, 29] is a method by which the autocorrelation can be quantified and evaluated. Information about the magnitude of deviations from the average level of a given activity and information about the period or length of these deviations can be obtained.

Regression Analysis

It is often meaningful to be able to express the relationship between the variable under study (the dependent variable) and the other variables which have influence over it (the independent variables). The most commonly accepted method of determining this relationship is that of least squares. A line, curve, or plane can be fitted to the data in such a manner as to minimize the vertical squared difference between the plotted data value and the value determined by the function being fitted. The result is then the "best fitting" line, curve, or plane. While this function shows the relationship between the independent variables and the dependent variables, it also enables predictions of the dependent variable to be made.

Correlation

Correlation theory can most easily be examined in terms of regression analysis. When all observations fall on the regression line developed from the data, perfect correlation exists between these variables for two variables, direct correlation exists if as one increases so does the other, while inverse correlation exists when the first variable increases with a decrease in the second. Perfect correlation occurs when both the amount and direction of change is identical for both variables, or the regression equation of the first variable on the second is identical to the regression of the second variable on the first.

Nonlinearity and multiple variables add computational complexity, but do not alter the logic of this type of analysis.

Analysis of Variance

Analysis of variance is used to test if two or more samples differ significantly with respect to a particular (usually qualitative) property. If observations are classified on the basis of a single property, the ratio of the variance between the groups and the average variances within the groups (the F ratio) is used to determine if a significant difference does exist between the groups with respect to the property.

The F Distribution

To compare variances of small samples, the F distribution is used. The F statistic is equal to the ratio of sample variances. Given a level of significance and the two sample sizes (from which can be determined the degrees of freedom), the critical value of F can be read from a table of F distribution. By comparing the value of the F statistic to the critical value of F, the hypothesis that the variables are significantly different can either be accepted or rejected.

Multiple Comparison

Analysis of variance uses the F test to determine if a significant difference exists between a statistic from different samples. If homogeneity does not exist, the method of multiple comparison quantifies the difference, while the method of multiple ranking[30] (to be discussed) directly identifies the "best" sample or plan on the basis of the measured statistic. Both multiple comparison and multiple ranking must follow analysis of variance for another reason—the computational reason that both methods use the mean square of the error. Use of confidence intervals rather than tests of hypotheses is a characteristic of the method.

Multiple Ranking

This is a method to find the "best" plan. It is a more direct method than multiple comparison, answering questions such as: With what probability can I say that a ranking of sample means represents the true ranking of the population means?

Sequential Analysis

Most decision-making procedures are carried out with the sample size predetermined and fixed. It is possible that this sample size is larger than it need be resulting in superfluous information and unnecessary expense. But this can be avoided if after each observation is examined the decision is made to: accept the hypothesis, reject the hypothesis, or postpone a decision on the hypothesis and make another observation. The method has several applications for the analysis of the results of computer simulations. Procedures for testing the position of the true mean in relation to a hypothesized mean and for comparing means of several experiments with a control mean have been developed by E. Paulson.[31] A heuristic approach to R. E. Bechhofer and S. Blumenthal's method[32] of selecting the population with the largest mean is described by W. E. Sasser et al.[33]

The Kolmogorov-Smirnov Test

The Kolmogorov-Smirnov Test is a nonparametric test to determine if a given sample is a sample from a particular distribution function. A chi-square test can also be developed to supply the same information.

Response-Surface Analysis

When a response is a continuous function of a single factor, the method of response surface analysis is relatively easily applied to find the maximum or minimum of this function in the practical range of interest. Several conditions must be satisfied before this technique can be effective. It must be assumed that the response function can be approximated by a simple polynomial over the range of interest and that the function has only a single maximum (or minimum) within this range. So the key to this method is seen to be the managerial skill with which the relevant area of interest is selected. The general area of the extreme point must be known.

The general aims of the procedure are to find the extreme point and also to determine the sensitivity of the response function in the area of the extreme point. When the response is dependent on more than one factor, the principles of the method remain the same, but now more than one path to the extreme point exists. The question now becomes how to reach the region of the optimum most economically.

Factor Analysis

Using the matrix of all correlations between the variables under consideration, the resolution of the set of variables linearly in terms of a small number of factors is possible. If this process is carried out satisfactorily, the factors will convey as much information about the system as did the original set of variables. The main aim of factor analysis is to provide the most economical description of the observed data.

A given matrix of correlations can be factored in an infinite number of ways. Factor solutions are usually generated according to statistical considerations, such as attempting to account for a maximum amount of the total variance, or according to the meaningfulness of the solution to the particular experimental context. It should be emphasized that factor analysis does not produce an exhaustive set of fundamental factors which are a complete description.

Graphical Techniques

A graphical description of a time series is easily developed and readily understood. Among the many possible graphical measures for comparing two time series are:[34] number, timing, and direction of turning points; amplitude of the fluctuations for corresponding time segments; average amplitude over the entire series; simultaneity of turning points for different variables; average values, probability distributions, and variation about the mean (variance, skewness, kurtosis) of variables; and exact matching of variables.

Due to the number of techniques to be considered, the description given of each has been brief. From these techniques, those suitable for each of the three types of validation procedure were selected. The results obtained from the technique were analyzed in the light of the particular technique's assumptions.[35]

VALIDATION RESULTS FOR LREPS

As previously indicated, efforts to validate a computer simulation model can be directed in two ways: to validate the design or method of construction of the model, and to validate the output of the model. The design or face validity, that is, determining the extent to which the assumptions of the model agree with known facts and also the internal consistency, was previously presented in this chapter. This section, therefore, emphasizes the results of the output validation procedures.

Long-Term Stability

The first aspect of validity subjected to detailed analysis is long-term stability. Stability is the ability of the model to generate endogenous data streams which show persistent behavior over the long run. The face validity analysis established the model's reasonableness over the short run—comparison of one year of history against the LREPS simulated output for the same year. The model's reasonableness over the long run—the ten-year planning horizon of the model—is tested using the stability analysis.

Endogenous data streams of sales weights for three products (a low volume, a medium volume, and a high volume) were examined in two different ways. First, the time series of the data stream was studied to determine the reasonableness of its variability over the time horizon. Spectral analysis was used for this test. The second type of analysis was to lag the original time series by K units and then the lagged time series was compared with the original set of observations. This comparison indicates the degree of correspondence between the two data streams. The techniques used for these analyses were graphical correlation, Theil's Inequality Coefficient, and spectral analysis. The results indicated that the model does generate persistent endogenous behavior and is stable over the long run.[36]

Output Versus Historical

The second major validation task was to compare the output of the simulation model for some time period with the actual historical data that were recorded for that time period. This type of analysis comes most readily to mind when considering validation. The results of comparing simulated endogenous data streams with the actual data streams are dependent upon the quality and length of the actual data streams.

Actual historical data for three products—dollar sales, sales weight, and inventory-on-hand—were available for one region on a daily basis, but only for a period of 103 days. The techniques used to perform the validation test included (1) graphical analysis, (2) analysis of variance, (3) multiple comparison, (4) the F test, (5) correlation, (6) regression analysis, (7) the chi-square test, (8) Theil's Inequality Coefficient, (9) spectral analysis, and (10) factor analysis.

The ability of the LREPS model to predict the behavior of the actual system was not established.[37] The results found with the various techniques were contradictory. However, no major defect in the model was established. The only conclusion that can be drawn is that the validity of the model's predictive capability has not been established. These tests would have to be repeated with a larger number of observations collected with a longer time increment. The 103 observations with a one-day time increment were not sufficient to draw conclusions regarding the model's predictive ability.

Sensitivity to Model Assumptions

The third and final part of the validation procedure was to determine the degree to which the characteristics of the endogenous data streams change when the form of one of the model's major assumptions is altered. Assumptions are usually made to simplify the complexity of real situations and thus facilitate the modeling process. Indeed, model construction may not be possible in many situations without incorporating rather stringent assumptions. It is, however, undesirable to have the model output dependent on the nature of the assumptions incorporated in the model. It seems reasonable that the endogenous data streams of a valid computer simulation model will not change significantly even with rather severe changes to the assumptions which are incorporated into the model.

Two of the major assumptions contained in the LREPS model were tested in this phase of the validation procedure. The first is related to the way in which demand from the consumer is generated. The second concerns the selection of products from the total product line over which this demand is allocated. Both of these assumptions were required in the initial version of LREPS because the industrial sponsor, like many other firms producing consumer goods, can expect to process hundreds of thousands of orders for hundreds of different products during the course of each year. The problem caused is that too much detail is impractical to process within the computer model design criteria of storage and running time, whereas too much aggregation of this detail will reduce the model's ability to test the effects of such changes as the introduction of new products, different inventory policies, or different demand patterns. Solution of the problem comes with the exercise of judgment by the model builders in introducing the simplifying assumptions.

This validation procedure investigated the effect of four changes in the assumptions related to product analysis and order generation. The normal blocking factor for order generation within LREPS is ten. In the validation analysis blocking factors of five and twenty were tested. The number of tracked products, ITP, used in the initial version of LREPS was a fixed set of fifty different items and these items were divided into four categories:

1. high movers or other products of special interest to management—category A1
2. high-volume items—category A
3. medium-volume items—category B
4. low-volume items—category C

A new sample of fifty products was tested and the effect of using only three product categories was also investigated.

The techniques used included (1) graphical analysis, (2) analysis of variance, (3) multiple comparison, (4) the F test, (5) correlation, (6) regression analysis, (7) the chi-square test, (8) Theil's Inequality Coefficient, (9) spectral analysis, and (10) factor analysis.

While there was not 100 percent support from all analyses for the hypothesis that no significant difference exists between the control simulation run and each of the four changes tested, neither was the hypothesis consistently rejected for any one change (even when considering only those few tests which rejected the hypothesis for one or more changes). The conclusion, therefore, was that these two major assumptions incorporated in LREPS—demand generation and product selection—do not have a significant influence on the model's endogenous data streams.

SUMMARY

This chapter described the three techniques used to validate the LREPS model: stability of endogenous variable data streams over time, sensitivity of model assumptions, and comparison of output to actual historical data. The results indicate that the LREPS model is stable over the long run. The model also satisfied the claims made concerning the generality of its structure—significant changes in specific major assumptions contained in the model did not result in significant changes in the output of the model.

While the results of these two validation procedures are positive, the ability of the model to duplicate actual historical data is still not established. But it must be emphasized that the failure to establish the predictive ability of the model does not necessarily indicate any shortcoming in the structure of the model. A more accurate evaluation of this important aspect of the model can be made only when a longer stream of actual historical data, collected at a time increment greater than one day, is available. The results of the validation procedures would undoubtedly be greatly improved for the LREPS model if two hundred observations of information collected weekly were available for use.

In addition to developing procedures for validation of LREPS, this research resulted in a generalized procedure for validation of computer simulation models.[38] The generalized procedure combines the three separate procedures presented in this chapter into a validity index which provides a basis for intramodel analysis and intermodel comparison.

7

EXPERIMENTAL DESIGN

This chapter presents a discussion related to the experimental design for the utilization of the LREPS model.[1] The chapter is divided into four major sections: (1) a review of existing simulations, (2) key considerations in experimentation, (3) strategic planning—designing experiments, and (4) tactical planning—running experiments.

As with test marketing or any other experimental investigation in the real world, experimentation with simulation requires careful design. The reason for simulation is that physical experimentation cannot be done on complex business systems. Physical experimentation has been in process for many years, and a very definitive body of knowledge has developed. In fact, simulation is basically just a type of experimental investigation, sharing the same problems as well as having some that arise due to its special characteristics. With simulation, experimentation on complex systems has become feasible, whereas before it was impractical if not impossible. Further, simulation allows for the accumulation of a great amount of experience in a relatively short period of time. The type of information it provides, however, is not basically different from that yielded by a physical experiment, and as R. W. Conway has stated:

> There is nothing inherent in the process that renders it less susceptible to the deleterious effects of poor experimental design or poor experimental techniques than its physical counterpart. There is nothing in the process that obviates the necessity of judgment, imagination, and scrupulous attention to detail on the part of the experimenter. Systems simulation promises to bring some of the advantages of an experimental science to the study of complex operating systems but it brings also the problems and limitations.[2]

The purpose of this chapter is to gain an understanding of the key aspects of experimental investigation. Since the primary objective in building LREPS is the conduct of experiments, some thought must be given to the particular type of experimental design features that must be built into it. In this way, effective and efficient experiments can be carried out with LREPS.

A REVIEW OF EXISTING SIMULATIONS: THEIR DESIGN AND ANALYSIS

Since the late 1950s, numerous large-scale computer simulation models have been built; and the variety and types of problems handled by these models have been all-encompassing.

A great deal can be learned about the methodology, validation, and experimentation required by examining other existing models. The purpose of this section, therefore, is to examine some of the better-documented computer simulations in order to gain an understanding of the problems, ramifications, and handling of experimentation. Specifically, interest will center on (1) procedures for selecting factors, (2) number of outputs being measured and methods used, (3) measurement techniques utilized, and (4) experimental designs employed. Other considerations relating to starting conditions and length of run also will be examined.

While several of the models reviewed here were discussed in the chapters on mathematical models and validation, emphasis at this point is placed on experimental design.

Cohen

K. Cohen in his doctoral dissertation "Computer Models of the Shoe, Leather, Hide Sequence" (1959) constructed two simulation models describing the aggregate behavior of shoe retailers, shoe manufacturers, and cattlehide leather tanners between 1930 and 1940. Exogenous variables included the BLS consumers' price index, disposable personal income, and the stocks of hides held by hide dealers. Endogenous variables included the retailers' selling price, sales, and shoe receipts; the tanners' selling price, production, and leather receipts; and the hide dealers' selling price.[3]

With the models he constructed, Cohen generated data for the endogenous variables for the ten-year period and visually compared them to the actual occurrences for the period. He did not develop any experiments using the models (as this was not his objective), but he did state that the main advantage of using computer simulation was to provide a concrete procedure for formulating and testing hypotheses.

Forrester

Using Industrial Dynamics, J. W. Forrester developed three hypothetical models of the firm. These include a production-distribution model, an advertising model, and a customer-producer employment model.[4] With each one, experiments were developed with the purpose of determining ways to improve management control for company success:[5]

> Unlike real life, all conditions but one can be held constant and a particular time-history repeated to see the effect of the one condition that was changed. Circumstances can be studied that might seldom be encountered in the real world. Daring changes that might seem too risky to try with an actual company can be investigated.[6]

Forrester was one of the first researchers to build large-scale models and place emphasis on experimental use, whereas up to this point, most researchers were focusing on the problems of building their models.

Using the production-distribution model, for example, Forrester introduced the following changes in order to learn the nature of the system response:

1. a simple step increase of 10 percent in the demand level,
2. a 10 percent unexpected rise and fall in retail sales over a one-year period,
3. irregular fluctuating retail sales pattern, and
4. reduction of clerical delays.

The impact or importance of these changes were based on comparative graphics. Other changes could also be examined. In essence, however, experimentation focused on use of the models but did not proceed to discuss the problems of designing experiments (what ought to be examined and what design to use) or analyzing the simulated output in a statistical manner.

Balderston

In 1962, F. E. Balderston and A. C. Hoggatt developed a simulation model of the West Coast lumber industry in order to "show how limits on market information, decentralization of market decisions, and institutional alignments affect and are affected by economic forces."[7]

Experimentation with this model involved hypotheses in three classes: those concerned with the impact of information cost and/or preference orderings upon market structure, those relating the same parameters to classical economic variables, and those relating market structure to economic results.[8] To test these hypotheses, unit cost was varied at four levels and preference orderings at two levels. Thus, eight computer runs were involved, each lasting sixty market periods (months). Eleven response variables (endogenous), each considered as a separate experiment, were measured using graphical analysis. Formal statistical testing using the Wilcoxon Two-Sample Test and the Kruskal-Wallis Test was applied to just one response variable (plant size) on day-sixty values for all three participants (manufacturers, wholesalers, and retailers). The hypothesis tests on the differences of mean plant size were conducted by grouping different computer runs together resulting in a total of twelve tests. Having treated average plant size with hypothesis testing, the distribution of plant size was then evaluated utilizing the Lorenz curve.

Cyert

R. M. Cyert and J. G. March, in 1963, developed a general model of price and output determination. Presented in *A Behavioral Theory of the Firm*, the approach was to (1) describe a general behavioral model of price and output determination in an oligopoly and (2) examine properties of the model by employing multiple regression procedures to identify the impact of samples of parameter values on selected output of the model.[9]

Experimentation consisted of varying 25 parameters through random selection of 100 random values for each of the 25 parameters in one firm while holding them at the mean value for the other firm. This was repeated for each of the three variations of the model.

The basic procedures of analysis then involved the following:

To this data we apply a multiple regression model to determine (within the linear constraints of that model) the contribution of variations in the output. The multiple regression procedure adds and drops variables systematically (reconsidering the entire set of variables at each stage) according to their contribution to the F-values associated with the regression. It identifies all variables that meet an arbitrary criterion of contribution, the criterion being the same for all 24 regression analyses.[10]

In essence, this analysis was considered by the authors as a first step in experimentation, and while it was complex, crude, and involved a host of assumptions, their approach was quite unique and proved most satisfactory in handling the problem of dealing with large numbers of parameters.

Bonini

In 1963, C. P. Bonini constructed a computer model of the behavioral theory of the firm based principally on the work of Cyert and March.[11] He was one of the first to deal in a comprehensive manner with experimentation, most researchers before him having stopped short of this point. The model developed was of a hypothetical firm which included manufacturing, sales, and an executive committee for planning and control of the whole firm.[12]

The objective of the model was to show the effects of organizational, informational, and environmental changes on the firm's decision-making process. Eight factors were carefully selected for experimentation, each having two values. The eight factors were selected to:

1. make preliminary tests to establish the reasonableness and stability of the model;
2. make changes in the external conditions not under the control of the firm and in the aggregation of factors used to simulate the systems in the model;
3. test the most crucial parameter, first—selected largely by intuition;
4. conduct experiments with factors in existing hypotheses (in economics, accounting, or the behavioral sciences). Presumably new hypotheses would also be formulated and tested.[13]

Experiments were then planned utilizing a fractional factorial design. In this way 64 computer runs were necessary rather than 2^8 (or 256).

This was accomplished by assuming that interactions higher than first order were zero and that standard statistical assumptions were valid.

With this design then, it was possible to estimate the main effects, all first-order interactions, and block effects which represented different starting conditions. For measurement purposes, six response variables (endogenous) were selected (each to be considered a separate experiment) to determine the effects of factors changes. These included price, inventory level, cost, sales, profit, and pressure. To characterize these response variables, three measures were then chosen, including the arithmetic mean, the standard deviation, and the trend. The standard technique of analysis of variance (F test) was then used to determine whether changes in the factors caused any statistically significant effects on the response variables.

Kaczka

E. E. Kaczka, in his doctoral dissertation "The Impact of Some Dimensions of Management Climate on the Performance of Industrial Organizations" (1966), constructed a simulation model. The central question investigated in this study was the following: "Does a managerial climate which is employee-oriented result in higher levels of organizational performance than a managerial climate which is task oriented?"[14]

To investigate this question, the research procedure employed was based on "(1) the design and implementation of a factorial experiment and its associated tests for statistical significance; (2) the transformation of the model of a business firm from prose to a mathematical-diagrammatic form and, in turn, this form to a computerized form."[15]

Managerial climate is described in the model by five factors which are investigated at two levels. Thirty-two (32) (or 2^5) factor combinations are considered so that a full factorial design is employed. To characterize the behavior of the model of the firm, six response variables were analyzed (mean, variance, trend) with each considered as a separate experiment using the analysis of variance (F test).

Since initial conditions can and do have impact on results, two different sets (blocks) of initial conditions were incorporated into the experimental design. Their use serves two purposes: "(1) They permit the measurement of the effect, if any, of different initial conditions on the firm's behavior. (2) They permit the testing of the major hypothesis over different input conditions."[16]

The length of run for the experiment was set at ten years or 120 time periods. The purpose for this length was to ensure that the model was stable.

Tuason

R. V. Tuason developed a simulation of the household coffee market in his doctoral dissertation research, "Experimental Simulation on a Pre-Determined Marketing Mix Strategy" (1965). The research question posed was: "Can an effective marketing mix strategy be predetermined for a firm marketing a frequently purchased consumer product by means of a parametric sensitivity analysis of time paths traced out in a simulation of sequential decision making?"[17] Tuason's hypothesis was that increased marketing efficiency could be obtained with experimental simulation of a predetermined strategy. Therefore, marketing management could get a greater return on time and money spent to try out market plans, since it would be possible to select the more promising strategy approaches from a number of policy alternatives with greater accuracy than would otherwise be the case.[18]

The model developed for the research consisted of the coffee manufacturer, who made decisions on price, deals, and product blends, his competitors—the supermarkets (retail outlets), and the consumer market.

Tuason based his plan for experimentation on two principal considerations adopted from classical statistics:

1. It is necessary to replicate all the experimentation treatments, that is, all the combination of experimental factors introduced into the research design, if the reproducibility of the experimentation results is to be assessed statistically.
2. The research design should be selected properly in order to estimate accurately the effects of the experimentation treatments.[19]

A factorial design of the 2^n type was selected:

The *raison d'être* then for a factorial design in this research stem from (1) the complexity of marketing systems phenomena, and (2) the effectiveness of the factorial experiment for a multi-factor, complex system. In fact, the existence of interraction among factors in complex systems can *only* be verified by the use of a factorial experiment.[20]

Three factors were then specified for testing the effectiveness of the strategy and two outputs specified for analysis. To measure the outputs, the analysis of variance (F Test—null hypothesis) was decided upon with either acceptance, rejection, or reservation of judgment resulting.

While the study was based on artificially generated data, it effectively demonstrated, as Bonini had done earlier, the importance of factorial design in simulation studies.

The simulation models which have been presented above can be described as follows:

First, most simulation models give greater emphasis to the model-building phase than to the experimentation phase. This would be expected with the earliest simulation models. More recent ones, however, might have pursued experimentation further.

Second, most of the experimentation conducted has been concerned with understanding the behavior in the present by comparing the fixed, real, or hypothetical system with the variable system resulting from changes in factor inputs. The next step beyond this is to evaluate the effect of future changes on the behavior and design of systems.

Third, when designs and techniques (other than graphical analysis) are employed, the most common experimental design is the full factorial design with the analysis of variance being the measurement technique. Only Bonini used a fractional factorial design. In all cases, the statistical assumptions underlying these designs and tests were assumed to be correct.

Fourth, those factors to be varied are most often determined on a qualitative and/or a priori basis. Only Cyert and March discuss a method for zeroing in on a select group of critical parameters.

Fifth, in all cases where more than one response (output) variable is measured, the approach is to consider each as a separate experiment.

Many other simulation models in business, economics, and the behavioral sciences, besides the ones discussed above, have been constructed. The most notable include the Shycon and Maffei simulation model[21] of a distribution system in 1960 and Amstutz's[22] simulation model of competitive market response (1967). Both simulation models are definite contributions in the model-building sense; however, neither discuss the concept or application of experimentation except in a general way.

KEY CONSIDERATIONS IN EXPERIMENTATION

In a computer simulation experiment, as in any experiment, the investigator is concerned with testing some hypothesis by changing a particular factor or input and observing the resultant response.

For the most part, the literature on experimentation is concerned with real world experiments and includes work by V. Chew,[23] W. G. Cochran and G. M. Cox,[24] O. L. Davies,[25] R. A. Fisher,[26] B. J. Winer,[27] and many others. Much less attention has been paid to experimentation relevant to mathematical models.

Certain writers including R. W. Conway,[28] Naylor et al.,[29] C. McMillian and R. F. Gonzalez,[30] and K. D. Tocher,[31] have discussed the relevance, importance, and considerations of experimentation with computer simulation models at various levels of presentation. Bonini,[32] G. S. Fishman and P. J. Kiviat,[33] and others have concerned themselves with particular or specific types of problems in computer simulation experiments.

The considerations involved in this type of experimentation are presented in numerous ways by these writers, depending on their orientation.

Conway[34] classifies the considerations of experimentation in two categories: (1) strategic planning—design of an experiment that will yield the desired information, and (2) tactical planning—determination of how each of the test runs specified in the experimental design is to be executed.

McMillian and Gonzalez[35] state that procedures have to be developed for: (1) determining the implications that changes of inputs (parameters, exogenous variables) will have generally, and (2) planning and executing experiments efficiently.

Naylor et al.,[36] who have given the most thorough treatment, state that experimentation, as used by LREPS, consists of two parts—the design of experiments and the analysis of simulated data. According to Naylor, having already defined the experimental problem, endogenous variables, and factors (exogenous variable) and parameters, the design of simulation experiments has two important goals. First, the factor levels, combinations of levels, and order of experiments must be selected. Second, care must be taken to ensure that the results will be reasonably free from random error.

The analysis of simulated data consists of three steps: collecting and processing simulated data, computation of test statistics, and interpretation of results.

Naylor presents a comprehensive review of the problems involved in experimental design including the problems of validity, stochastic convergence, size, motive, and the many-response problem.[37]

A host of considerations and problems are tied one to another in experimentation with simulation models. Experimental design depends on the number of factors and their characteristics. It also depends on measurement techniques. Likewise, measurement techniques depend on the type of simulated data, the assumptions that are made. The number and level of factors depend on the objectives, computer costs, and so on. Based on the treatment given to this topic by the writers discussed thus far, the following is a synthesis of those considerations pertinent to experimentation with LREPS developed within Conway's framework:

1. Strategic Planning—Designing Experiments
    objectives of experimentation
    factor characterization and specification
    outputs (response variable) designation
    measurement technique determination
    experimental design alternatives
2. Tactical Planning—Running Experiments
    starting conditions—accounting for and minimizing their effects on the output

    randomization (stochastic convergence)—accounting for and minimizing its effect on the output

A brief discussion of each of these considerations is presented in the next two sections.

STRATEGIC PLANNING: DESIGNING EXPERIMENTS

Selection of appropriate experimental design and measurement techniques will generally be the last decision made in planning an experiment. The investigator will reach these decisions by evaluating the many alternative design and measurement techniques relative to the nature of the experimental objectives, factors, and outputs.

Objectives of Experimentation

Learning more about the system being investigated (in this case, LREPS) is the primary goal of any experimental investigation. George Box[38] states that this goal can be achieved by the objectives of (1) optimization—find the combination of factor levels at which the response variable is maximized (or minimized), (2) investigation—determine the underlying mechanisms governing the process under study through analysis of the relationship of the response to the factors. This requires that careful and precise consideration be given to the present level of knowledge and to the questions and uncertainties which exist. Only in this way will the experimental data yield pertinent results.

Associated with each of these objectives is a set of experimental designs, which was discussed above. If optimization is the experimental objective, then the single-factor method or the method of steepest descent (ascent) will be used. If investigation is the objective, then full-factorial, fractional-factorial, rotable, or response-surface designs will be used with analysis of variance, regression analysis, and so on.

Factor Characterization and Specification

A factor is a variable which can be set by the experimenter with the purpose of yielding some response from the model. Factors are also called independent variables, exogenous (input) variables, treatments, and parameters. The chief consideration is the selection of those factors which are to be changed for purposes of experimental investigation so that critical runs can be made in a reasonable time. For example, to completely test three variables at two levels using a full-factorial design requires 2^3 or eight simulation runs, while a complete testing of five variables at two levels requires 2^5 or thirty-two runs. Consequently, appropriate selection of truly critical factors is of utmost importance.

According to Naylor[39, 40, 41] factors in experimentation are characterized in five ways (J. L. Overholt[42] also presents a similar characterization), and recognition of the type of factor is necessary for good design and analysis. These five factors are discussed below.

First, a factor can be defined as controlled or uncontrolled. A factor is controlled if the experimenter purposefully selects its level.

Second, a factor can be observed or unobserved. If the levels of a factor are measured and recorded as part of the data, it is considered to be observed. In most situations, the only observed factors are those that are controlled.

Third, the effect of the factor is either a subject for study or the factor is included only to increase the precision of the experiment. The distinction between factors of interest and those included to increase precision is important for it serves to emphasize the fact that for almost all experiments the factors of basic interest are not the only ones to significantly affect the outcome.

The fourth factor relates to the quantitative versus qualitative response relationship. If the levels of a factor have a meaningful relationship with a response, it is considered quantitative; otherwise, a factor is qualitative. This characterization of factors is most salient, since regression analysis and curve fitting techniques are appropriate when factors are quantitative, while analysis of variance is appropriate for qualitative factors.

Fifth and finally, a factor is fixed if all the levels of particular interest are included in the experiment. Where only a random sample from the population of levels is included, the factor is said to be random. With random factors, inferences of a probabilistic nature can be made about factor levels which do not appear. Naylor[43] calls the factor selection problem one of size or too many factors. This arises in both the real-world and computer-simulation experiments. Numerous writers propose criteria similar to the scientific method approach.

As presented earlier, Bonini[44] proposed the selection of eight factors to: (1) perform preliminary tests of model reasonableness, (2) evaluate changes in the external conditions not under firm control, (3) test crucial parameters selected largely by intuition, and (4) conduct experiments with factors existing as well as new hypotheses.

Cochran and Cox[45] propose that the objectives of the study be explicitly stated, the experiment be described, and the method of analysis be outlined before the experiment is started.

Overholt[46] presents several additional considerations in factor selection including (1) objectives of the sponsor, (2) the recognition that certain factors have a bearing and are important, (3) examination of the factors in the proper breadth, (4) translation of variables if necessary so that they are compatible with the simulation, (5) treatment of uncertainty through use of "optimistic" and "pessimistic" inputs or through random sampling where the population can be estimated, (6) development of a hierarchy of solutions, (7) evaluating tentative designs to determine the feasibility of using the proposed factors, and

(8) recognition of deadlines and other constraints which limit the number of factors which can be tested in a given time.

Response Variables

Strategic planning outputs or responses are the endogenous variables or results obtained in the simulation experiment and depend upon the settings or levels of the factors used in the experiment. The problems with responses are twofold: which are to be observed, and when to observe them. Generally, there is a desire to observe more than one output or response. In the simulations reviewed, all experimenters observed at least two and generally more responses.

Naylor[47] calls this the multiple response problem, and one approach to solving it is to treat an experiment with many responses as many experiments each with a single response. This is the approach that was followed by the simulations reviewed. Another approach is to combine (e.g., by addition, etc.) the responses and treat them as a single response. The other problem, when to measure each response, is generally a judgmental decision.

Measurement Techniques

Measurement techniques and design alternatives are closely allied since any well-designed experiment requires that consideration be given to methods of analyzing the data once they are obtained; and as Naylor and others have stated, most of the classical experimental design techniques are described in the expectation that the data will be analyzed by either analysis of variance and/or regression analysis.

The great bulk of experimental design techniques in the literature, such as full-factorial, fractional-factorial, Latin-square, and so forth, have the analysis of variance as the intended method of data analysis. With analysis of variance, individual factor effects (main effects) as well as interaction effects can be ascertained from the data. Specific measurement tests with the analysis of variance include the F-Test, multiple comparisons, multiple rankings, spectral analysis, and sequential analysis. The F-Test is used to test the null hypothesis (that alternatives are the same) and if the null hypothesis is rejected, then further analysis using multiple comparisons and multiple rankings is usually appropriate.

The use of the F-test alone is subject to question in regard to evaluation of observed differences. Hypothesizing that model changes will not alter system behavior (null hypothesis) is not appropriate, according to some researchers, since changes in rules and other parameters result in system behavior change, however slight. Failure to reject the null hypothesis only indicates that the test is not sensitive to the differences for the given sample size or length of run.[48]

Multiple comparisons[49] will tell how alternatives differ. Multiple rankings[50] rank the alternatives. Three important assumptions of these techniques include normality, equality of variance,[51] and statistical independence. While the first two do not necessarily have to be met, the third, statistical independence, must be.[52] Yet, in almost all simulations, some degree of dependence or autocorrelation exists.[53] This problem has been attacked in several different ways. First, many investigators simply assume independence without checking to see if this assumption is really met. Of those simulation models previously reviewed, all accepted independence on face value. Second, linear transformations are performed on the original time series to reduce or eliminate the autocorrelation. Traditional analysis is then applied assuming the transformed observations are uncorrelated.[54] This procedure, however, throws away a considerable amount of valuable information about the behavior of the process, and the transformed time series may in fact be inappropriate for comparison purposes.[55] Third, the sample record length can be divided into intervals that are longer than the interval of major autocorrelation. These intervals are then treated as if they were independent.[56] The key problem with this approach is that the selection of the sample record length and sampling interval is almost arbitrary, since in most cases there is neither enough prior or posterior justification to make the choice more scientifically.[54] Fourth, the computer experiment can be replicated with sample means and variances computed across the ensemble rather than over time. This method will undoubtedly lead to excessive computer time and also fail to yield the information desired.[58] Fifth, a method proposed by M. J. Gilman[59] takes into consideration the presence of autocorrelation and requires that sampling stop when the variance of the sample mean falls below a predetermined level.[60]

Sixth, and finally, spectral analysis or some equivalent technique can be used which is based on a model in which the probabilities of component outcomes in a time series depend on previous outcomes in the series.[61] Spectral analysis is frequently employed in the physical sciences and more recently has been used to analyze the behavior of economic time series.[62]

Although there has been a fair amount of discussion by authors concerning the use of spectral analysis as a technique in experimentation, so far its application has been limited to validation of simulation models. An example of this is Naylor, Wallace, and Sasser's application of spectral analysis to validation of a computer simulation model of the textile industry.[63] Most simulation models, including all of the ones reviewed here, do not consider spectral analysis since the assumption of independence has been considered as correct; hence, the analysis of variance technique is used. To test for autocorrelation of time series, the Durbin-Watson statistic can be computed.[64]

While spectral analysis is useful in dealing with the problem of autocorrelation, sequential sampling[65] is a technique which focuses on minimizing the number of observations (sample size or length of computer run) necessary for obtaining the information which is required from the experiment with predetermined accuracy. The sample size n is considered to be a random variable dependent on the outcome of the first n-1 observations, rather than being set in advance.

Other measurement techniques include regression analysis, and the category of techniques classed as nonparametric methods (chi-square, Wilcoxon Two-Sample Test, Kruskal-Wallis Test, and others). In general, these techniques are not as widely applied in simulation experiments (one excellent example is Cyert and March,[66] who used regression analysis for determination of critical parameters; another is Balderston and Hoggatt,[67] who used nonparametric techniques).

Experimental Design Alternatives

The discussion thus far has centered on alternative measurement techniques. Before data can be analyzed, however, experiments must be designed. Many different experimental designs exist, some of which have been briefly mentioned. J. S. Hunter and T. H. Naylor single out four different designs which may be particularly relevant, including full-factorial, fractional-factorial, rotable, and response-surface designs.[68]

Based on the literature review already presented, the full-factorial design was the design most frequently employed. In this type of design, the total number of design points is the product of the number of levels of each factor. If there are K factors with n values each, then the number of design points is n^k. For example, an experiment with five factors having two levels each would require $2^5 = 32$ design points (32 computer runs). This design allows for analysis of every interaction between factors and is therefore generally used in behavioral simulations since higher-order interactions may be important. On the other hand, the number of factors which can be examined is somewhat limited since a full-factorial design can require an unmanageably large number of design points (and hence the number of computer runs) if more than a few factors are investigated.

If excessive computer time is a problem, then a fractional-factorial design may be more appropriate. Designs of this type such as Latin-square or Greco-Latin-square require only a fraction of the trials or computer runs required by the full-factorial design without much loss in information. Little information is generally lost because higher-order interactions are ignored. The focus is on main effects and two-factor interactions.

Most often, fractional designs are used for screening or identifying the most important variable influencing a response. The one problem with this type of design is the confounding of effects which can occur in any design which utilizes fewer trials than the full-factorial design. Without a full design, higher-order interaction effects, if there are any, become part of main effects. Thus confounding occurs since the statistic used to measure the existence of an observed effect can say that it, an effect, exists but its nature cannot be determined; that is, whether it is a main effect, a higher-order interaction effect, or some additive combination of the two.

Only when the interaction effect is negligibly small or is assumed to be zero is there justification for stating that the observed effect estimates the main effect. To ensure against this problem, a fractional-factorial design will be arranged so that estimates of the effects thought to be important are confounded by effects thought to be unimportant.

Rotable designs[69, 70] have been developed for fitting second- (and higher-) order polynomials to output data. So long as first-order regression equations are being used to fit the data generated by an experiment, full- or fractional-factorial designs are acceptable. However, to fit a second- (and higher-) order polynomial to the output data requires a rotable design. Generally, a rotable design will have less design points than a full factorial but more than a fractional factorial. The fractional-factorial design is not appropriate in this case since it will lead to parameter estimates of the coefficients which have relatively low precision.[71, 72] A. C. Hoggatt provides an excellent example of rotable designs in his simulation experiments with marketing models.[73]

Response-surface designs are designs which are appropriate when response-surface exploration by regression analysis is the aim of the experiment.[74] In the discussion of factorial designs and analysis of variance, the factors are either qualitative or assumed so. When the factors are quantitative, and the response y is related to the factors by some mathematical function f, then regression analysis is the more appropriate technique of data analysis and response-surface designs are more appropriate designs. The functional relationship between the response and the quantitative factors is called the response surface.[75, 76]

Reduction in required experiment size is the chief advantage of response-surface designs over comparable factorial designs without a reduction in the information obtained.

The designs presented thus far are of the investigative type. Often, however, there is a desire to optimize. With LREPS, for example, optimization could mean minimizing the total cost of the system. (Alternatively, it could mean maximizing customer service.) Two optimum seeking methods include the method of steepest descent (ascent), and the single factor method.

According to Burdick and Naylor,[77] Hunter and Naylor,[78] and others, in the method of steepest descent (ascent), the following steps are involved: beginning with a design point in the factor space, the first step is to take a linear approximation. Since the response surface may not be a known function, a linear fit by least squares may be obtained using a simplex-, a fractional-factorial, or a first-order rotable design. The next step is to explore along the direction of steepest descent (ascent) as determined above. "Design points would be chosen along this direction until a point is reached at which no further progress seems likely. At this point a new local exploration is performed with the possible result that a new direction of steepest descent (ascent) will be obtained."[79] The local linear fit should become nearly horizontal after several cycles. As a final step, exploration of the apparent minimum (maximum) will be done by fitting a local quadratic approximation to the response surface using, for instance, a second-order rotable design or a three-level fractional-factorial design. If the approximating quadratic is positive definite (negative definite), then the minimum (maximum) of the response surface may have been reached.

The single-factor method,[80] an alternative optimum-seeking method, involves varying the levels of a single factor while the levels of all other factors are held constant. Once the results of the first factor are optimized, other factors are varied in turn. After this single-factor search is completed, the cycle is repeated until no further optimization in the response variables occurs.

Both the single factor and steepest descent (ascent) have advantages over one another which require close analysis before final selection.

TACTICAL PLANNING: RUNNING EXPERIMENTS

The purpose of experimentation is to measure the effects of experimental changes that are made in the model. Other effects, however, may have an impact, including the effects of starting conditions, and randomization or stochastic convergence. Steps should be taken to ensure that there is control of these effects to the degree possible.

Starting Conditions

With a dynamic simulation model, a question arises as to the values to be assigned to the model's variables and parameters at the point in time when the simulation of the system is to begin. Determining how to start the model and how to obtain measurements that are not biased by the method of starting or stopping is a key procedural question. According to Naylor et al., "This question is not easily answered for most systems, and the investigator usually must resort to the trial and error methods for determining a set of initial values for the system that will not lead to distorted results in later time periods."[81]

Conway suggests three alternatives to handling this problem:

1. Test each system starting "empty and idle."
2. Test each system using a common set of starting conditions that is essentially a compromise between the two different sets of reasonable starting conditions.
3. Test each system with its own "reasonable" starting conditions.

The second strategy is clearly more efficient than the first; the choice between the second and third is less obvious. While presumably less time would be lost in achieving near-equilibrium conditions by using the third strategy, one must also consider the possibility that the use of different starting conditions is biasing the results. In general, one should compare alternatives under as close to identical conditions as possible. In deference to this canon I would avoid using the third strategy.

I would be reluctant to report an investigation in the following manner:

1. I wished to compare two systems: A and B.
2. I anticipated that System A would yield a greater mean value of attribute M than would System B.
3. I performed an experiment in which the initial value of attribute M for System A was set greater than that for System B.
4. The experimental results demonstrate that the mean value of attribute M for System A is significantly greater than that for System B.

Constructing a "good compromise" set of starting conditions to materially shorten the necessary stabilization period is not a trivial task, even when possessing considerable knowledge of the nature of the equilibrium conditions for each alternative. But at least there is the consolation that it is almost impossible to do worse than "empty and idle" conditions so that any effort will allow some reduction in computing time.[82]

Stochastic Convergence

In stochastic models, observation of the effects of experimental changes is made more difficult by the random processes in the model. Stochastic properties are built into the model in fact in order that the model will be more representative of the real world and the random fluctuation which occurs therein. To handle this random fluctuation or random error in real-world experiments, factors such as blocks or concomitant variables, which are not of basic interest to the investigator, are included. In simulation experiments, ironically, the random error cannot be handled in the same manner since additional factors cannot be included for error-reduction purposes. Once the model is specified, all the uncontrolled factors are absorbed in the probabilistic specifications for the exogenous inputs.[83]

Two approaches for error reduction do exist. The first involves increasing the sample size; the second, the use of Monte Carlo techniques. Most experiments are intended to provide information about population parameters such as expected or mean communications cost, inbound and outbound transportation cost, inventory cost, order-cycle time, and so forth. The sample averages derived from the experiment, however, will be subject to random error and therefore not necessarily be equal to its respective population average. Increasing the size of the sample will, however, increase the probability that the sample average will be close to the population average. "The convergence of sample averages for increasing sample size is called stochastic convergence."[84]

Sample size can be increased in three ways: increase the total length of the simulation run, replicate runs of a given length using different sets of pseudo-random numbers, and reduce the minimum time unit.[85]

The chief problem, however, is that stochastic convergence is a slow process:

> A measure of the amount of random fluctuation interest in a chance quantity is its standard deviation. If σ is the standard deviation of a single observation, then the standard deviation of the average of n observations is $\sigma/\sqrt{n}$. Thus, in order to halve the random error one must quadruple the sample size n. . . . It can easily happen that a reasonably small random error requires an unreasonably large sample size.[86]

Monte Carlo techniques in many cases therefore offer a viable alternative for reducing error since stochastic convergence proceeds so slowly. With Monte Carlo techniques, the underlying principle is the utilization of knowledge about model structure, properties of the probability distributions of the exogenous inputs, and properties of the observed variates actually used for inputs to increase the precision.[87]

SUMMARY

In using simulation to develop more realistic, less aggregative dynamic models of a firm, a physical distribution system, and so on, the purpose is to achieve innovations in theory in these areas. In 1960, the *American Economic Review* published a symposium on simulation. Martin Shubik in that December issue made the following statement:

> Simulation studies promise to provide the way to add the richness (in terms of explicit consideration of information costs, marketing variables, organizational structure, and so forth) needed to obtain adequate theories of the firm, pricing, and market structure. The new methodology is beginning to offer the opportunity both to construct more complex theories and to validate them.[88]

Other authors, including Cohen and Cyert, have made similar prognoses. As of 1971, this has not occurred. The chief reasons include:

1. The lack of adequate data. Generally the data required to build a highly disaggregative computer model are not available.
2. A lack of knowledge about the decision processes actually followed by firms. Obtaining knowledge of this type requires not only empirical data of the decision processes of actual firms but also a thorough grasp of the contributions of the behavioral sciences (psychology, sociology, political science, business administration) to decision theory.[89]
3. A lack of emphasis on experimentation. As in any experiment, careful thought should be given to the problem of experimental design and analysis of results.[90]

8

LREPS UTILIZATION

INTRODUCTION

This chapter, in two sections, presents an overview of the utilization of LREPS. The first section discusses the utilization of the LREPS model to assist management in applied systems planning. The second section discusses current and planned project team efforts to extend the scope of LREPS for systems planning and to utilize LREPS in basic business research. The initial utilization of LREPS was oriented toward applied systems planning to physical distribution situations as defined by the project sponsor. The following types of situations are representative of the tests that can be conducted over a planning period utilizing LREPS:

1. location problems
2. inventory control policies
3. modification of physical distribution system components
4. distribution channel alternatives
5. new product introductions
6. sales forecasts impacts
7. customer service standards
8. distribution center service areas
9. partial line warehouse stocking policies
10. changing customer order characteristics
11. contingency planning
12. environmental and act of nature analysis

Numerous other planning situations are within the capabilities of the LREPS model. The above list is merely a sample of the potential systems planning applications.

Applications of LREPS can concentrate upon the target, controllable, or environmental variables. For a specified target variable, such as desired level of customer service, sales, or system cost, the model will seek a physical distribution system structure capable of achieving the desired target. For example, the model can be set to seek a system structure that provides a specified level of customer service. For this situation, the location algorithm could be set to add or delete automatically the facility locations for a given order processing system, a given inventory management policy, for each product and transportation capability until the target level is achieved.

An example of the output generated by the LREPS model, that is useful in evaluating applications concentrating on target variables, is illustrated in figure 8-1A.[1] The output example illustrates the level of detail available for each distribution center and demand unit evaluated. The most significant aspects of the data for evaluating a specified level of customer service, for example, would be the various components of total cost and service measures over the planning horizon.

Systems planning with the controllable variables consists of holding the environmental variables constant from experiment to experiment, with respect to level and rate of change, while one or more of the controllable variables are adjusted in a heuristic manner. An example would be the testing and measurement of several different inventory policies for all or a subset of the tracked products given the other physical distribution system components.

Of specific interest for this type of problem is the output generated for the inventory condition of each distribution center evaluated. Given expected sales, for example, sensitivities in inventory on hand, number of stockouts, percent sales units backordered, average stockout delay, average lead time, and inventory turns would indicate the specific effects of variations in inventory policies. Figure 8-1B illustrates information output capabilities related to inventory condition of the distribution center.

The effect of changing the customer and/or the product mix represents additional examples that can be tested and measured for a given arrangement of other system components. Of interest in situations involving changes in customer mix and/or customer purchase order patterns is the output information illustrated in figure 8-1C.

Figure 8-1
Representative Information Output LREPS

SECTION A—TOTAL SYSTEM AND INDIVIDUAL DISTRIBUTION CENTER DATA

Summary for Selected Period—One Facility in Solution

Sales $ $\frac{\$}{7079.8}$	Cost $ $\frac{\$}{607.3}$	Profit Contrib. $ $\frac{\$}{6472.5}$	Order Cycle Time $\frac{}{6.2}$	Inventory on Hand $\frac{}{227.0}$

Sales Information:

Dollars $\frac{}{7079.8}$	Weight $\frac{}{4574}$	Cube $\frac{}{580}$	Cases $\frac{}{400}$	Lines $\frac{}{80,100}$	Orders $\frac{}{13,650}$

Component Cost Information:

Outbound $\frac{}{123.3}$	Inbound $\frac{}{30.7}$	Throughput $\frac{}{180.2}$	Commics. $\frac{}{12.6}$	Fac. $\frac{}{200.0}$	Invn. $\frac{}{60.5}$	Total $\frac{}{607.3}$

Order Cycle Time Information:

Total Order Cycle $\frac{}{6.2}$	Backorder Penalty (BP) $\frac{}{0.3}$	Order Cycle W/O-BP $\frac{}{5.9}$	Standard Deviation Cycle $\frac{}{0.6}$	Average Transit Time $\frac{}{2.0}$	Standard Deviation Transit Time $\frac{}{0.3}$	Desired to Actual Service Ratio $\frac{}{0.91}$

Proportion Within Order Cycle Time:

Days	3 Days	5 Days	7 Days	9 Days	11 Days
Orders	0.10	0.70	0.85	0.95	1.0
Dollars	0.15	0.75	0.88	0.98	1.0

SECTION B—PRODUCT TRACK INFORMATION

Summary for Selected Period Per Product and Total All Products by Individual Warehouse and Demand Units

Manufacturing Replenishment:

	Plant 1	Plant 2	Plant N
Reorder Avg. Days Lead Time	55 / 1.5	60 / 6.0	45 / 7.5

Distribution Center Period Performance:

Inventory On Hand	Total Stockouts	Total Reorders	% Case Units Backordered	Inventory Turns/Year
200	135	899	1.0	6.1

Avg. Stock-out Delay	Standard Deviation of Avg. Stockout Delay
6.3	3.2

SECTION C—DEMAND UNIT DATA

Demand Unit	Sales Dollars	PD Costs	Weight	Cube	Sales Units	Lines	Orders
Unit 1	283.2	200.0	180.3	23.2	16.0	3204.0	546.0
Unit 2	709.1	650.0	480.5	60.3	42.0	8120.0	1465.0
Unit N	141.1	100.0	92.1	12.6	8.0	1610.0	268.0

Once a best policy for a given system structure is established, other system component variables can be varied to evaluate the suitability of the selected variable level under a range of different conditions. This type of sensitivity analysis centers around the asking of "what if" types of questions.

Finally, different assumptions concerning the environmental variables can be tested to determine the consequences of such events as strikes, introduction of jumbo jet aircraft, a change in freight rates, and so on. This form of testing enables the selection of system alternatives that are highly flexible, that is, are suitable for all conceivable changes in the environmental variables.

To illustrate current applications of LREPS in applied systems planning three areas of application are briefly reported. First, an example of the application of LREPS to physical distribution situations is presented. The second area develops a build-up forecasting technique that will generate short-term market forecasts for products by utilizing the order allocation capabilities of LREPS. Finally, the third area involves discussion of the application of a financially oriented LREPS model to applied systems planning.

Applications—Physical Distribution (LREPS-PD)

In this category the following three examples of applications to systems planning are presented: evaluation of customer service capabilities, facility planning, and evaluation of new product introduction.[2]

Evaluation of Customer Service Capabilities

One major problem in physical distribution planning is the determination of customer service capacity. In actual practice the service policy is an area subjected to considerable opinion and limited facts. Naturally, marketing desires high levels of physical response to customer orders. This generally means that the resultant physical distribution system will either employ numerous field warehouses or very fast and high cost order processing and transportation capability. From a cost viewpoint, high levels of customer service are expensive. In addition, the marginal service value of each dollar invested in a system to achieve higher and higher levels of customer service experiences a diminishing return. What is the proper balance?

Simulated planning in the area of customer service places primary emphasis on target variables. Two applications of the model, described below, will illustrate two approaches to the problem of optional customer service at minimum cost, and with a forecasted increase in demand.

For the first application, the planning situation called for a ten-year evaluation of warehousing requirements given a 50 percent sales growth forecast. The existing system consisted of six regional distribution centers with 80 percent of all orders being serviced within a five-day total order cycle.

A preliminary analysis of the system using LREPS presented three design alternatives: expand the existing facilities, add two new facilities, and add three new facilities. Simulation of these alternatives was performed, given the minimum 80 percent service level, expected increase in sales, and the objective to minimize total cost.

Over the planning horizon, the simulation indicated that total system cost was similar for each alternative as shown in figure 8-2. Alternative 1 experienced the highest transport costs with the lowest inventory costs. The situation was reversed for Alternative 3. The most significant difference between the alternatives, as illustrated in figure 8-3, was the customer service capabilities. All three systems achieved the target level of 80 percent of all orders filled within 5 days. Alternative 3 however realized approximately 95 percent service level, hence was 15 percent more effective than Alternative 1 at about the same total cost. In anticipation of increased demand, a target variable, the utilization of the optional service and cost constraints of the LREPS Model produced a flexible plan for expanding service capabilities.

Another useful application of LREPS is to simulate the relationship of inventory and location versus different inventory policies. In this second application, the customer wanted to add a second warehouse in an effort to improve existing service capabilities and average order cycle by reducing transit time. A second alternative was to alter existing inventory policies by increasing safety stock at the existing warehouse, with the hope of improving the average order-cycle time via a reduction in backorders. The target variable involved was an average order-cycle time of 4.6 days with 75 percent of all orders being filled within 5 days.

Simulation of these two alternatives indicated that the addition of a warehouse reduced the average order-cycle time to 4.1 days, which was equivalent to increasing the orders filled within 5 days to 92 percent. Alternative 2, increasing safety stock, decreased the order-cycle time by

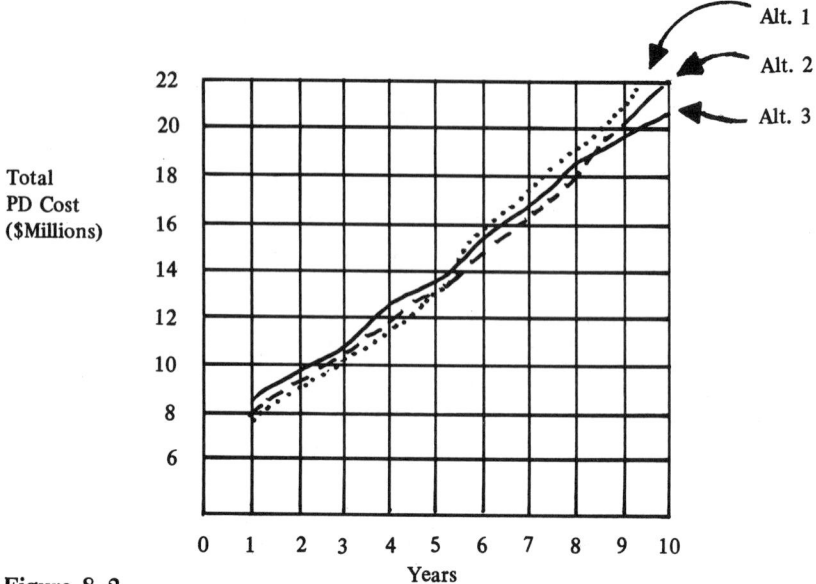

Figure 8–2
Total Cost—Illustration I

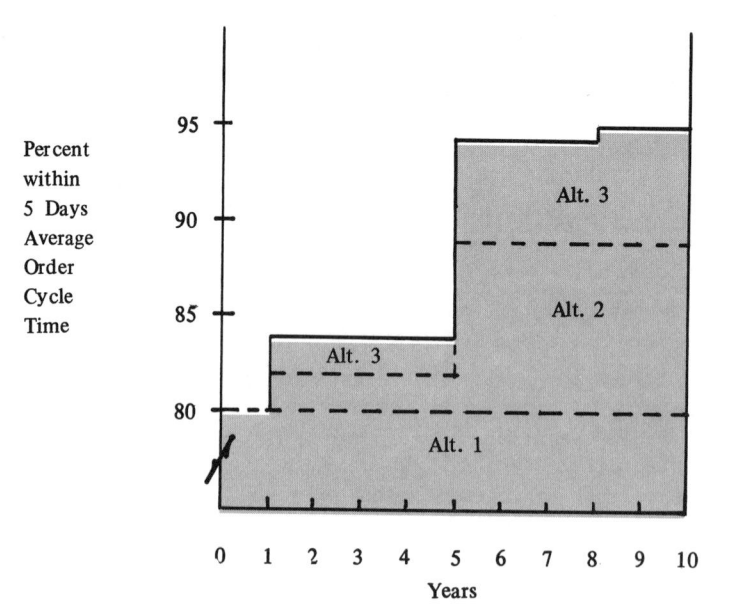

Figure 8–3
Order Cycle Time—Illustration I

only .3 days and, equivalently, increased the percentage of orders filled within 5 days by only 12 percent to 87 percent. In addition, over the ten-year period, the second warehouse provided the lowest cost alternative.

The service-cost relationships are illustrated in figures 8-4 and 8-5 respectively. Although the addition of a warehouse generated the higher cost for the first two years, over the long term it resulted in the lowest cost at the highest service level. The striking result of this analysis revealed that a combination of the two alternatives would produce the desired goals over the ten-year planning horizon. By increasing inventory at the current location, the customer could realize a 12 percent increase in service capabilities at the lowest total cost, and with the establishment of a warehouse by year four would realize an additional 5 percent improvement in service still at a least cost relationship.

Facility Planning

The classical physical distribution planning problem for a firm concerns how many warehouse facilities should be included in a system, how large each should be, where they should be located, and which market area or customers should be serviced by each facility. This planning problem is appropriately approached from the viewpoint of total cost, and the solution can be expected to change with time.

The capability of LREPS to approach the location problem in terms of a continuous ten-year planning horizon offers a new dimension to the analysis. First, total cost measurement of location and inventory planning on an integrated systems basis is possible.[3, 4] Second, the potential of various ownership arrangements as to private and public warehouse facilities can be tested.[5] Third, alternative stocking policies and multichannel supply lines based upon inventory, customer, and order composition can be tested. Finally, and perhaps most important, alternatives of facility investment with related risk can be traded off, against less-than-most-economical distribution thereby obtaining measures of cash flow and investment for each alternative. In essence, full extension of the facility plan over the planning horizon can help plan where to locate, when to locate, sequence of location, impact of expansion on current facilities, and holds forth the potential to postpone expansion by adjusting distribution patterns when economically justified.[6]

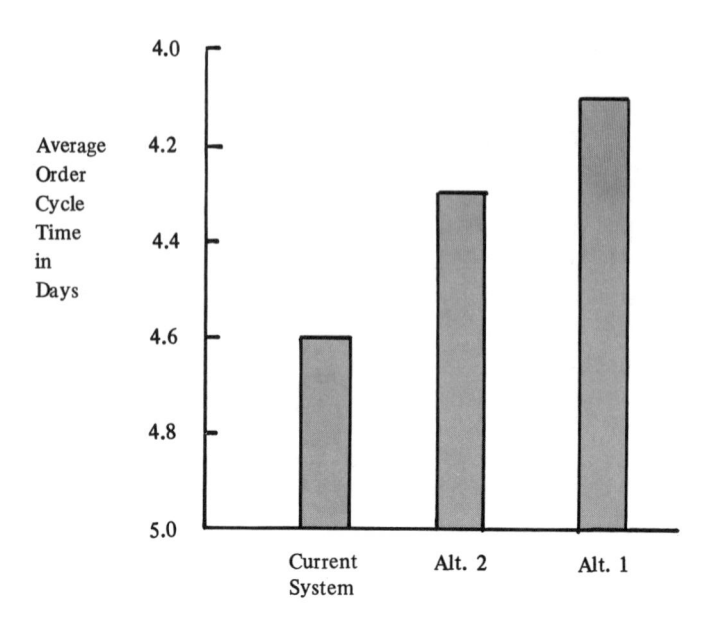

**Figure 8–4
Total Cost—Illustration II**

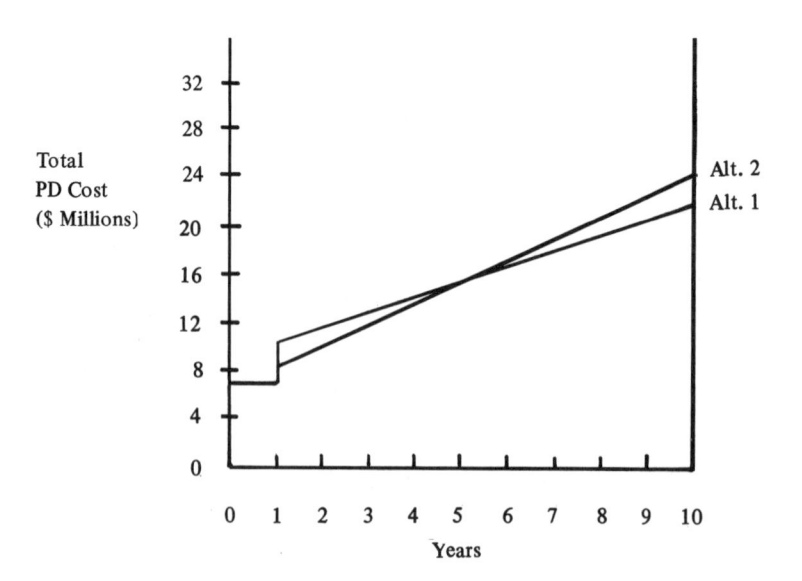

**Figure 8–5
Order Cycle Time—Illustration II**

An application of the LREPS model to facility planning involved simulation of total system service relationships on: the number and sequencing of warehouse locations, inventory cost related to performance delays for an eight-location structure, and market area adjustment to postpone timing of warehouse additions. In this application, a specific marketing situation was simulated over a ten-year planning horizon. The objective was to determine the distribution configuration and inventory policy to achieve the shortest possible average order-cycle duration. Given an initial configuration of six distribution center locations, an expansion plan was developed from a list of thirty-five additional potential distribution center locations. From the list of potential distribution centers the facility location algorithms of LREPS selected the sequence and number of distribution center locations. The algorithm determined the expansion sequence by selecting each additional distribution center based on an approximation of achieving maximum added service at minimum added cost. During the simulation runs inventory performance was held constant, for example, 85 percent of all customer orders being filled within the average order-cycle time. As expected, improvement in the average order-cycle time increased at a decreasing rate as additional distribution centers were added.

Based upon the information presented in figure 8-6 the client elected to evaluate the eight distribution center configuration. For this configuration and a constant average service level of 5 days order-cycle time, the percentage of orders filled was allowed to vary for different levels of safety stock. For this particular situation the annual inventory cost would increase from $7 million for 85 percent fulfillment within the 5 days to $14 million for 100 percent fulfillment (figure 8-7).

Finally, a sensitivity analysis was performed of the service and cost of the two additional distribution centers relative to market area assignment. In this analysis market area assignments to specific distribution centers were allowed to shift a maximum of twice during the ten-year planning horizon. The objective was to determine if a tradeoff in increased transportation cost by less than optimum market area assignment versus postponed plant investment could be achieved at little or no sacrifice in customer service. The results in this situation suggested a plan to postpone the first facility by one year and the second facility by two years.

A second illustration of facility planning involves selecting the best plan for distribution within the United States of consumer product line manufactured overseas. The alternatives tested in this situation were:

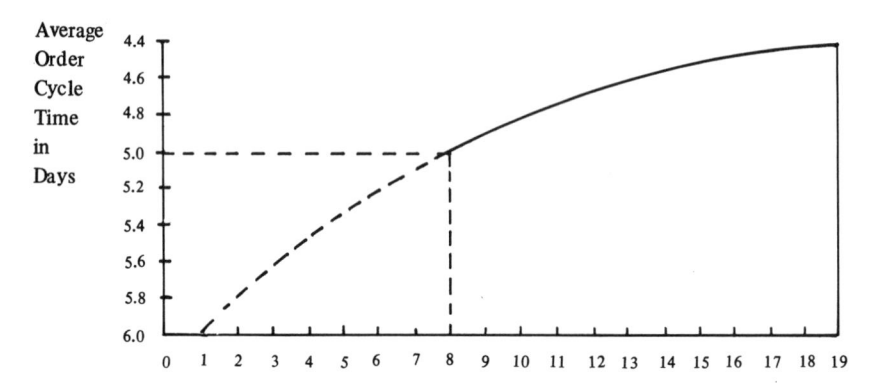

Figure 8–6
Relationship Distribution Centers to Order Cycle Time—Illustration III

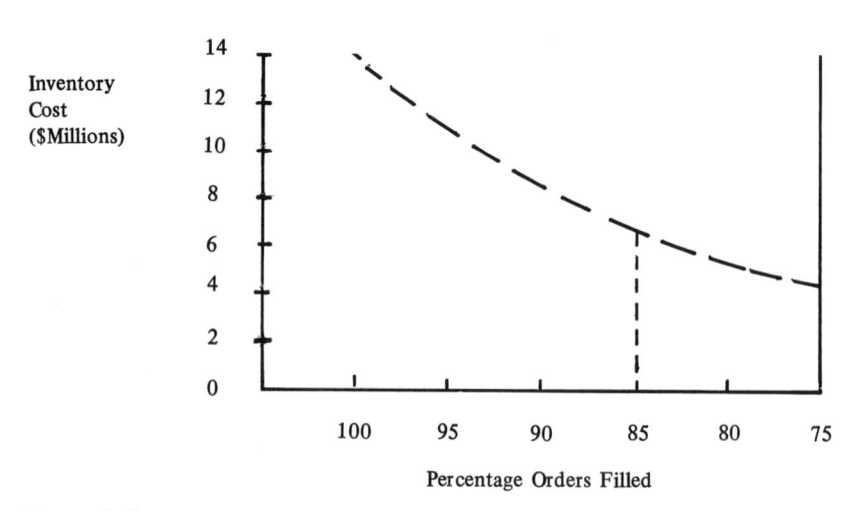

Figure 8–7
Percentage Orders Filled in 5.0 Average Order Cycle Days—Eight Warehouse Configuration—One Year—Illustration III

distribution to all customers from the one existing location in the Midwest, direct shipments from the overseas plant to customers/distributors, and regional distribution centers utilized in conjunction with the existing location in the Midwest.

In this situation, simulation of several years' sales activity indicated that a combination of shipping direct to a selected set of large distributors and continuing to ship through the midwestern distribution center for the remaining customers would be the most appropriate alternative. As the market demand shifts for the particular product line, additional distributors will become large enough to warrant direct shipment from overseas. The simulation also indicated that increased volume would probably warrant location of a regional distribution center(s) on the West Coast.

Evaluation of New Product Introductions

Given a physical distribution system, the impact of alternative plans for introducing new products can be tested under an unlimited variety of conditions. To date, physical distribution contingency planning as an aspect of new product introduction represents a relatively untapped area of inquiry. Three types of new product planning hold a great deal of promise.

First, a series of new product penetration simulations can be structured in terms of level of initial market acceptance and degree of contiguousness in geographical areas of acceptance. From such a series of simulations a plan built around postponement, which provides maximum flexibility and distribution economy under a wide variety of different contingencies, can be identified.

A second type of new product introduction planning deals with an evaluation of potential customer order characteristics. Given a new product line, in what assortment, size, and frequency can we expect to receive orders during the introductory stage of market acceptance? What will be the impact upon operations if these critical order factors change over time? Finally, to what extent can quantity pricing be supported on the basis of measurable distribution cost differentials?

A final type of planning in the area of new product introduction is more operational in nature. Assume a product or product line gains rapid market acceptance and holds forth the potential for continued rapid growth. Under such conditions of rapid growth, products are in high demand and short supply. The capability to simulate short supply allocation on a continuous basis in order to achieve greatest payoff in terms of key customer, critical market, or maximum profits can avoid some critical mistakes.

The introduction of new products and the evaluation of the product life cycle for existing products have been simulated with LREPS in conjunction with several of the previously mentioned problem situations.

The three situations and illustrations reviewed above introduce the type of physical distribution problems that can be simulated using a model with the scope and range of LREPS. Given a competitive planning situation, a physical distribution system capable of meeting well-defined objectives can be designed. However, the planning potential only starts with the design of such a system. Using LREPS, the resultant system can be subjected to changes in marketing strategy, customer ordering patterns, sales forecast variation, product mix, new channel arrangements, and a host of environmental changes and potential acts of nature. The extra value of dynamic simulation results from such areas of sensitivity analysis.

Applications—Marketing (LREPS-MK): Product Forecasting

The determination of sales volumes for future time is one of the most important processes in evaluating a company's prospects for the years ahead. Indeed, the sales forecast is the core of the firm's planning effort. But even firms with the most sophisticated forecasting systems must wait until anticipated sales become actual sales before evaluating their forecasting capabilities. Research has been started to provide firms with a way to deal with this problem of timing by developing both a suitable forecasting archetype and an approach for tailoring the details of the forecasting model to meet specific needs.

There are three traditional bases for categorizing forecasting models: the length of the forecasting period, the level of the forecast, and the technique utilized. If the forecasting period is less than one year, it can be arbitrarily defined as short term. Forecasting and planning for periods lengthier than one year can be called long term in nature. The level of the forecast could be the economy, the industry, or the firm. And within the firm there are the product group, product, region, and product-region levels.

Techniques can be described as either statistical or judgmental. A mathematical-nonmathematical dichotomy may be more appropriate than a statistical-judgmental one because, after all, management must subjectively evaluate the reliability of any forecast, regardless of the technique used.

All basic work has been completed toward development and comparison of alternative simulated sales forecasting approaches utilizing LREPS.[7] This model represents the initial set of routines for LREPS' marketing model, LREPS-MK.

The objective of this research is to build a model with flexibility along the three dimensions of technique, time interval, and detail, utilizing the unique allocative capability of the LREPS order file generator. The result is a build-up (from detailed to aggregate levels) forecasting mechanism. Emphasis arbitrarily is placed on a short-term mechanism because long- and short-range forecasting and planning have different purposes.

Using this model framework, the firm can determine which combination of forecasting technique, prediction interval, and level of detail is most suitable. This determination can be made by experimenting with alternative sales patterns and then comparing forecasting accuracy.

To guide the initial portion of this research and to lay a foundation for experimentation, these questions were formulated:

1. What are the criteria for selecting the most useful forecasting system? More specifically, how should a short-term (one year) forecasting mechanism be chosen? Although each firm is in a situation that is unique in certain ways, perhaps certain guidelines could prove to be universally applicable.
2. What is the current "state of the art" of forecasting? What techniques are currently available for use in predicting sales volumes? Will the shortened time period (one year) decrease the number of alternatives available?
3. What should be the desired accuracy of the forecasted time series, and what are the criteria for evaluating accuracy? Statistical measures, such as the mean-square deviation and mean absolute difference, and prediction of turning points are examples of error measurement methods.

Researching these questions led to the conceptualization and development of the basic forecasting module within LREPS. Exponential smoothing was chosen as the appropriate technique for short-term forecasting. The ZIP regional system and the broad range of possible tracked products found in LREPS allow the simultaneous use of many techniques. However, only exponential smoothing was deemed suitable for this research. So to maintain maximum flexibility, the smoothing constant was allowed to vary by product and by region. At one extreme, the same smoothing constant can be used for all products and regions. At the other extreme, each product area could be assigned a different smoothing constant.

The second dimension, level of forecasting detail, is operable at four levels. These are the firm, the product, the DU (ZIP Sectional Center), and the product-DU. More levels are theoretically possible, but were not modeled.

One of the unique features of this model is that it facilitates the development of aggregate forecasts by accumulating lower-level estimates. For example, product forecasts can be generated by summing all product-DU forecasts for that product. Alternatively, the forecast can be made at the product level, but product-DU projections would then be only arbitrary factions of this product total. Even though the aggregate forecasts might be equal under the two approaches, the detailed forecasts under the build-up method should prove to be more accurate and, thus, more useful.

Variations in the prediction interval are quite easy to achieve. The forecasting module within the LREPS model simply is called at different times during the simulation run. Frequent callings generate frequent forecasts, but for shorter periods, and vice versa. Again, different product-DUs can be assigned unequal forecasting intervals.

An application of this basic forecasting model is currently in process; however, only preliminary findings have been developed. Several questions were devised which served to focus this research on specific topics. These questions are:

1. What are the "best" values for the smoothing constants of the predictive equations for the sample data? These values can be determined through experimentation—evaluated on the basis of forecasting accuracy and physical distribution costs—or by examining previous research aimed at this problem.
2. What prediction interval (day, week, month, and so forth) is most appropriate? What is the functional relationship between

physical distribution costs and the size of the prediction interval?
3. What is the nature of the build-up function which provides the national forecast from the local forecasts? In other words, how much detail is required for a satisfactory forecast?
4. What is the relationship between physical distribution costs and system service levels? Cost traditionally has been considered to be an increasing function (at an increasing rate) of the service level.
5. What is the sensitivity of the optimal solution (minimized constrained physical distribution costs) to a series of changes in certain LREPS variables and/or parameters?

The questions are ordered in a way which suggests a possible sequencing of the experimentation. The analyses of previously described questions 1, 2, and 3 were carried out concurrently. That is, smoothing constant values, prediction intervals, and build-up functions were derived simultaneously. Initial values were selected on the basis of research by Packer[8] and others. Various changes were then made to yield different combinations of these three factors. The result was a convergence on a heuristically optimum combination for these sample data.

The second set of experiments was designed to isolate the effect of physical distribution service on costs. Since the structure of the components of total cost could have changed, these cost components also were traced.

Last, several combinations of system variables and parameters were inputted to the LREPS model, and results were studied to learn the sensitivity of the output to these changes.

In summary, this application consists of starting on a bottom-up basis, a product sales forecast generated by time frame sequence per demand unit using random order processing. Simulation of actual filling and logistical support of these orders introduces the variations of distribution performance not normally evaluated in sales forecasts at the customer or local market area level. This procedure provides the potential to integrate forecast and prediction with variances due to operating performance to develop a most likelihood projection of sales by product for each specific geographical market area or demand unit.[9]

Applications—Financial (LREPS-F)

Preliminary research has been completed which had as its objective the development of better understanding of the interaction between decisions in the distribution warehousing area and changes in a firm's critical financial variables.[10] The goal was to develop a model that would improve the informational input to distribution management decisions as well as the capability of financial management to anticipate system changes most likely to occur. Financial variables were used to measure the significance of addition of a warehouse, the use of public versus private warehousing, and changes in sales growth rate with each given warehouse system.

For the purpose of this research, *financial variables* include the following:

1. Each item in the balance sheet and income statement
2. A set of different financial ratios
3. Several proxy measures of risk which are based on the regression of quarterly sales and adjusted quarterly net income. Adjusted net income is defined by net earnings, after taxes plus depreciation less annual principle repayments on long-term debt. The specific statistics from this regression analysis are:
    a. The formula $X = \alpha/\beta$ formed by transforming the linear regression equation, which is a measure of the level of quarterly sales below which adjusted net income would become negative.
    b. Total variance, which is the total dispersion of adjusted net income over the twenty quarter period and is a measure of the stability of earnings.
    c. Residual variance, which is the amount of total variance which is not explained by the relationship between sales and net income and is a measure of the uncertainty of earnings beyond the instability which occurs because of variable sales levels.

The ratios are included as traditional measures of financial position and performance. The ratios included in this report were selected on the following bases:

1. Those ratios identified by Carlson as effective predictors of "financial efficiency" in univariate analysis.[11]

2. Those ratios identified in three or more of the studies in the literature review as effective predictors of corporate failure.
3. Ratios which measure certain aspects of financial position not measured by the ratios identified in (1) and (2) are judgmentally included by the researcher.

The ratios included in the report and the formulas for calculating them are presented in appendix 4.

The special statistics are used as a measure of the more academic financial parameter, risk. The financial statements are included primarily as tools for explaining the shifts in return, risk, and financial position reflected in the ratios and special statistics.

The specific objective of the research was to study the relationship between warehousing decisions and changes in financial variables. However, certain financial variable changes may occur indirectly from warehousing decisions through the more direct effects which the decisions have on distribution variables. Therefore, measures of distribution variables are generated as possible tools for explaining the observed changes in financial variables.

The two frameworks within which distribution systems are most commonly measured are service and costs. For this research, the service levels were measured from two approaches: stockout frequencies and order-cycle time. The measures of stockout frequencies used here were: number of stockouts, average days per stockout, and standard deviations days per stockout.

The measures of order-cycle time used for this research were:

1. percent of total sales dollars delivered to customers within 4, 5, 6, and 7 days from the time the order is placed, and
2. percent of total orders delivered to customers within 4, 5, 6, and 7 days from the time the order is placed.

The service level reports were developed quarterly and for the end of the five-year period. Costs were reported quarterly and at the end of the five-year period for the total distribution system and for each of its functional areas. The functional areas included are:

1. inbound transportation
2. outbound transportation
3. warehouse operations expense (throughput cost)

4. warehouse facilities expense
   a. straight-line depreciation
   b. interest
5. communications expense
6. inventory expense

Several effects of the warehousing alternatives were identified which could improve the quality of informational input to the decision-making process. Further, the research technique of exogenously changing only one variable between experiments resulted in by-products from the research of interest to both the distribution and finance areas.

The relative attractiveness of two instead of one warehouse in terms of return and profitability is completely dependent upon the individual situation. The impact of the decision to add an additional warehouse on financial position revolves around the effect of the decision on inventories and accounts payable.[12]

The results of experimentation indicate that the relative attractiveness of public versus private warehousing depends upon the individual company and situation.[13] Further, experimental results exhibit the classic relationship between fixed expense, contribution margins, and the total leverage function. The decision to use public warehousing in all experiments resulted in drops in the required level of sales to break even on net income and in the variability of earnings and cash flows. It also resulted in increases in the *Net Working Capital ÷ Total Assets* and debt service coverage ratios. These changes, individually and in total, reflect a much improved defensive posture against market and economic reversals. The change in earnings variance and the *Net Working Capital ÷ Total Assets* ratio also indicate that the firm will not benefit as much from bullish market conditions using public warehousing.

Decisions concerning warehousing are certainly not the only decisions in the distribution area which are felt in the financial system. An interesting application would be to use LREPS-F to study the total impact on the finance variables of decisions made in the transportation, inventory communications, and throughput components. For example, the existence of tradeoffs between the costs of these various components has received a large amount of attention in the distribution area.[14]

The initial section in this chapter presented examples of utilization of existing capabilities of LREPS model(s). The next section presents current and planned research and development related to LREPS.

LREPS RESEARCH AND DEVELOPMENT

LREPS research and development can be classified into two broad categories. First, in line with the objective of utilization of the model(s) for applied systems planning the current emphasis of research and development involves continuous improvement of the existing LREPS physical distribution model, LREPS-PD, and extending the scope of the LREPS model to enable systems planning for a larger variety of business and public sector problem situations. The second category of research and development is in basic research with primary emphasis on physical distribution and business logistics systems. Selected aspects of each of the above categories of research and development are briefly discussed in the following sections.

R&D: Applied Systems Planning

The areas of research and development that involve extending the capabilities of LREPS for applied systems planning include: physical distribution, logistics, marketing and finance, and the public sector.

LREPS: Physical Distribution

The current development effort to improve the LREPS model for physical distribution system planning, LREPS–PHYSICAL DISTRIBUTION (LREPS-PD), centers around model design and operation. In this regard, for example, many individual modules within LREPS-PD, such as the cost routines, are being improved. In addition, additional options are being incorporated in the model. For example, a linear programming algorithm is being implemented as an option in addition to the current heuristic LOCATE algorithm.

The universal features are also being improved by reprogramming LREPS-PD with increased limits on key variables. For example, the limit of the number of market areas or individual customers, referred to as demand units, is being increased from 400 to 10,000, and the number of distribution centers that can be assumed to be in the system at one time is being increased from 20 to greater than 100. Other examples include increasing the number of tracked products, and the number of manufacturing points.

Operational characteristics of the computer model have also been improved relative to the original version of LREPS-PD. This development effort has already resulted in a 50 percent reduction of computer processing time and cost. In addition the model was originally programmed in FORTRAN IV for the CDC 6500. It now is also operational in COBOL for a Burroughs 2500.

LREPS: Logistics

The current research and development efforts also include extension of the scope of the original LREPS model to include systems planning capabilities in logistics. The objective is to develop a strategic planning model to aid firms in design and analysis of the total logistics system. In this context logistics include: physical distribution, and production and materials input subsystems. This research task has been divided into three phases:

1. development of materials input model, LREPS-MI;
2. development of the production model, LREPS-P; and
3. integration of the three subsystems models to enable testing of the total business logistics system, LREPS-LG.

Initial research and development efforts have concentrated on the initial task of development of the materials input model, and to date the conceptual system for LREPS-MI has been completed.[15] The model capabilities will be similar to those included in LREPS-PD and should therefore assist management in determining the best time and sequencing to implement material input system modifications. The LREPS-MI model draws upon the LREPS-PD conceptual model utilizing modified versions of the Supporting Data, Operating, and Report Generator Systems to enable testing the effect on materials system performance of changing within a planning horizon such variables as purchase price, materials mix, supplier mix, quality of materials, and production schedule.

The production planning model, LREPS-P, is currently in the process of development. LREPS-P will attempt to draw upon the extensive research and development reported in the literature to design routines that will enable testing of tradeoffs among production, work force, and inventory on the cost, service, and flexibility target variables.[16, 17] Among the variables that are being considered for the model are: inprocess inventories, facility network, production rate and capacity, hiring and firing, overtime, communication, and interplant transportation. As improvements made in LREPS-PD, LREPS-MI, and LREPS-P are operationalized, the data base, inputs/outputs, and transformations will be programmed to enable use of any one of the three models individually or as an integrated total logistics model, LREPS-LG.

LREPS: Marketing and Finance

The scope of the LREPS model will also be extended to include more aspects of the marketing (LREPS-MK) and financial (LREPS-F) functions of the firm. Although considerable research and development would have to be completed before operational models would be available for strategic planning in marketing and finance, current and planned research involves improving the capabilities of the LREPS model in each of these two functional areas.

In the marketing area, for example, current research and development holds forth the potential for incorporating in LREPS a new form of sales forecasting as previously discussed.[18] Additional planned research to expand the model to provide capability of systems planning of the marketing function includes modules to enable testing the effect of modifying such controllable variables as advertising, price, and so on, by product and by geographical market area.

As previously reported in this chapter the initial version of a LREPS financial model, LREPS-F, has been developed and utilized for experimentation. Future research and development in the finance area will be directed toward the general problem of adding manufacturing and physical supply subsystems to LREPS-F. In addition, the concept of flexibility or robustness[19, 20] will be explored in more depth. The essence of this concept is that in selecting an alternative from a group of possible decisions, overt consideration should be given to how well each decision alternative can adapt to whatever the future states of nature might be. The more flexible a decision is, the more attractive it would be for possible selection. The use of multiple experimental runs of the LREPS-F model is an avenue by which the concept of flexibility could become a parameter in financial analysis.[21]

The model could also be used to test the criticism of many academicians that the financial management of most corporations is unreasonably conservative.[22] Instead of initializing the balance sheet items in the model based on the industry average financial ratios, they could be initialized based on the median of the poorest quartile for each ratio. The objective of the experimentation would be to determine how bad conditions would have to get before the companies would be in serious trouble; and to compare these results to the similar results based on the industry averages.

Finally, cash management within the firm is an area which recently has been receiving much attention in financial circles. Managers and academicians are becoming increasingly concerned with getting optimum productivity from liquid assets without sacrificing liquid protection. A model such as LREPS-F could serve as an avenue to experimentally compare under a wide range of situations and conditions the various quantitative cash management models which have been proposed in recent years.

LREPS: Public Sector

The components included in the LREPS model also exist in many nonbusiness situations.[23, 24] The LREPS model could therefore conceivably be applicable to strategic applied systems planning for the following: land use studies, solid waste disposal systems, airport systems, fire station systems, hospital systems, equipment pools, and school systems.

The demand unit in the above situations would probably be stated in terms of small geographical or political units, such as subdivisions, sections, street boundaries, individual households, or any special grid system required for a given situation. The demand could be stated in terms of pseudo products (service), and the target variables would probably still be defined within the broad categories of demand for services, cost, service level, and flexibility of the system. In each of these situations the objective would be to aid in applied systems planning.

A particular applied systems planning problem that is being investigated because it appears to be suitable and of current interest is the problem of disposal and recycling of solid wastes. This recycling problem situation can be viewed as a channels-of-distribution problem. W. G. Zikmund and W. J. Stanton view recycling of solid waste as a backward channel or service distribution problem from customer to manufacturer. The authors state that "one of marketing's important roles is to determine the most efficient channel of distribution necessary to move the trash to the firm that will technically recycle the materials."[25] Of course, from the perspective of the materials manager the recycling problem would be considered similar to other input systems with raw material, the trash, being supplied for conversion recycling into a new finished product. In either case, whether viewed as a backward channel or standard materials input system the LREPS model could be utilized to test the effect of such variables as the number, type, and location of middlemen (collection points) in the system. The importance of modes of transportation, communications delays, and the role of inventories also could be tested to determine the effect on the demand, cost, service, and flexibility performance variables. The demand units of the LREPS model would serve as the household pickup (supply) points of solid waste, the distribution centers would act as collection points (middlemen), and the manufacturing centers would replicate the recycling plants. The application of LREPS to this problem of recycling glass and regional solid waste management is actively being investigated.[26]

R&D: Basic Research

While business planners are interested in the applied systems planning aspects of LREPS, the basic researcher will also find the model of interest. The main potential for basic research centers around the following four features of the model.

First, the model is dynamic in structure. The entire area of dynamics holds forth the potential for more penetrating evaluation of time linkages in systems analysis. Dynamics coupled with stochastic relationships introduce a realism that has not for the most part been fully explored in business situations.[27]

Second, the LREPS model integrates the spatial elements of location and the temporal elements of inventory on an echelon and multichannel basis.[28] In addition to achieving true total cost perspective, this particular capability introduces the potential to design and test systems that are in fact many different product flow paths from manufacturing to consumption. Thus, the capability to simplex systems based upon the economics of distribution flow is introduced to the researcher.

Third, the echelon nature of LREPS provides a mechanism wherein research in the economics of vertical marketing systems can be examined under experimental conditions. For example, the concept of separation, which suggests that trading and supply are best performed via separate and unique channel structures, can be tested within the capacity of LREPS for a wide variety of different marketing situations.[29] In addition, many other aspects of channel management as they relate to product flow can be tested in an effort to substantiate existing potential principles.[30]

Fourth, LREPS holds forth the potential for a new form of sales forecasting.[31] Starting on a bottom-up basis the sales forecast by product in time usage sequence can be generated at a local market level using random order generation. Simulation of actual filling and logistical support of these orders introduces the variations of system performance not normally included in sales forecasts. Such performance and use patterns across simulated time can then be aggregated to consecutively higher levels of organizational integration. In terms of historical patterns such a procedure has the potential of integrating forecast and prediction with operational variances to capture a total projection of future likelihood of sales by product type in specific geographical areas.

SUMMARY

The results presented indicate that the LREPS model has successfully combined and reported, possibly for the first time, a model which includes all of the physical distribution components, a strategic planning horizon, and the sequential decision process.

The implications are even more exciting. The entities and components included in the LREPS model could enable it to be truly as general as the title implies—Long-Range Environmental Planning Simulator. In theory, the model should be applicable to any problem in which:

1. there is a cost holding the resource, and the future demand for the resource is uncertain (the Inventory Component);
2. the number of inventory nodes is a decision variable over time (the Location Component);
3. the cost of holding and processing the resource at the inventory node is significant (the Warehouse Component);
4. the movement of the resource and the transmittal of information requires a cost in dollars and/or time for the demand units acquiring the resource at the inventory node and for the inventory node replenishment of the resource (the Inbound and Outbound Transportation Component, and the Communications Component);

5. the demand for the resource exists in either its original form or in processed form (the Demand Unit and Demand Allocation);
6. the objective of the system is to provide the resource to the demand units in terms of an acceptable average and variance of the availability and cost of the resource.[32]

In excess of thirty calendar months, twelve man years, over three hundred years of simulated business operations, and thousands of dollars of research support have been invested in LREPS. The focal point—physical distribution planning—has yielded most expected and many unexpected results. However, one singular thought has been discussed over and over by members of the research group. Namely, the potential of greater understanding of business situations available from controlled simulation experimentation is in its infancy.

APPENDIX 1
Data Base Information

Data Base Information

The data base of the LREPS operating system is listed on the following pages.
The coding scheme for each column of information is:
1. Column one, "NAME,'" contains the name or mnemonic of the variable. If the variable is multidimensional, a more descriptive name of the array is footnoted at the bottom of the page.

2. Column two, "COL," refers to the dimensions of the variable. If the variable has only one dimension, then this column is blank. Multidimensioned variables are given a number from one to n for each of the n dimensions of the variable.

3. Column three, "DLT," refers to the delta-time unit or frequency with which a variable can be changed. "C" refers to cyclic; "A" refers to annual; "Q'" refers to quarterly; and "D" refers to daily.

4. Column four, "TYPE," designates the variable as either exogenous, "X," or endogenous, "N." The "N" variables could have been set exogenously at the beginning of the simulation cycle. During cycle execution, the "N" variables are only altered within the operating system.

5. The next four columns, "M&C," "OPS," "D&E," and "MEAS," indicate the data base variables used or altered by the model's major subsystems. "U" signifies that the data base variable is only used by the specified subsystem. "S" signifies that the data base variable is used and altered in the subsystem.

6. Column six, "MODE," signifies whether a variable is "R," a real, fractional variable; "I," an integer variable; or "P," a packed variable containing more than one piece of information per computer word.

7. Column seven, "CONTENTS," is a description of the contents of each of the variables in the data base. If the variable is multidimensional, then each dimension or column of the variable is described.

Note: Data Base Information from E. J. Marien, "Development of a Dynamic Simulation Model for Planning Physical Distribution Systems: Formulation of the Computer Model" (Ph.D. dissertation, Michigan State University, 1970).

238   APPENDIX 1

APPENDIX 1.—Data Base Information.

Name	COLT	TYPE	M&C	OD&PES	MEAS	MODE	Contents
DU[1]	1	C	X	U		R	Special customer indicators
	2	C	X			R	Rectangular x-coordinate converted from latitude for hub city
	3	C	X			R	Rectangular y-coordinate converted from longitude for hub city
	4	A	X			P	Weighted index used for sales allocation
	5	O	N	U		I	Customer service time ring numbers T1 & T4 for majorly assigned DC and T4 for regional PDC
	6	O	N	S		I	Sorted DU code for DUs assigned to in-solution DC
	7	O	N	U		I	Cumulative weighted index used for selecting randomly DUs for sales allocation
	8	O	N	U		I	Code identifying the row of the in-solution DC array to which the sorted DU code is linked
	9	O	N	S		R	Exponentially averaged quarterly dollar sales
	10	O	N	S	U	R	Calculated highway distance from the full line DC
	11	O	N	S	U	R	Calculated highway distance from the partial line DC
	12	O	N	S		R	Quarter-to-date dollar sales for the full line DC
	13	D	N	S	U	R	Quarter-to-date dollar sales for the partial line DC
	14	D	N	S		R	Quarter-to-date sales in pounds for the full line DC
	15	D	N	S	U	R	Quarter-to-date sales in pounds for the partial line DC
	16	D	N	S		R	
DCP[2]	1	C	X	U		R	Rectangular x-coordinate converted from the latitude
	2	C	X	U		R	Rectangular y-coordinate converted from the longitude
	3	C	X	U	U	R	Constant "a" coefficient used for calculating the outbound transportation rates
	4	C	X	U	U	R	Variable "b" coefficient used for calculating the outbound transportation rates based on distance
	5	C	X	U	U	R	Real transportation rate modifier "R1" for the above "a" coefficient
	6	C	X	U		R	Real transportation rate modifier "R2" for the above "b" coefficient
	7	C	X	U		P	Customer service time variance pointers for T1, T2, T4
	8	O	X		U	I	Type of DC plus PDC assignment code
	9	O	X			P	Mileage ring set indicators for customer service time elements T1 and T4
	10	O	N	S		R	Exponentially averaged quarterly dollar sales
	11	O	N	S		R	Exponentially averaged quarterly weight sales
	12	O	N		U	R	Time when a DC was added, deleted or its capacity changed
DCIS[3]	1	O	N	S	S	R	Approximated backorder penalty time (T3)
	2	O	N	S	U	I	Code of the potential DC location that is in-solution
	3	O	N	S		I	Number of demand units assigned to this DC
	4	O	N	S	U	R	Sales modification factor used in determining DC simulated sales dollars—exponentially averaged
	5	O	N	S	U	R	Sum of the weighted indices for the demand units in this DC's geographic area
	6	O	N	S		R	Total physical distribution cost for the past quarter's activities
	7	O	N		U	R	Average total order cycle time
	8	O	N	S	S	R	Indicator of the sales dollar capacity of this distribution center
	9	D	N	S	S	R	Normal average order cycle time that is computed from the sum of the T1 + T2 + T4 for all orders in the last quarter
	10	D	N	S	S	R	Standard deviation of the normal average order cycle time which is computed from the sum of the square of T1 + T2 + T4 for all orders in the last quarter

Data Base Information

Name	COLT	TYPE	MOPS	OD&ES	MEAS	MODE	Contents
DCIS[3]	11	D	N	S	S	S	R	Average outbound transportation time (T4) which is computed from the sum of the T4's for all orders in the last quarter
	12	D	N	S		S	R	Standard deviation of T4 which is computed from the sum of the square of T4 for all the orders in the last quarter
	13	D	N	S		S	R	Percent of case units backordered of the total case units sold for the tracked products
	14	D	N	S		S	R	Average stockout delay, given a product stocked out, which is computed from the sum of the individual product delays
	15	D	N	S		S	R	Standard deviation of the stockout delay which is computed from the sum of the square of the individual product delays
	16	D	N	S		U	R	Quarter-to-date dollar sales
	17	D	N	S		U	R	Quarter-to-date weight sales
	18	D	N	S		U	R	Quarter-to-date cube sales
	19	D	N	S		U	R	Quarter-to-date case sales
	20	D	N	S		U	R	Quarter-to-date line sales
	21	D	N	S		U	R	Quarter-to-date order sales
REG[4]	1	O	X	U			I	Maximum number of DCs allowed in system
	2	O	X	U			I	Maximum number of DCs that can be added
	3	O	X	U			I	Maximum number of DCs that can be deleted
	4	O	X	U			R	QTD tracked product, weight sales
	5	O	X	U			R	Desired level of customer service
	6	O	X	U			R	Maximum allowed dollar investment in DCs
	7	O	X	S	U		R	Maximum allowed dollar investment for in-process DCs
	8	O	X	S			R	Sum of the weighted indices for the region's demand units
	9	O	X	S			I	Number of DCs in the process of being added
	10	O	X	S			I	Number of DCs in the process of being deleted
	11	O	X	S			R	Total dollar investment for DCs in solution
	12	O	X	S			R	Total dollar investment for in-process DCs
	13	O	X	S		S	R	Actual service achieved for the last quarter
	14	O	X	S			R	Exponentially averaged sales modification factor
	15	O	X	S	U		R	Ratio of total product sales to the tracked product sales in pounds
	16	O	X	S			R	Total physical distribution cost for activities over the last quarter
	17	O	X	S		S	I	Number of DCs that are presently in-solution
MCC[5]	1	O	X	U			I	T2 variance pointer for processing and preparing reorders at the MCC stage
	2	O	X	U			I	MCC scheduled shipment dispatch policy that is given in number of days later than the MCC
	3	Q	X	U		U	R	Cost of preparing and processing a multiple-product reorder at a MCC
DCMCC[6]	1	D	N	S		U	I	Total number of multiple-product reorders
	2	D	N	S		U	I	Accumulated total reorder lead time plus later used for calculating the average reorder lead time
	3	D	N	S		S	P	Packed computer word containing the products that are presently on reorder at the MCC from the DC
	4	D	N	S			I	Number of multiple product reorders that are outstanding at the MCC
	5	D	N	S			R	Total weight on order at the MCC plus an indicator of whether a shipment had been dispatched within the past scheduled shipment review period

240   APPENDIX 1

APPENDIX 1.—Continued

Name	COLT	DLPT	TYM&C	MOPS	D&ES	MEAD	MODE	Contents
PRCT[7]	1	C	X	U			I	Indicator of the categories handled by partial line DCs
	2	C	X	U			I	Beginning product model code for this category
	3	C	X	U			I	Ending product model code for this category
	4	C	X	U		U	I	Total number of products that this category is representing
	5	O	X	U			R	Type of inventory policy
	6	O	X	U			R	Review period length for above policy
	7	O	X				R	Safety stock factor for above policy
PRDC[8]	1	O	N	S			P	Packed computer word containing reorder point 1 (ROP1) and reorder point 2 (ROP2)
	2	O	N	S			R	Replenishment S-level
	3	D	N	S		S	R	Time-integrated inventory on hand plus outstanding reorder quantities used in calculating the average total inventory per day
	4	D	N	S			R	Inventory on hand
	5	D	N	S			I	Number of days that a product has been stocked out given a stockout
	6	D	N	S			R	Reorder quantity (ROQ) plus an indicator that a reorder is presently outstanding
PRCTDC[9]	1	D	N	S		S	I	Quarter-to-date stockouts
	2	D	N	S		S	I	Quarter-to-date single-product reorders
	3	D	N	S		S	R	Time-integrated stocked-out case units which will be divided by total case unit sales to get the approximated customer service time T3 by category—tracked product basis
	4	D	N	S		S	R	Total number of case units sold for the tracked products
CGSCS		C	X	U		U	R	Cost of goods sold per case unit by tracked product
CUBCS		C	X	U		U	R	Average cube per case unit by tracked product
WTCU		C	X	U		U	R	Average weight per case unit by tracked product
OBTNRM[10]	1	C	X	U		U	R	R3 modifier of the "a" coefficient by region
	2	C	X	U		U	R	R4 modifier of the "b" coefficient by region
DCP1[11]	1	C	X	U			P	Packed computer word containing the tracked products linked to a specific MCC
	2	C	X	U			R	Proportion of total weight that will be supplied via this link
	3	Q	X	U			P	Inbound reorder transmission time and transit time factors
MCCWB		C	X	U			R	Maximum weight breaks for shipment dispatches from each MCC
DCWB		C	X	U			R	Maximum weight breaks for the DC shipment accumulators
RING		C	X	U			R	Alternative customer mileage ring sets for 1, 2 and 3 day average service times
DCASGN		C	X				P	Packed computer words containing the feasible DCs, in decreasing priority, that can service a specific DC
CSTBLK		C	X	U		U	I	Number of order blocks per major customer type per order group
CLF		Q	X	U			R	Potential DC cost of living factors

Data Base Information

Name	COLT	TYPE	M&C	OP&S	MEADS	MODE	Contents
IUDF[12]	1	X	U	X		I	PD facility changes flag
	2	X	U	X		I	Transportation related changes
	3	X	U	X		I	Inventory management policy changes
	4	X	U	X		I	Unitization or materials handling changes
	5	X	U	X		I	Communication's related changes
DCCAPC	Q	X	U	X	U	R	Capacity constraint by size of DC
DCP2	Q	X	U	X	U	R	Potential DC-MCC freight rates by weight class
COMMCR[13]	1	X	U	X	U	R	Fixed cost factor
	2	X	U	X	U	R	Variable cost per order
	3	X	U	X	U	R	Variable cost per line item
COMMCD[14]	1	X	U	X	U	R	Fixed cost factor
	2	X	U	X	U	R	Variable cost per order
	3	X	U	X	U	R	Variable cost per line item
CSPLTP		X	U	X	U	R	Regional customer dollar split percentages
THRUPC		X	U	X	U	R	Throughput cost rate per pound by DC size and type
INVEST	Q	X	U	X	U	R	Average investment dollars by size and DC type
COMMC[15]	1	X	U	X	U	R	Fixed cost factor
	2	X	U	X	U	R	Variable cost per order
	3	X	U	X	U	R	Variable cost per line item
DCCOST[16]	1	N	U	X	S	R	Outbound transportation cost
	2	N	U	X	S	R	Inbound transportation cost
	3	N	U	X	S	R	Throughput cost
	4	N	U	X	S	R	Communications cost
	5	N	U	X	S	R	Facility cost
	6	N	U	X	S	R	Inventory carrying and handling cost
REGSAC	Q	N	U	X	S	R	Regional, quarterly dollar and weight sales accumulators
DOMSAL	Q	N	U	X	S	R	Domestic, quarterly dollar and weight sales accumulators
OCTDIS[17]	1	D	S	X	S	R	Proportion of sales dollars within 3, 5, 7, 9 and 11 days
	2	D	S	X	S	R	Proportions of orders within 3, 5, 7, 9 and 11 days
WTACUM	D	N	S	X	U	R	Accumulators of the weight shipped from each of the in-solution DCs by weight class
DCMCCI	D	N	S	X	U	R	Accumulators of the weight shipped from each of the MCCs to the in-solution DCs by weight class
TPDEM[18]	1	D	S	X	S	R	Quarter-to-date total domestic demand for each tracked product
	2	Q	S	X	S	R	Exponentially averaged total domestic product demand for each tracked product

APPENDIX 1.—Continued

Name	DLT	TYPE	M&PC	OP&S	MODE	MADE	MOE		Contents
NSCH	C	X	U				I		Day and event numbers for the scheduled fixed-time events
PARM	O	X	U				R		Service time variance functions for generating customr and reorder lead time variances
DCREGP	O	X	U				I		Regional priority list of DCs to be added via the DC location algorithm
ITNSP	C	X	U	U			I		Total number of tracked products for cycle
ITNPC	C	X	U	U			I		Total number of inventory categories
NDUS	C	X	U	U			I		Total number of DUs being processed
IREGNO	D	N		U			I		Number of region being processed
TDSFLG	C	X					R		Flag indicating whether the domestic daily sales quota is a constant or modified variate
DICC	C	X					I		Daily inventory carrying charge–proportion
MXINVS	C	X		U			I		Maximum domestic dollar investment for in-solution DCs
MXIPDS	C	X					I		Maximum domestic dollar investment in facilities that can be deleted
NWKDYS	C	X					I		Number of simulated workdays per year
ADTMRD	C	X					R		Delay time to add a RDC-F facility
ADTMPD	C	X					R		Delay time to add a RDC-P facility
ADTMCP	C	X					R		Delay time to add a CSP facility
DLTMRD	C	X					R		Delay time to delete a RDC-F facility
DLTMPD	C	X					R		Delay time to delete a RDC-P facility
DLTMCP	C	X					R		Delay time to delete a CSP facility
TDSF	A	X		U	U		R		Total annual domestic sales dollar forecast
IYEAR	A	N	S				I		Year of simulated time
SDSM	Q	X	U	U			R		Maximum dollar shipment size that can be considered for daily shipments from the PDCs
CSDP	O	X	U				R		Percent of customer orders less than dollar SDSM that can be shipped daily from a PDC
MAXDCS	O	X	U				I		Maximum number of DCs allowed domestically
MXIPAS	O	X	U				I		Maximum number of in-process DCs domestically
MXIVPS	O	X					I		Maximum domestic dollar investment allowed in process
NMINPS	O	N	S				I		Number of in-process DCs being added domestically
INVSTS	O	N	S				I		Domestic dollar investment in DCs being added to system
NUMDCS	O	N	S				I		Number of DCs in PD system
PDTCST	O	N	S		S		R		Total cost for PD system over last quarter
DOMAST	O	N	S		S		R		Domestic average total order cycle time for past quarter
NMBDLS	O	N	S				I		Number of in-process DCs being deleted domestically
IDUNO	D	N			S		I		Number of DU being processed
IDUNOI	D	N		U	U		I		Number of DU being processed based on present DC assignment
IDCNO	D	N		U			I		Number of in-solution DC being processed
IDCNOI	D	N		U	U		I		Code of potential DC being processed
IDCAGN	D	N	S				I		Code of DC being set in solution
DSQ	D	N	S				R		Domestic daily sales dollar forecast
IORD	D	N					I		Number of order being processed
IBLOCK	D	N		U			I		Number of order block that has been randomly selected
OBM	D	N		U			R		Order block modifier to attain a customer's sales allocation
ICTYPE	D	N					I		Major customer type being processed
IPBLKS	D	N					I		Number of past customer order blocks processed

Data Base Information

	C O L T	T Y P E	M & C	O P S	D & E	M E A S	M O D E	Contents
IBLKS	D	N	S	S			R	Number of order blocks for this major customer
WIACC	D	N	S	S			R	Variable used to accumulate weighted indices by DU and DC
CSTSAL	Q	N	S				R	Sales dollar allocation by major customer
CSTSAC	D	N	S	S			R	Sales dollar accumulator by major customer
DCSALS	D	X		S			R	DC simulated sales for day
NATCON	O	X	U				I	Flag as to domestic constraints on DC decisions or not
REGCON	O	X	U				I	Flag as to regional constraints on DC decisions or not
TYPEAD	O	X	U				I	Flag as to type of algorithm to be used in ADC of DCs
NDCADD	O	X	U	U			I	Maximum number of DCs that can be added domestically and quarterly
TMINPR	O	X					R	Delay time to expand an existing DC facility
NMCCS	Q	X	U			U	I	Number of in-solution MCCs
NREGS		X					I	Number of in-solution regions
ORDGRP[19] 1	D	X		U			R	Order block sales dollar summary
2	D	X		U			R	Order block sales weight summary
3	D	X		U			R	Other order sales summary data
4	D	X		U			R	Order block tracked product detail
RDCPC	D	N		S			R	Percent of order block allocated to full-time DC
PLPC	D	N		S			R	Percent of order block allocated to RDC-P
IDCTEMP	D	X	U			U	I	Temporary storage of PDC-identification number
DAYCON	O	X					R	Customer total OCT decision parameter used for SMP
CM	O	N				S	R	Inventory category extrapolation modifier
RCF	O	N				S	R	DC-type rate correction factor
DIST	O	N				S	R	DC to DU road distance
WT	O	N				S	R	DC to DU quarterly, accumulated weight
POOLFC	O	N				S	R	PDC pooled shipment rate mod factor
IVOLP	O	N				S	R	Number of PDC weight categories
IVOLR	O	N				S	R	Number of RDC weight categories
FC	O	N				S	R	Total fixed cost for all geographic units
FCO	O	N				S	R	Total variable cost/order for all geographic units
VCL	O	N				S	R	Total variable cost/line for all geographic units
PDSCHG	O	N					I	Indicator of PD system change(s)
SUMWT	O	N	S				R	Total QTD regional weight sales
DCACTS	O	N	S				R	DC actual level of service proportion used for calculating DC sales modification factor
DEM	O	N	S				R	DC tracked product average daily demand
SLT	O	N	S				R	Standard deviation of reorder lead time
SRP	O	N	S				R	Standard deviation of review period length
SPD	O	N	S				R	Standard deviation of tracked product avg daily demand per DC
BUF	O	N	S				R	DC tracked product buffer stock
EOQ	O	N	S				R	DC tracked product economic order quantity
ORDCST	O	N	S				R	Tracked product ordering cost
XINC	A	N					R	Monthly domestic sales forecast increment

APPENDIX 1.—Continued

Name	TYPE	DYP&C	MOD&S	DEAD&S	MODE	MODE	Contents
SRATIO	Q	N	S			R	DC dollar to sales capacity ratio
RLIST	Q	N	S			R	Array used for M&C working lists of regions and DCs
DCSUM	Q	N	S			R	Sum of DC expected DU sales for eligible DCs
NDCIN	Q	N	S			R	Number of DCs put into process this quarter

[1]Demand Unit–DU(COL)
[2]Potential DC Location–DCP(COL)
[3]DCs in Solution–DCIS(COL)
[4]Regional–REG(COL)
[5]Manufacturing Control Center–MCC(COL)
[6]DC-MCC Link–DCMCC(COL)
[7]Product Detail by Inventory Category–PRCT(COL)
[8]Product Detail by DC–PRDC(COL)
[9]Product Category by DC–PRCTDC(COL)
[10]Outbound Transp Negotiated Rate Modifiers–OBTNRM(COL)
[11]Potential DC-MCC Product Link–DCPI(COL)
[12]PD Update Flags for System Changes–IUDF(COL)
[13]Regional COMM Costs–COMMCR(COL)
[14]Domestic COMM Costs–COMMCD(COL)
[15]Potential DC COMM Costs by Size and DC Type–COMMC(COL)
[16]In-Solution DC Cost for PD Activities–DCCOST(COL)
[17]Normal Order Cycle Time Proportions–OCTDIS(COL)
[18]Domestic Product Demand–TPDEM(COL)
[19]Order Block Detail by Group–ORDGRP(COL)

APPENDIX 2
LREPS System Activity Flowchart

LREPS System Activity Flowchart 247

LREPS: Supporting Data System

248　Appendix 2

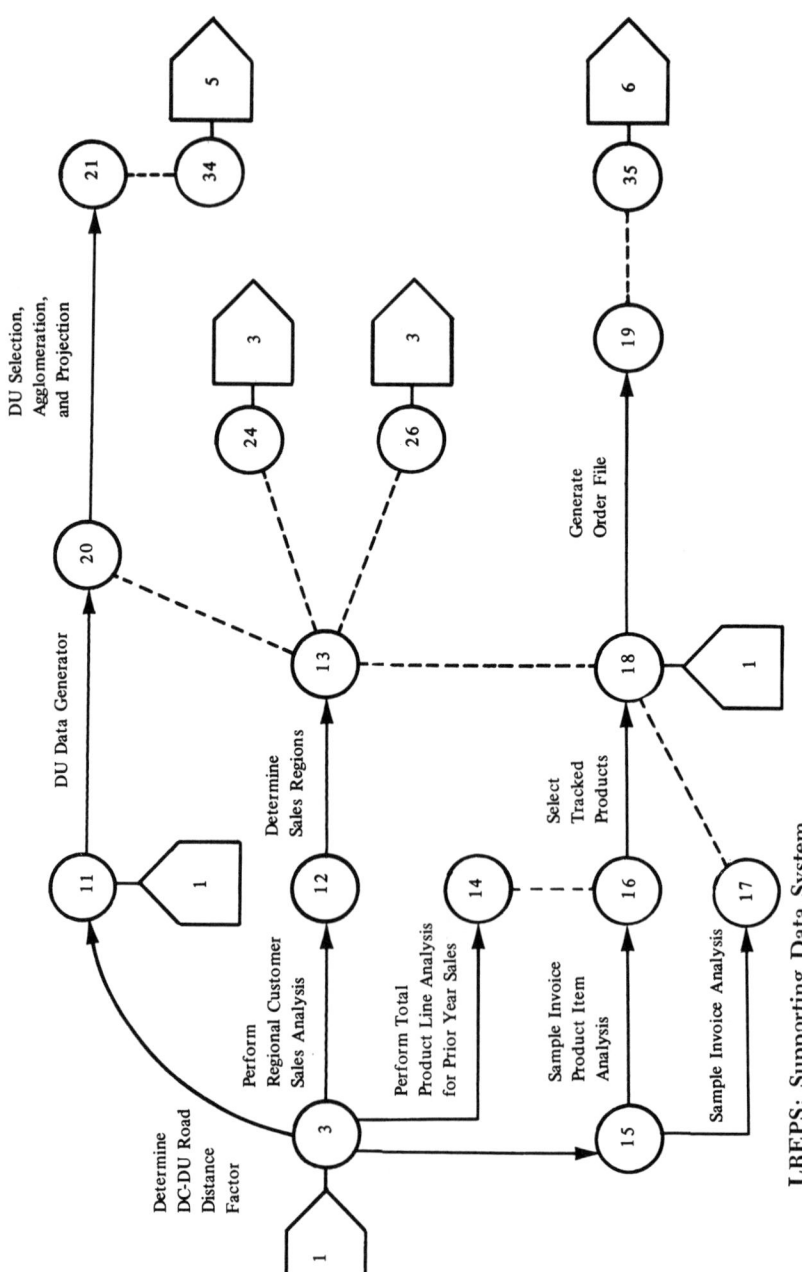

LREPS: Supporting Data System

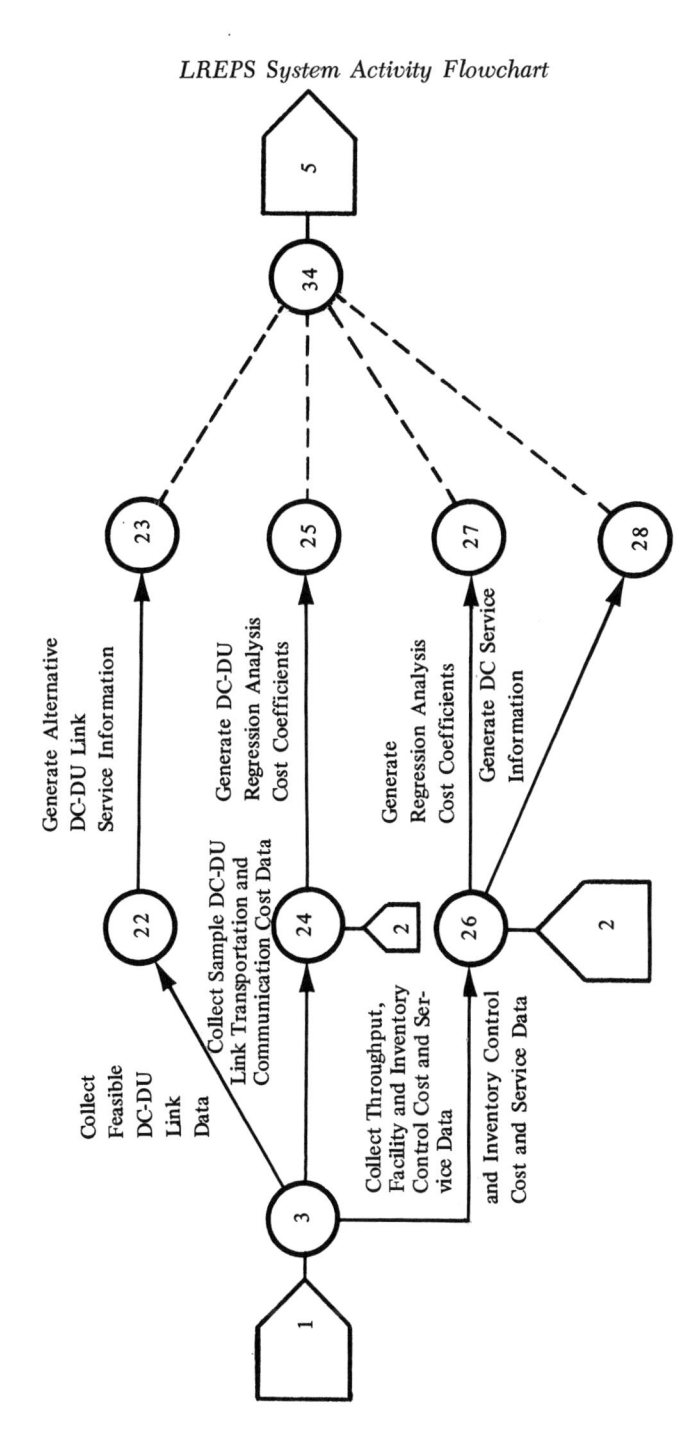

LREPS System Activity Flowchart 249

LREPS: Supporting Data System

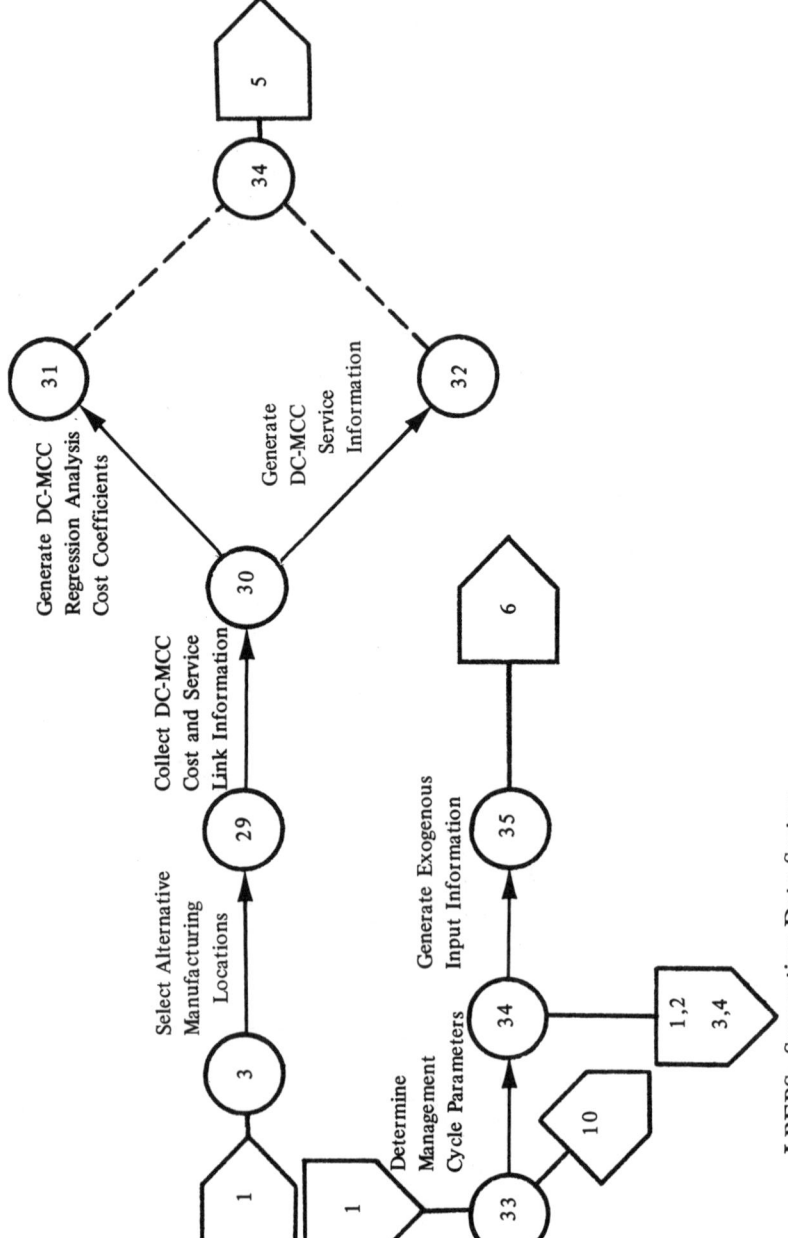

250 APPENDIX 2

LREPS: Supporting Data System

LREPS System Activity Flowchart

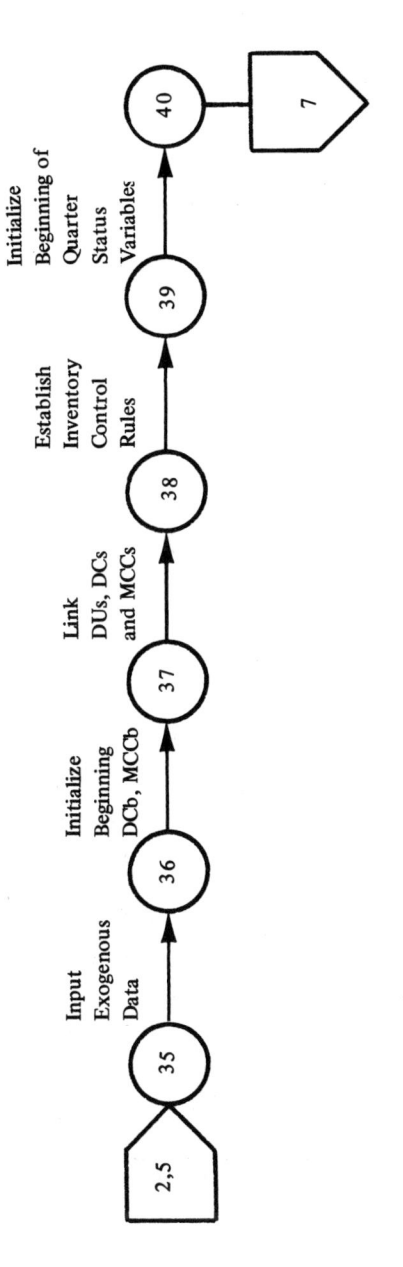

251

```
(2,5) → ( 35 ) → ( 36 ) → ( 37 ) → ( 38 ) → ( 39 ) → ( 40 ) → ( 7 )
```

- 35: Input Exogenous Data
- 36: Initialize Beginning DCb, MCCb
- 37: Link DUs, DCs and MCCs
- 38: Establish Inventory Control Rules
- 39: Initialize Beginning of Quarter Status Variables

**LREPS: Operating System
Beginning of Cycle Initialization**

APPENDIX 2

LREPS: Operating System
Daily Activities

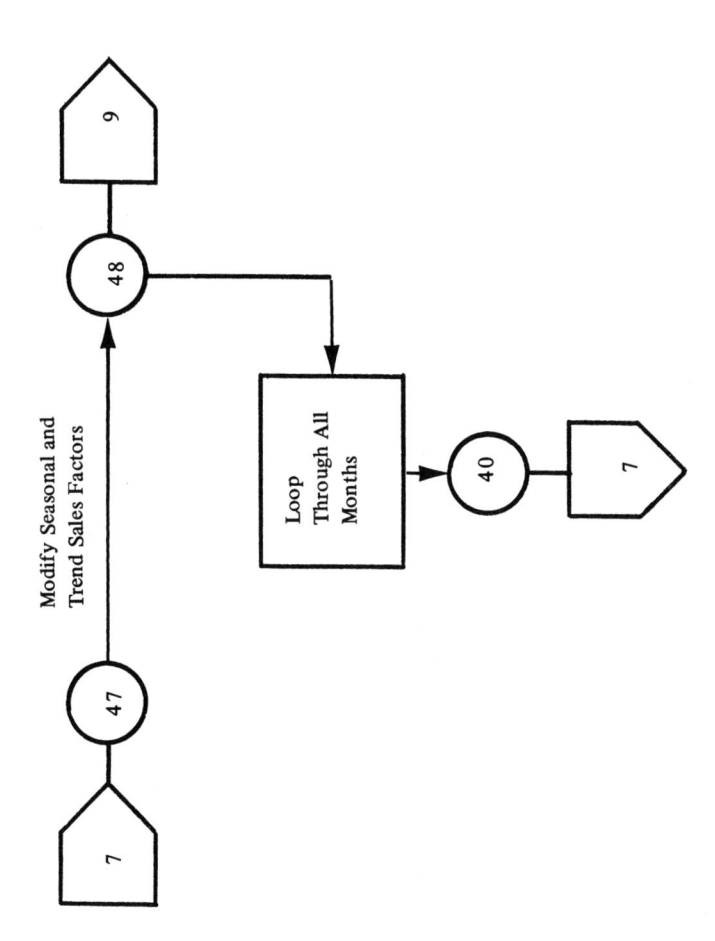

LREPS System Activity Flowchart

LREPS: Operating System Monthly Activities

254　Appendix 2

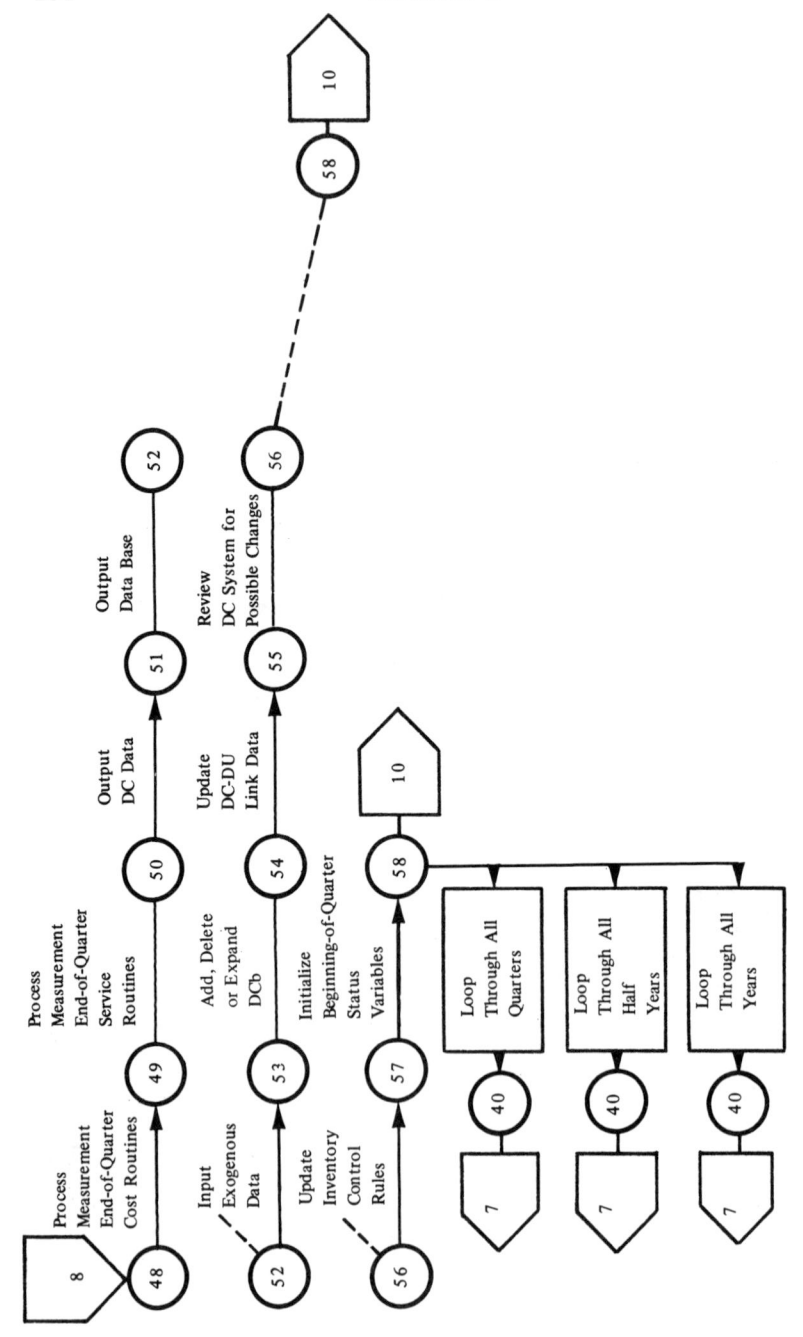

LREPS: Operating System Quarterly, Semiannual, and Annual Activities

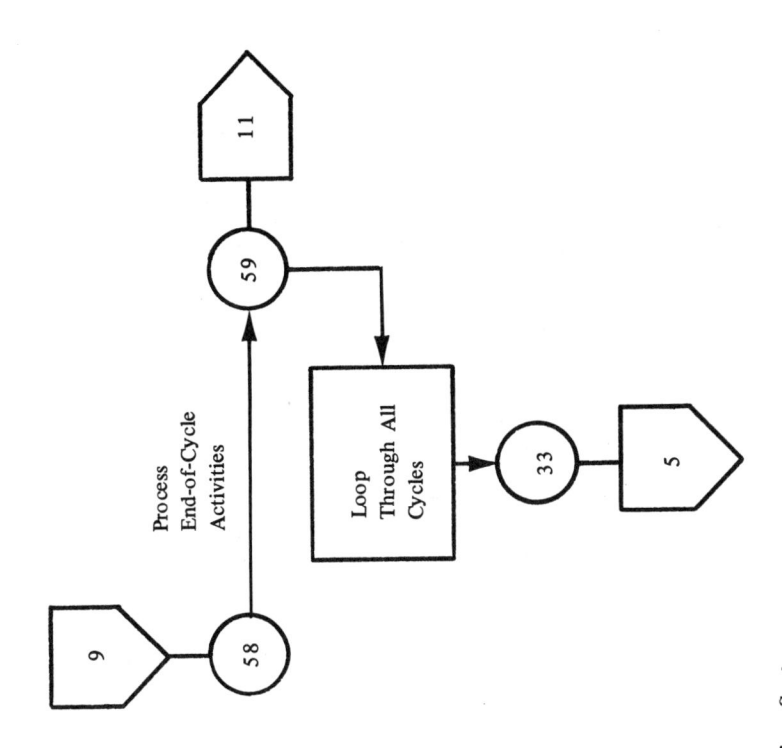

LREPS System Activity Flowchart 255

**LREPS: Operating System
End-Of-Cycle Activities**

256   APPENDIX 2

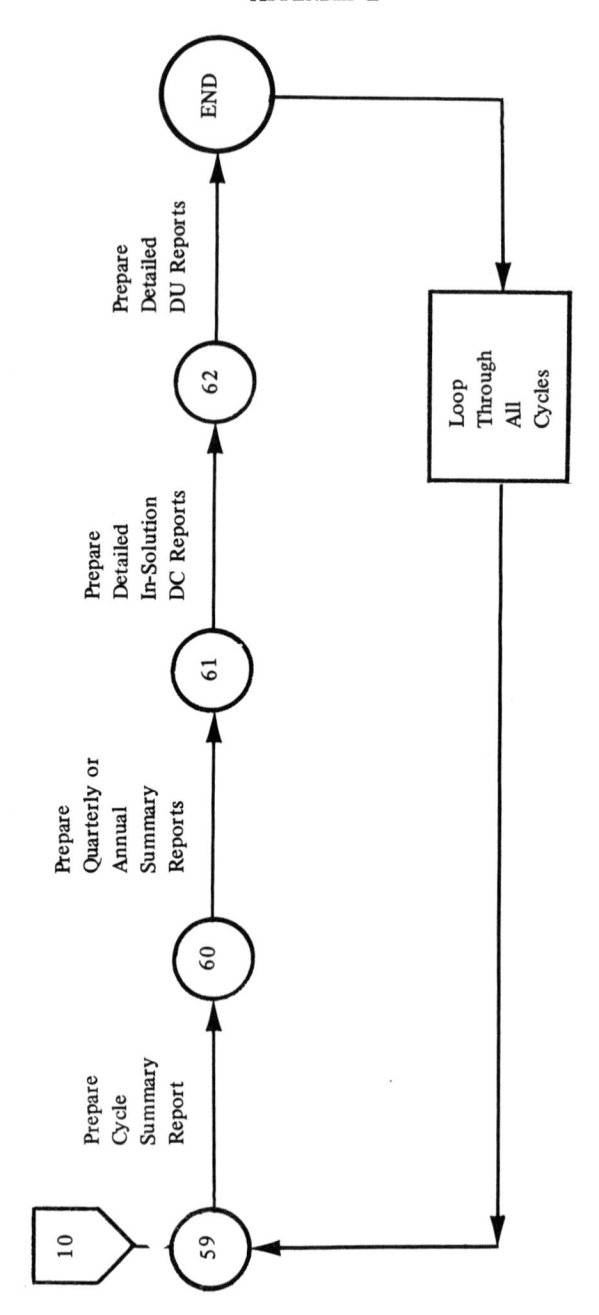

```
         ┌─────┐
         │ END │ ←──────────────┐
         └──┬──┘                │
            ↑                   │
   Prepare                      │
   Detailed                     │
   DU Reports                   │
         ┌──┐             ┌──────────┐
         │62│             │   Loop   │
         └──┘             │ Through  │
            ↑             │   All    │
                          │  Cycles  │
   Prepare                └──────────┘
   Detailed                     │
   In-Solution                  │
   DC Reports                   │
         ┌──┐                   │
         │61│                   │
         └──┘                   │
            ↑                   │
   Prepare                      │
   Quarterly or                 │
   Annual                       │
   Summary                      │
   Reports                      │
         ┌──┐                   │
         │60│                   │
         └──┘                   │
            ↑                   │
   Prepare                      │
   Cycle                        │
   Summary                      │
   Report                       │
   ┌──┐   ┌──┐                  │
   │10│──▷│59│ ←────────────────┘
   └──┘   └──┘
```

LREPS: Report Generator System

APPENDIX 3

Example of LREPS Report Output Format

Example of LREPS Report Output Format

TABLE OF CONTENTS

END OF CYCLE SUMMARY(IES)
QUARTERLY SUMMARIES
DISTRIBUTION CENTER DETAIL REPORTS
  SALES REPORT
  COST REPORT
  ORDER CYCLE TIME REPORT
  REORDER REPORT
  INVENTORY CONDITION REPORT
  AVERAGE INVENTORY REPORT
  IDENTIFICATION REPORT
  NORMAL ORDER CYCLE TIME REPORT (DOLLARS)
  NORMAL ORDER CYCLE TIME REPORT (ORDERS)
  WEIGHT CLASS ACCUMULATIONS REPORT (DC TOTALS)
  WEIGHT CLASS ACCUMULATIONS REPORT (MCC1)
DEMAND (CUSTOMER) UNIT REPORTS
  (ESSENTIALLY THE SAME LEVEL OF DETAIL AS THE
  DC DETAIL REPORTS CAN BE PRINTED OUT BY CUSTOMER)
MANUFACTURING REPORTS
  (ESSENTIALLY THE SAME LEVEL OF DETAIL AS THE
  DC DETAIL REPORTS CAN BE PRINTED OUT BY MANUFACTURING
  UNIT)

Note: This appendix presents an example of the type of information that is available by time period (week, month, quarter, or year) for up to a ten-year planning horizon for each node in the system (plant, distribution center, customer).

APPENDIX 3

```
LONG RANGE ENVIRONMENTAL PLANNING SIMULATOR                    PAGE
MICHIGAN STATE UNIVERSITY                               DATE 09/09/71
              LOCATION: END OF CYCLE SUMMARY
     DC        SALES      COST      PROFIT    OC TIME    INV OH
LOCATION   1   XXXXX     XXXXX      XXXXX       XX       XXXXX
LOCATION   2   XXXXX     XXXXX      XXXXX       XX       XXXXX
LOCATION   3   XXXXX     XXXXX      XXXXX       XX       XXXXX
LOCATION   4   XXXXX     XXXXX      XXXXX       XX       XXXXX
LOCATION   5              WAS NEVER IN SOLUTION
LOCATION   6   XXXXX     XXXXX      XXXXX       XX       XXXXX
LOCATION   7              WAS NEVER IN SOLUTION
LOCATION   8              WAS NEVER IN SOLUTION
LOCATION   9              WAS NEVER IN SOLUTION
LOCATION  10              WAS NEVER IN SOLUTION
   •                              •
   •                              •
   •                              •
LOCATION  NL              WAS NEVER IN SOLUTION
```

```
LONG RANGE ENVIRONMENTAL PLANNING SIMULATOR                    PAGE
MICHIGAN STATE UNIVERSITY                               DATE 09/09/71
              QUARTER: END OF CYCLE SUMMARY
         LOCATION 1            LOCATION 2    • • •   LOCATION NL
QTR   SALES   COST   OCT    SALES   COST   OCT    SALES   COST   OCT
 1    XXXXX   XXX    XX     NOT IN SOLUTION       XXXXX   XXX    XX
 2    XXXXX   XXX    XX     NOT IN SOLUTION       XXXXX   XXX    XX
 3    XXXXX   XXX    XX     NOT IN SOLUTION       XXXXX   XXX    XX
 4    XXXXX   XXX    XX     XXXXX   XXX    XX     NOT IN SOLUTION
 5    XXXXX   XXX    XX     XXXXX   XXX    XX     NOT IN SOLUTION
 6    XXXXX   XXX    XX     XXXXX   XXX    XX     NOT IN SOLUTION
  •     •      •      •       •      •      •       •      •      •
  •     •      •      •       •      •      •       •      •      •
  •     •      •      •       •      •      •       •      •      •
40    XXXXX   XXX    XX     XXXXX   XXX    XX     NOT IN SOLUTION
```

```
LONG RANGE ENVIRONMENTAL PLANNING SIMULATOR                    PAGE
MICHIGAN STATE UNIVERSITY                               DATE 09/09/71
              SUMMARY FOR QUARTER 1
     DC        SALES      COST      PROFIT    OC TIME    INV OH
LOCATION   1   XXXXX     XXXXX      XXXXX       XX       XXXXXX
LOCATION   2   NOT IN SOLUTION
   •             •          •          •         •          •
   •             •          •          •         •          •
   •             •          •          •         •          •
LOCATION  NL   XXXXX     XXXXX      XXXXX       XX       XXXXX
   TOTALS      XXXXX     XXXXX      XXXXX       XX       XXXXX
```

```
LONG RANGE ENVIRONMENTAL PLANNING SIMULATOR                    PAGE
MICHIGAN STATE UNIVERSITY                               DATE 09/09/71
              LOCATION 1: SALES REPORT
QTR   DOLLARS   WEIGHT    CUBE    CASES    LINES    ORDERS
 1    XXXXX     XXXXX    XXXXX    XXXXX    XXXXX    XXXXX
 2    XXXXX     XXXXX    XXXXX    XXXXX    XXXXX    XXXXX
  •      •        •        •        •        •        •
  •      •        •        •        •        •        •
  •      •        •        •        •        •        •
40    XXXXX     XXXXX    XXXXX    XXXXX    XXXXX    XXXXX
```

```
LONG RANGE ENVIRONMENTAL PLANNING SIMULATOR                    PAGE
MICHIGAN STATE UNIVERSITY                               DATE 09/09/71
              LOCATION 1: COST REPORT
QTR   OBC     IBC     TPC    COM     FAC     INV     TOT
 1    XXXXX   XXXXX   XXXXX  XXXXX   XXXXX   XXXXX   XXXXX
 2    XXXXX   XXXXX   XXXXX  XXXXX   XXXXX   XXXXX   XXXXX
  •     •       •       •      •       •       •       •
  •     •       •       •      •       •       •       •
  •     •       •       •      •       •       •       •
40    XXXXX   XXXXX   XXXXX  XXXXX   XXXXX   XXXXX   XXXXX
```

```
LONG RANGE ENVIRONMENTAL PLANNING SIMULATOR                    PAGE
MICHIGAN STATE UNIVERSITY                               DATE 09/09/71
              LOCATION 1: ORDER CYCLE TIME REPORT
QTR   TOT OCT   BO PEN   NOCT   SD NOCT   OBT    SD OBT
 1      XX        XX      XX      XX       XX      XX
 2      XX        XX      XX      XX       XX      XX
  •      •         •       •       •        •       •
  •      •         •       •       •        •       •
  •      •         •       •       •        •       •
40      XX        XX      XX      XX       XX      XX
```

```
LONG RANGE ENVIRONMENTAL PLANNING SIMULATOR                PAGE
MICHIGAN STATE UNIVERSITY                             DATE 09/09/71
              LOCATION 1: REORDER REPORT
         MULTI PRODUCT REORDERS         AVG LEAD TIME
QTR  MCC 1   MCC 2           MCC-NM   MCC 1   MCC 2        MCC-NM
 1    XXX     XXX   • • •     XXX      XX      XX    • • •   XX
 2    XXX     XXX             XXX      XX      XX            XX
 •     •       •               •        •       •             •
 •     •       •               •        •       •             •
 •     •       •               •        •       •             •
40    XXX     XXX   • • •     XXX      XX      XX    • • •   XX
```

```
LONG RANGE ENVIRONMENTAL PLANNING SIMULATOR                PAGE
MICHIGAN STATE UNIVERSITY                             DATE 09/09/71
              LOCATION 1: INVENTORY CONDITION REPORT
QTR   IOH     TSO      TRO     PCUBO   AVG SD   SD ASD   INVTURNS
 1   XXXXX    XXX      XXX      XX      XX       XX        XX
 2   XXXXX    XXX      XXX      XX      XX       XX        XX
 •     •       •        •        •       •        •         •
 •     •       •        •        •       •        •         •
 •     •       •        •        •       •        •         •
40   XXXXX    XXX      XXX      XX      XX       XX        XX
```

```
LONG RANGE ENVIRONMENTAL PLANNING SIMULATOR                PAGE
MICHIGAN STATE UNIVERSITY                             DATE 09/09/71
              LOCATION 1: AVERAGE INVENTORY REPORT
       PIECES OR UNITS                      DOLLARS
QTR  SKU: 1   SKU: 2  • • •  SKU: NU  SKU: 1   SKU: 2  • • •  SKU: NU
 1    XXXX    XXXX            XXXX    XXXX    XXXX            XXXX
 2    XXXX    XXXX            XXXX    XXXX    XXXX            XXXX
 •     •       •               •       •       •               •
 •     •       •               •       •       •               •
 •     •       •               •       •       •               •
40    XXXX    XXXX   • • •    XXXX    XXXX    XXXX   • • •    XXXX
```

```
LONG RANGE ENVIRONMENTAL PLANNING SIMULATOR                PAGE
MICHIGAN STATE UNIVERSITY                             DATE 09/09/71
              LOCATION 1: IDENTIFICATION REPORT
QTR   NO OF DUS    S-M FACTOR    DU WI SUM    DOL SIZE IND
 1      XXXXX          XX           XX           XXXXX
 2      XXXXX          XX           XX           XXXXX
 •        •             •            •             •
 •        •             •            •             •
 •        •             •            •             •
40      XXXXX          XX           XX           XXXXX
```

```
LONG RANGE ENVIRONMENTAL PLANNING SIMULATOR                PAGE
MICHIGAN STATE UNIVERSITY                             DATE 09/09/71
         LOCATION 1: NORMAL ORDER CYCLE TIME DOLLAR PROPORTIONS
              PROPORTION OF SALES DOLLARS WITHIN DAYS
QTR    1 DAY     2 DAYS     3 DAYS      • • •         ND
 1      XX         XX         XX                      XX
 2      XX         XX         XX                      XX
 •       •          •          •                       •
 •       •          •          •                       •
 •       •          •          •                       •
40      XX         XX         XX        • • •         XX
```

```
LONG RANGE ENVIRONMENTAL PLANNING SIMULATOR                PAGE
MICHIGAN STATE UNIVERSITY                             DATE 09/09/71
         LOCATION 1: NORMAL ORDER CYCLE TIME ORDER PROPORTIONS
              PROPORTION OF ORDERS WITHIN DAYS
QTR    1 DAY     2 DAYS     3 DAYS      • • •         ND
 1      XX         XX         XX                      XX
 2      XX         XX         XX                      XX
 •       •          •          •                       •
 •       •          •          •                       •
 •       •          •          •                       •
40      XX         XX         XX        • • •         XX
```

APPENDIX 3

```
LONG RANGE ENVIRONMENTAL PLANNING SIMULATOR              PAGE
MICHIGAN STATE UNIVERSITY                          DATE 09/09/71
   LOCATION 1:    WEIGHT CLASS   INTERVAL  ACCUMULATIONS IN POUNDS
  QTR     WCI1        WCI2         WCI3         • • •         NO
   1      XXXX        XXXX         XXXX                      XXXX
   2      XXXX        XXXX         XXXX                      XXXX
   •       •           •            •                         •
   •       •           •            •                         •
   •       •           •            •                         •
  40      XXXX        XXXX         XXXX         • • •        XXXX
```

```
LONG RANGE ENVIRONMENTAL PLANNING SIMULATOR              PAGE
MICHIGAN STATE UNIVERSITY                          DATE 09/09/71
DCC-MCC WEIGHT CLASS INTERVAL ACCUMULATIONS IN POUNDS
   TO LOCATION 1          FROM              LOCATION 3
  QTR     WCI1        WCI2         WCI3         • • •         NI
   1      XXXX        XXXX         XXXX                      XXXX
   2      XXXX        XXXX         XXXX                      XXXX
   •       •           •            •                         •
   •       •           •            •                         •
   •       •           •            •                         •
  40      XXXX        XXXX         XXXX         • • •        XXXX
```

GLOSSARY OF ABBREVIATIONS

AVG	AVERAGE
AVG SD	AVERAGE STOCKOUT DELAY
BO PEN	BACK ORDER PENALTY TIME
COM	COMMUNICATIONS COST
DC	DISTRIBUTION CENTER
DOL SIZE IND	DOLLAR SIZE INDICATOR
DU WI SUM	SUM OF THE DU WEIGHTED INDICES
FAC	ALLOCATED FACILITIES COST: LAND, EQUIP
IBC	INBOUND SHIPPING COST
INV	INVENTORY COST
INV OH	AVG CUBIC INVENTORY ON HAND
IOH	AVG CUBIC INVENTORY ON HAND
MCC	MANUFACTURING CONTROL CENTER
NO OF DUS	NUMBER OF DEMAND UNITS
NOCT	NORMAL ORDER CYCLE TIME
OBC	OUTBOUND SHIPPING COST
OBT	OUTBOUND TRANSIT TIME
OC TIME	ORDER CYCLE TIME
PCUBO	PERCENT CASE UNITS BACK ORDERED
PROFIT	SALES LESS DISTRIBUTION COST
QTR	QUARTER
S-M FACTOR	SALES MODIFICATION FACTOR
SD ASD	STANDARD DEVIATION AVG SD
SD NOCT	STANDARD DEVIATION NOCT
SD OBT	STANDARD DEVIATION OBT
TOT	TOTAL
TOT OCT	TOTAL ORDER CYCLE TIME
TPC	THROUGHPUT COST
TRO	TOTAL REORDERS
TSO	TOTAL STOCKOUTS

APPENDIX 4

Overview of Functions in LREPS—Finance

Overview of Functions in LREPS—Finance

Table A4–1
Financial Ratios Included in LREPS-F

Ratio	Formula
$\dfrac{\text{Current assets}}{\text{Current liabilities}}$	$\dfrac{\text{CASH} + \text{ACCRC} + \text{INVTY} + \text{MKTSC}}{\text{ACCPY} + \text{TXPAY} + \text{STDBT}}$
Acid ratio	$\dfrac{\text{Cash} + \text{ACCRC} + \text{MKTSC}}{\text{ACCPY} + \text{TXPAY} + \text{STDBT}}$
Cash turnover	$\dfrac{\text{Quarterly sales}}{\text{Average weekly cash balance}}$
$\dfrac{\text{Working capital}}{\text{Total assets}}$	$\dfrac{\text{CASH} + \text{ACCRC} + \text{INVTY} + \text{MKTSC}}{\text{TOTAS}}$
$\dfrac{\text{Net working capital}}{\text{Total assets}}$	$\dfrac{\text{Current assets} - \text{Current liabilities}}{\text{TOTAS}}$
$\dfrac{\text{Fixed asset}}{\text{Turnover}}$	$\dfrac{\text{Quarterly sales}}{\text{Average weekly level of fixed assets}}$
$\dfrac{\text{Debt}}{\text{Equity}}$	$\dfrac{\text{TOTAS} - \text{SHEQT}}{\text{SHEQT}}$
$\dfrac{\text{Debt}}{\text{Total assets}}$	$\dfrac{\text{TOTAS} - \text{SHEQT}}{\text{TOTAS}}$
Return on assets	$\dfrac{\text{EAFIT}}{\text{TOTAS}}$
Return on equity	$\dfrac{\text{EAFIT}}{\text{SHEQT}}$
Debt service coverage	$\dfrac{\text{EAFIT} + \text{CSDBT} + \text{SLDPX}}{\text{CSDBT} + \text{Principal Repayments}}$

Note: "Overview of Functions in LREPS—Finance" is adapted from M. L. Lawrence, "Development of a Dynamic Simulation Model for Planning Physical Distribution Systems: Warehouse Analysis" (Ph.D. dissertation, Michigan State University, 1971).

Table A4-2
Financial Statement Items and the Associated Operations Systems Routines

Item	Code	Associated Routines
Cash	CASH	PAYAC, ARADJ, LAMGT, CSMGT, FTXPY, CPBUD, DIVPY, INTRS, MKSCY, PRRPY, TOPRX
Marketable securities	MKTSC	CSMGT
Accounts receivable	ACCRC	DLSLS, ARADJ
Inventory	INVTY	IDCGS, INRPL
Fixed assets	PLNEQ	CPBUD, TOPRX
Total assets	TOTAS	(RESIDUAL)
Accounts payable	ACCPY	PAYAC, INRPL
Taxes payable	TXPAY	FTXRT, FTXPY
Deferred taxes	DEFTX	FTXRT
Short-term loans	STDBT	LAMGT
Current maturities—long-term loans	LTDTC	PRRPY
Long-term loans	LTDBT	PRRPY
Equity	SHEQT	EAFIT, DIVPY
Sales	SALES	DLSLS
Cost of goods sold	CSTGS	IDCGS
Gross margin	GMARG	(RESIDUAL)
Administrative and selling expense	ADSLX	TOPRX
Outbound transportation expense	OTBDX	TOPRX
Inbound transportation expense	INBTX	TOPRX
Throughput expense	THPTX	TOPRX
Communications expense	COMMX	TOPRX
Straight line depreciation	SLDPX	TOPRX, FTXRT
Interest on debt	CSDBT	INTRS
Net operating income	NOINC	(RESIDUAL)
Marketable securities income	MSINC	MKSCY
Marketable securities expense	MKSCX	CSMGT
Net income	EBFIT	(RESIDUAL)
Federal income taxes	FINCT	FTXRT
Net income, after taxes	EAFIT	NETIN

A summary of the financial flows is presented in tables A4-2 and A4-3. Table A4-2 lists the items in the balance sheet and income statement, their code names, and the code name of routines in the model which directly cause change in that item.

Table A4-3 presents a schematic of the finance-associated routines, approximately in the order in which they occur in the model. The information presented in table A4-3 includes: the code name of the routines, the event which activates the routine, the name of the routine, the code name of the finance variables and finance-related variables which link to it in the model, both input and output, and a brief explanation of the routine. In table A4-4, each code name used in this section is listed in alphabetical order along with the variable or routine which it represents.

Table A4-3
A Summary Overview of the Finance Associated Routines and Their Associated Variables

Routine Name	Code	Event	Associated Routines	Associated Variables Input	Associated Variables Output	Explanation
Daily sales	DLSLS	DAILY	IDCGS	GENRL	SALES	Generate daily sales and assign to OCs and DUs
Inventory depletion, cost of goods sold	IDCGS	DAILY	DLSLS	SALES	CSTGS INVTY	Calculate cost of units sold and subtract from inventory
Inventory replenishment	INRPL	DCSHPAR		GENRL	INVTY ACCPY	Record arrival of inventory, increase accounts payable
Payment of accounts	PAYAC	END-OF-DAY	INRPL	INVTY ADSLX OTBDX INBOX THPTX COMMX	ACCPY CASHA	Pay accounts scheduled for payment today
Accounts receivables adjustments	ARADJ	END-OF-DAY	DLSLS	SALES ACCRC	CASHA ACCRC	Randomly generate receipts; add today's sales to receivables

Table A4-3—continued

Routine			Associated Routines	Associated Variables		Explanation
Name	Code	Event		Input	Output	
Liquid assets management	LAMGT	END-OF-DAY		LIQAS	STDBT CASHA	Compare LIQAS to acceptable limits, adjust with short-term loans if required
Cash management	CSMGT	END-OF-DAY		CASHA	CASHA MKTSC MSCTX	Compare CASHA acceptable limits, adjust with MKTSC if required
Accumulating variable update	AVUPD	END-OF-DAY		MKTSC STDBT LTDBT	ADDMS ADDSD ADDLD	Add amount in each security, loan account to appropriate accumulating variable for income and costing purposes
Operating expense routines	TDPRX	END-OF-WEEK		GENRL PLNEQ	ADSLX OTBDX INBTX THPTX COMMX SLDPX CASH ACCPY	Calculate all operating expenses for week, make appropriate adjustments to cash and accounts payable
Interest	INTRS	END-OF-MONTH	AVVPD	ADDSD ADDLD	CSDBT CASH	Multiply daily interest rates by accumulated loans if required

Overview of Functions

Routine			Associated Routines	Associated Variables		Explanation
Name	Code	Event		Input	Output	
Marketable securities income	MKSCY	END-OF-MONTH	AVVPD	ADDMS	MSINC CASH	Multiple daily return by accumulated M.S. dollar days
Accumulated depreciation	SYDDP	END-OF-MONTH		PLNEQ	SYDDX	Sum-of-years digits depreciation for tax purposes
Net income	NETIN	END-OF-MONTH		ALL INCOME STATEMENT	ITEMS	Calculate net income, after taxes, based on straight line depreciation
Federal income taxes	FTXRT	END-OF-MONTH	SYDDP		TXPAY DFTAX	Calculate taxes payable based on SYDDP; add ⅓ of (SYDDP-SLDPX) to deferred taxes
Tax payment	FTXPY	END-OF-QUARTER		TXPAY	TXPAY CASH	Pay taxes; subtract from cash and taxes payable
Principal repayment	PRRPY	END-OF-QUARTER		LTDTC	LTDBT	Pay ¼ of current maturities; transfer same from LTDBT TO LTDTC
Dividend payment	DIVPY	END-OF-QUARTER		EAFIT	CASH SHEQT	70 percent of net earnings after taxes
Capital budgeting	CPBUD	END-OF-YEAR		SLDPX SALES	CASH PLNEQ	Replacement + net equipment

Table A4-4
Financial Variable and Routine Code Glossary

Code	Description
ACCPY	Accounts payable
ACCRC	Accounts receivable
ADSLX	Administration and selling expense
ARADJ	Accounts receivable adjustment routine
AVUPD	Accumulating variable update routine
CASH	Cash
COMMX	Communications expense
CPBUD	Capital budgeting routine
CSDBT	Interest on debt
CSMGT	Cash management routine
CSTGS	Cost of goods sold
DEFTX	Deferred taxes
DIVPY	Dividend payment routine
DLSLS	Daily sales
EAFIT	Net income, after taxes
EBFIT	Net income
FINCT	Federal income taxes
FTXPY	Tax payment routine
FTXRT	Federal income taxes routine
GMARG	Gross margin
IDCGS	Inventory depletion, cost of goods sold routine
INBTX	Inbound transportation expense
INRPL	Inventory replenishment
INTRS	Interest routine
INVTY	Inventory
LAMGT	Liquid management assets routine
LTDBT	Long-term loans
LTDTC	Current maturities—long-term loan
MKSCY	Marketable securities income routine
MKSCX	Marketable securities expense
MKTSC	Marketable securities
MSINC	Marketable securities
NETIN	Net income routine
NOINC	Net operating income
OTBDX	Outbound transportation expense routine
PAYAC	Payment of accounts routine
PLNEQ	Fixed assets
PRRPY	Principal repayment
SALES	Sales
SHEQT	Equity
SLDPX	Straight line depreciation
STDBT	Short-term loan
SYDDP	Accumulated depreciation routine
TDPRX	Operating expense routine
THPTX	Throughput expense
TOTAS	Total assets
TXPAY	Taxes payable

NOTES

Chapter 1

1. P. F. Drucker, "Long-Range Planning," *Management Science*, April 1959.
2. M. A. Geisler and W. A. Steger, "The Combination of Alternative Research Techniques in Logistics Systems Analysis," in *Operations Management Selected Readings*, edited by G. K. Groff and J. F. Muth, pp. 324-32 (Homewood, Illinois: Richard D. Irwin, Inc., 1969).
3. A. A. Kuehn, "Logistics of Physical Facilities in Distribution," *Readings in Physical Distribution Management*, edited by D. J. Bowersox, B. J. La Londe, E. W. Smykay (New York: The Macmillan Company, 1969).
4. G. Gordon, *Systems Simulation* (Englewood Cliffs, New Jersey: Prentice-Hall, Inc., 1969), p. 18.
5. D. J. Bowersox, E. W. Smykay, and B. J. La Londe, *Physical Distribution Management* (New York: The Macmillan Company, 1968), p. 5.
6. R. LeKashman and J. F. Stolle, "The Total Cost Approach to Distribution," *Business Horizons*, Winter 1965, pp. 33-46.
7. M. Flaks, "Total Cost Approach to Physical Distribution," *Business Management* 24 (August 1963): 55-61.
8. For examples see: Ronald H. Ballou, "Quantitative Methods—What They Are and How You Can Use Them," *Handling & Shipping*, December 1967, pp. 39-43; Harvey N. Shycon and Richard B. Maffei, "Simulation—Tool for Better Distribution," *Harvard Business Review*, November-December 1960, pp. 65-75; B. F. Rowan, "Linear Programming: A Straight Line to Distribution Efficiency," *Handling & Shipping*, November 1965, pp. 56-60; and Bowersox, Smykay, and La Londe, *Physical Distribution Management*, ch. 12.

Chapter 2

1. T. H. Naylor, J. L. Balintfy, D. S. Burdick, K. Chu, *Computer Simulation Techniques* (New York: John Wiley & Sons, 1966), pp. 10-12.
2. A. H. Packer, "Simulation and Adaptive Forecasting as Applied to Inventory Control," *Operations Research*, July 1967, p. 672.
3. A. A. Kuehn and M. J. Hamburger, "A Heuristic Program for Locating Warehouses," *Management Science* 9 (July 1963): 543-666.

Chapter 3

1. G. A. Steiner, *Top Management Planning* (New York: The Macmillan Company, 1969), pp. 22-24.
2. C. Hadley, *Nonlinear and Dynamic Programming* (Reading, Mass.: Addison-Wesley, 1964), p. 159.

3. W. Hausman, "Sequential Decision Problems: A Model to Exploit Existing Forecasters," *Management Science* 16, no. 2 (October 1969): B-93.
4. J. L. Heskett, "A Missing Link in Physical Distribution System Design," *Journal of Marketing*, October 1966, pp. 37-41.
5. Naylor et al., *Simulation Techniques*, p. 18.
6. D. J. Bowersox, "Forces Influencing Finished Inventory Distribution," in *Readings in Business Logistics*, edited by D. McConaughy for American Marketing Association, p. 88 (Homewood, Illinois: Richard D. Irwin, Inc., 1969).
7. Naylor et al., *Simulation Techniques*, p. 4.
8. C. McMillan and R. F. Gonzalez, *Systems Analysis: A Computer Approach to Decision Models* (Homewood, Illinois: Richard D. Irwin, Inc., 1968), p. 25.
9. J. W. Forrester, *Industrial Dynamics* (Cambridge, Mass.: The M.I.T. Press, Massachusetts Institute of Technology, 1961), pp. 13-19.
10. Geisler and Steger, "Alternative Research Techniques," pp. 324-32.
11. Ibid., p. 332.
12. Kuehn, "Logistics of Facilities."
13. Ibid., p. 263.
14. Bowersox, Smykay, and La Londe, *Physical Distribution Management*, p. 326.
15. M. K. Starr, "Evolving Concepts in Production Management," in *Operations Management Selected Readings*, edited by G. K. Groff and J. F. Muth (Homewood, Illinois: Richard D. Irwin, Inc., 1969).
16. Heskett, "Missing Link," p. 137.
17. Ibid., p. 143.
18. Ibid., p. 140.
19. W. J. Baumol and P. Wolfe, "A Warehouse Location Problem," *Operations Research* 6 (March-April 1958): 252-63.
20. A. A. Kuehn and M. J. Hamburger, "Heuristic Program," pp. 543-666.
21. D. J. Bowersox, "An Analytical Approach to Warehouse Location," *Handling & Shipping* 11 (February 1962).
22. Heskett, "Missing Link," p. 140.
23. Ibid., p. 143.
24. R. A. Howard, "Dynamic Programming," *Management Science* 12, no. 5 (January 1966): 317.
25. Ibid.
26. R. H. Ballou, "Dynamic Warehouse Location Analysis," *Journal of Marketing Research* 5 (August 1968): 271-76.
27. Ibid., p. 271.
28. Ibid.
29. Forrester, *Industrial Dynamics*.
30. Ibid., p. 14.
31. R. E. Bellman and S. E. Dreyfus, *Applied Dynamic Programming* (Princeton, New Jersey: Princeton University Press, 1962).
32. Hadley, *Nonlinear Programming*.
33. Bowersox, "Analytical Approach."
34. Bowersox, Smykay, and La Londe, *Physical Distribution Management*, p. 29.
35. P. Kotler and R. L. Schultz, "Marketing Simulations: Review and Prospects," *Journal of Business* (The Graduate School of Business of the University of Chicago: the University of Chicago Press) 43, no. 3 (July 1970): 237-95.
36. Steiner, *Top Management Planning*, p. 21.
37. Forrester, *Industrial Dynamics*, p. 7.
38. J. F. Magee, "Quantitative Analysis of Physical Distribution Systems," in *Readings in Business Logistics*.
39. Ibid., p. 76.

40. R. H. Ballou, "Quantitative Methods—What They Are and How You Can Use Them," *Readings in Physical Distribution Management*, edited by D. J. Bowersox, B. J. La Londe, and E. W. Smykay, pp. 235-42 (New York: The Macmillan Company, 1969).
41. Magee, "Quantitative Analysis."
42. Bowersox, Smykay, and La Londe, *Physical Distribution Management*.
43. H. M. Wagner, *Principles of Operations Research* (Englewood Cliffs, N. J.: Prentice-Hall, Inc., 1969).
44. Kuehn and Hamburger, "Heuristic Program."
45. Ibid.
46. H. N. Shycon and R. B. Maffei, "Simulation—Tool for Better Distribution," *Readings in Physical Distribution Management*, pp. 243-60.
47. Ibid., p. 244.
48. Ibid., p. 249.
49. Ballou, "Dynamic Warehouse."
50. Ibid., p. 271.
51. Ibid.
52. Bellman and Dreyfus, *Dynamic Programming*.
53. Ballou, "Dynamic Warehouse."
54. Forrester, *Industrial Dynamics*.
55. Ibid., p. 22.
56. Ibid., p. 23.
57. Ibid.
58. J. W. Farrell, "Distribution Dynamics at Work: Carrier Air Conditioning Company," *Traffic/Physical Distribution Management* 9, no. 6 (June 1970).
59. Packer, "Adaptive Forecasting," p. 672.
60. R. C. Brown, *Statistical Forecasting for Inventory Control* (New York: McGraw-Hill, 1959).
61. Packer, "Adaptive Forecasting," p. 662.
62. F. Hanssmann, "A Survey of Inventory Theory from the Operations Research Viewpoint," *Progress in Operations Research* (New York, 1961).
63. R. H. Ballou, "Multi-Echelon Inventory Control for Interrelated and Vertically Integrated Firms" (Ph.D. dissertation, Univ. Microfilms, Inc., 1965).
64. Naylor et al., *Simulation Techniques*, p. 16.
65. Gordon, *System Simulation*, p. 4.
66. P. J. Kiviat and A. A. B. Pritsker, *Simulation with GASP II, A FORTRAN-Based Simulation Language* (Englewood Cliffs, N.J.: Prentice-Hall, 1969).
67. Naylor et al., *Simulation Techniques*, p. 126.
68. Ibid., p. 127.
69. Ibid.
70. Forrester, *Industrial Dynamics*.

Chapter 4

1. Naylor et al., *Simulation Techniques*, p. 10.
2. McMillan and Gonzalez, *Systems Analysis*, p. 11.
3. Ibid., p. 31.
4. Van Court Hare, Jr., *Systems Analysis: A Diagnostic Approach* (New York: Harcourt, Brace & World, Inc., 1967).
5. W. T. Morris, "On the Art of Modeling," *Management Science* 13, no. 12: B-707-17.
6. P. J. Kiviat, *Digital Computer Simulation Modeling Concepts* (Santa Monica, California: The Rand Corporation, 1967), p. 18.

7. Ibid., pp. 19-20.
8. Naylor et al., *Simulation Techniques*, p. 29.
9. M. Asimow, *Introduction to Design* (Englewood Cliffs, N.J.: Prentice-Hall, Inc., 1962).
10. Forrester, *Industrial Dynamics*.
11. Naylor et al., *Simulation Techniques*.
12. W. K. Holstein and W. L. Berry, "Work Flow Structure: An Analysis for Planning and Control," *Management Science* 16 (February 1970): 324-37.
13. Van Court Hare, Jr., *Diagnostic Approach*, p. 157.
14. Ibid., p. 160.
15. Ibid., p. 200.
16. Ibid., p. 210.
17. Morris, "Art of Modeling," p. 715.
18. Ibid., p. 716.
19. S. K. Gupta and J. Rosenhead, "Robustness in Sequential Investment Decisions," *Management Science* 15 (October 1968): 18-29.
20. O. K. Helferich, "Development of a Dynamic Simulation Model for Planning Physical Distribution Systems: Formulation of the Mathematical Model." Ph.D. dissertation, Michigan State University, 1970, chaps. 4-6.
21. Wagner, *Principles of Operations Research*.
22. Kuehn and Hamburger, "Heuristic Program."
23. Ballou, "Dynamic Warehouse."
24. R. C. Brown, *Statistical Forecasting*.
25. Packer, "Adaptive Forecasting."
26. Naylor et al., *Simulation Techniques*.
27. A. Amstutz, *Computer Simulation of Competitive Market Response* (Cambridge, Mass: The M.I.T. Press, Massachusetts Institute of Technology, 1967).
28. E. J. Marien, "Development of a Dynamic Simulation Model for Planning Physical Distribution Systems: Formulation of the Computer Model" (Ph.D. dissertation, Michigan State University, 1970).

Chapter 5

1. Marien, "Dynamic Simulation Model."
2. Naylor et al., *Simulation Techniques*, pp. 239-40.
3. Daniel Teichroew and J. F. Lubin, "Computer Simulation—Discussion of Techniques and Comparisons of Languages," *Communications ACM* 10 (October 1966): 725-31.
4. H. S. Krasnow and R. A. Merikallio, "The Past, Present and Future of General Simulation Languages," *Management Science* 2 (November 1964): 254-67.
5. Naylor et al., *Simulation Techniques*, p. 241.
6. Howard S. Krasnow, "Computer Languages of System Simulation," in *Digital Computer User's Handbook*, edited by Melvin Klerer and Granino Korn, section I, p. 261 (New York: McGraw Hill Book Co., 1967).
7. Naylor et al., *Simulation Techniques*, p. 241.
8. Krasnow and Merikallio, "Past, Present and Future," p. 254.
9. P. J. Kiviat and A. A. B. Pritsker, *Simulation with GASP II*, pp. 1-21.
10. Krasnow and Merikallio, "Past, Present and Future," p. 254.
11. Naylor et al., *Simulation Techniques*, pp. 240-41.
12. Teichroew and Lubin, "Computer Simulation," pp. 736-38.
13. Ibid., p. 738.
14. Naylor et al., *Simulation Techniques*, p. 241.
15. Teichroew and Lubin, "Computer Simulation," p. 732.

16. Naylor et al., *Simulation Techniques*, p. 241.
17. Ibid.
18. Teichroew and Lubin, "Computer Simulation," p. 732.
19. Ibid., p. 731.
20. Ibid., p. 732.
21. Naylor et al., *Simulation Techniques*, p. 241.
22. Krasnow and Merikallio, "Past, Present and Future," p. 254.
23. D. Teichroew, T. D. Truitt, and J. F. Lubin, "Discussion of Computer Simulation Techniques and Comparison of Languages." *Simulation* 9 (October 1967): 244.
24. Teichroew and Lubin, "Computer Simulation," p. 732.
25. Krasnow and Merikallio, "Past, Present and Future," p. 238.
26. Krasnow, "Computer Languages," pp. 263-64.
27. Krasnow and Merikallio, "Past, Present and Future," pp. 265-67.
28. Teichroew and Lubin, "Computer Simulation," p. 733.
29. Krasnow, "Computer Languages," p. 276.
30. Krasnow and Merikallio, "Past, Present and Future," p. 238.
31. Teichroew and Lubin, "Computer Simulation," p. 730.
32. Ibid., p. 733.
33. Naylor et al., *Simulation Techniques*, p. 241.
34. Teichroew and Lubin, "Computer Simulation," p. 733.
35. Naylor et al., *Simulation Techniques*, p. 241.
36. Krasnow and Merikallio, "Past, Present and Future," p. 257.
37. Krasnow, "Computer Languages," p. 261.
38. Naylor et al., *Simulation Techniques*, p. 241.
39. Kiviat and Pritsker, *Simulation with GASP II*, pp. 258-63.
40. P. J. Kiviat, R. Villanueva, and H. M. Markowitz, *SIMSCRIPT II* (Englewood Cliffs, N.J.: Prentice-Hall, Inc., 1968).
41. *Control Data 6400/6500/6600 Computer Systems: FORTRAN Extended Reference Manual*, Control Data Corporation, Palo Alto, California, printed in the United States of America, 1969.

Chapter 6

1. One basic procedure is to determine the model's face validity. That is, the extent to which the assumptions of the model agree with known facts and also the internal consistency or "deductive veracity" of the model. In other words, the model must make sense.
2. G. P. E. Clarkson, *Portfolio Selection: A Simulation of Trust Investment* (Englewood Cliffs, New Jersey: Prentice-Hall, Inc., 1962).
3. K. R. Popper, *The Logic of Scientific Discovery* (New York: Basic Books, 1959).
4. R. Carnap, "Testability and Meaning," *Philosophy of Science III*, 1936.
5. R. Van Horn, "Validation," in *The Design of Computer Simulation Experiments*, edited by Thomas H. Naylor, p. 233 (Durham, N.C.: Duke University Press, 1969).
6. T. H. Naylor and J. M. Finger, "Verification of Computer Simulation Models," *Management Science* 14 (October 1967): 92-101.
7. Ibid., p. B-93.
8. G. S. Fishman and P. J. Kiviat, *Digital Computer Simulation: Statistical Considerations* (Santa Monica, Cal.: The Rand Corporation) Rm-3281-PR, 1962.
9. Ibid.

10. K. J. Cohen, *Computer Models of the Shoe, Leather, Hide Sequence* (Englewood Cliffs, N.J.: Prentice-Hall, 1960), p. 60.
11. Ibid., pp. 62-63.
12. Ibid., p. 63.
13. R. M. Cyert, E. A. Feigenbaum, and J. G. March, "Models of a Behavioral Theory of the Firm," *Behavioral Science* 4, no. 2 (April 1959): 81-95.
14. C. P. Bonini, *Simulation of Information and Decision Systems in the Firm* (Englewood Cliffs, N.J.: Prentice-Hall, 1962), p. 52.
15. Clarkson, *Portfolio Selection*, p. 55.
16. A. M. Turing, "Can a Machine Think?" in *The World of Mathematics*, edited by J. R. Newman (New York: Simon and Schuster, 1956).
17. F. E. Balderston and A. C. Hoggatt, *Simulation of Market Processes* (Berkeley, California: Institute of Business and Economic Research, 1962), p. 33.
18. A. C. Hoggatt, "Statistical Techniques for the Computer Analysis of Simulation Models," in *Studies in a Simulated Market*, edited by L. E. Preston and N. R. Collins (Berkeley, California: Institute of Business and Economic Research, 1966).
19. G. E. P. Box and K. B. Wilson, "On the Experimental Attainment of Optimum Conditions," *Journal of the Royal Statistical Society*, B, XIII, 1951, pp. 1-45.
20. Hoggatt, "Statistical Techniques," p. 94.
21. Forrester, *Industrial Dynamics*, p. 13.
22. Ibid., p. 115.
23. Ibid.
24. Ibid., p. 118.
25. Amstutz, *Competitive Market Response*, p. 18.
26. Ibid., p. 369.
27. H. Theil, *Applied Economic Forecasting* (Amsterdam: The North Holland Publishing Co., 1966).
28. G. S. Fishman and P. J. Kiviat, *Spectral Analysis of Time Series Generated by Simulation Models* (Santa Monica, California: The Rand Corporation), RM-4393-PR, 1965.
29. T. H. Naylor, K. Wertz, and T. H. Wonnacott, "Spectral Analysis of Data Generated by Simulation Experiments with Economic Models," *Econometrica* 37 (April 1969): 333-52.
30. T. H. Naylor, K. Wertz, and T. H. Wonnacott, "Methods for Analyzing Data from Computer Simulation Experiments," *Communications of the ACM* 10 (November 1967): 707.
31. E. Paulson, "Sequential Estimation and Closed Sequential Decision Procedures," *The Annals of Mathematical Statistics* 35 (September 1964): 1048-1958.
32. R. E. Bechhofer and S. Blumenthal, "A Sequential Multiple-Decision Procedure for Selecting the Best One of Several Normal Populations with a Common Unknown Variance, II: Monte Carlo Sampling Results and New Computing Formulae," *Biometrics* 18 (March 1962): 52-67.
33. W. E. Sasser, D. S. Burdick, D. A. Graham, and T. H. Naylor, "The Application of Sequential Sampling to Simulation: An Example Inventory Model," *Communications of the ACM* 13 (May 1970): 287-96.
34. R. M. Cyert, "A Description and Evaluation of Some Firm Simulations," *Proceedings of the IBM Scientific Computing Symposium on Simulation Models and Gaming* (White Plains, N.Y.: IBM, 1966).
35. P. Gilmour, "Development of a Dynamic Simulation Model for Planning Physical Distribution Systems: Validation" (Ph.D. dissertation, Michigan State University, 1970).
36. Ibid., ch. 5.
37. Ibid., ch. 6.
38. Ibid., p. 188.

Chapter 7

1. R. T. Rogers, "Development of a Dynamic Simulation Model for Planning Physical Distribution Systems: Experimentation" (Ph.D. dissertation forthcoming, Michigan State University).
2. R. W. Conway, B. M. Johnson, and W. L. Maxwell, "Some Problems of Digital Systems Simulation," *Management Science* 6 (October 1959): 103-104.
3. Cohen, *Computer Models*, p. 4.
4. Forrester, *Industrial Dynamics*, p. 13.
5. Ibid., p. 31.
6. Ibid., p. 43.
7. F. E. Balderston and A. C. Hoggatt, "Simulation Models: Analytic Variety and the Problem of Model Reduction," *Symposium on Simulation Models* (Cincinnati, Ohio: South-Western Publishing Company, 1963), p. 183.
8. Balderston and Hoggatt, *Simulation of Market Processes*, p. 49.
9. Richard M. Cyert and James G. March, *A Behavioral Theory of the Firm* (Englewood Cliffs, New Jersey: Prentice-Hall, Inc., 1963), p. 149.
10. Ibid., p. 176.
11. Ibid.
12. C. Bonini, *Information and Decision Symptoms*, p. 29.
13. Ibid.
14. Eugene Edwin Kaczka, *The Impact of Some Dimensions of Management Climate on the Performance of Industrial Organizations: A Computer Simulation Study* (Ann Arbor, Michigan: Microfilms, Inc., May 1966), p. 14.
15. Ibid., p. 171.
16. Ibid.
17. R. V. Tuason, "Experimental Simulation on a Pre-determined Marketing Mix Strategy" (Ph.D. dissertation, Northwestern University, 1965), p. 38.
18. Ibid.
19. Ibid., p. 45.
20. Ibid., p. 48.
21. Shycon and Maffei, "Tool for Better Distribution," pp. 65-75.
22. Amstutz, *Competitive Market Response*.
23. Victor Chew, ed., *Experimental Design in Industry* (New York: John Wiley & Sons, 1958).
24. W. G. Cochran and G. M. Cox, *Experimental Designs* (New York: John Wiley & Sons, 1957).
25. O. L. Davies, ed., *Design and Analysis of Industrial Experiments* (New York: Hafner Publishing Company, 1960).
26. Ronald A. Fisher, *The Design of Experiments* (London: Oliver and Boyd, 1951).
27. B. J. Winer, *Statistical Principles in Experimental Design* (New York: McGraw-Hill Book Company, 1962).
28. R. W. Conway, "Some Tactical Problems in Digital Simulation," *Management Science* 10 (October 1963): 47-61.
29. Naylor et al., *Simulation Techniques*.
30. McMillan and Gonzalez, *Systems Analysis*.
31. K. D. Tocher, *The Art of Simulation* (Princeton, New Jersey: D. Van Nostrand Company, 1963).
32. Bonini, *Information and Decision Systems*.
33. Fishman and Kiviat, "Spectral Analysis."
34. Conway, *Tactical Problems*, p. 47.
35. McMillan and Gonzalez, *Systems Analysis*.

36. Naylor et al., *Simulation Techniques*, pp. 40-41.
37. Ibid., pp. 332-40.
38. George Box, "Use of Statistical Methods in the Education of Basic Mechanisms," *Biometrics* 13 (1957).
39. Donald S. Burdick and Thomas H. Naylor, "Design of Computer Simulation Experiments for Industrial Systems," *Communications of the ACM* 9, no. 5 (May 1966): 330-32.
40. Thomas N. Naylor, Donald S. Burdick, and W. Earl Sasser, "Computer Simulation Experiments with Economic Systems: The Problem of Experimental Design," *Journal of the American Statistical Association* 62 (December 1967).
41. Naylor et al., *Simulation Techniques*.
42. John L. Overholt, "Factor Selection," in *Design of Computer Experiments*, edited by Thomas H. Naylor, pp. 59-80 (Durham, N.C.: Duke University Press, 1969).
43. Naylor et al., *Simulation Techniques*.
44. Bonini, *Information and Decision Systems*.
45. Cochran and Cox, *Experimental Designs*.
46. Overholt, "Factor Selection," pp. 64-67.
47. Naylor et al., *Simulation Techniques*.
48. Conway, "Tactical Problems," p. 53.
49. D. R. Cox, "A Remark on Multiple Comparisons," *Technometrics* 7 (May 1965): 223-24.
50. R. E. Bechhofer, "A Single-Sample Multiple Decision Procedure for Ranking Means of Normal Populations with Known Variances," *Ann. Math. Stat.* 25 (1954): 16-39.
51. For multiple ranking, the use of Bechhofer's procedure: "A single-sample multiple-decision procedure for ranking means of normal populations with known variances," *Ann. Math. Stat.* 25 (1954), assumes that variances are known and may or may not be equal. Using Bechhofer, Dunnett, and Sobel's procedure assumes that variances are unknown: "A two-sample decision procedure for ranking means of normal population with a common unknown variance." *Biometrica* 41 (1954): 170-76.
52. H. Scheffé, *The Analysis of Variance* (New York: John Wiley & Sons, 1959).
53. McMillan and Gonzalez, *Systems Analysis*.
54. R. W. Conway, "An Experimental Investigation of Priority Assignment in a Job Shop," RM-3789 (DDC N. AO429 970) (Santa Monica, California: Rand Corporation, February, 1964).
55. Fishman and Kiviat, *Digital Computer Simulation*.
56. Ibid.
57. Ibid.
58. Naylor, Burdick, and Sasser, "Computer Simulation Experiments with Economic Systems," p. 1328.
59. Michael J. Gilman, "A Brief Survey of Stopping Rules in Monte Carlo Simulations," *Digest of the Second Conference on Applications of Simulation* (December 2-4, 1968).
60. Thomas H. Naylor, *Computer Simulation Experiments with Models of Economic Systems* (New York: John Wiley & Sons, 1971), p. 295.
61. Donald Watts, "Time Series Analysis," in *The Design of Computer Simulation Experiments*, edited by Thomas H. Naylor, pp. 165-79 (Durham, N.C.: Duke University Press, 1969).
62. C. W. G. Granger and M. Hatanaka, *Spectral Analysis of Economic Time Series* (Princeton, N.J.: Princeton University Press, 1964).

63. Thomas H. Naylor, William H. Wallace, and W. Earl Sasser, "A Computer Simulation Model of the Textile Industry," *Journal of the American Statistical Association* 62 (December 1967): 1338-64.
64. J. Durbin and G. S. Watson, "Testing for Serial Correlation in Least Squares Regression," *Biometrica* 38 (1951): 159-78.
65. A. Wald, *Sequential Analysis* (New York: John Wiley & Sons, 1947).
66. Cyert and March, *Behavioral Theory*.
67. Balderston and Hoggatt, *Simulation Models*.
68. J. S. Hunter and T. H. Naylor, "Experimental Designs for Computer Simulation Experiments," *Management Science* 16, no. 7 (March 1970): 422-34.
69. Ibid., pp. 427-28.
70. Cochran and Cox, *Experimental Designs*, ch. 8A.
71. Hunter and Naylor, "Experimental Designs for Computer Simulation."
72. Cochran and Cox, *Experimental Designs*.
73. Lee E. Preston and Norman R. Collins, *Studies in a Simulated Market* (Berkeley, California, 1966), Research Program in Marketing, Graduate School of Business Administration, University of California.
74. Donald S. Burdick and Thomas H. Naylor, "Response Surface Designs," in *Design of Computer Experiments*, edited by Thomas H. Naylor (Durham, N.C.: Duke University Press, 1969).
75. Davies, *Design and Analysis*.
76. Cochran and Cox, *Experimental Design*.
77. Burdick and Naylor, "Response Surface Designs."
78. Hunter and Naylor, "Experimental Designs for Computer Simulation."
79. Burdick and Naylor, "Response Surface Designs," p. 86.
80. Ibid.
81. Naylor et al., *Simulation Techniques*, p. 38.
82. Conway, "Tactical Problems," p. 51.
83. Burdick and Naylor, "Computer Simulation Experiments," p. 335.
84. Hunter and Naylor, "Experimental Designs for Computer Simulation," p. 431.
85. A. V. Gafarian and C. I. Ancker, "Mean Value Estimation from Digital Computer Simulation," SP 2005/000/01 (Santa Monica, California: System Development Corporation, July 16, 1965).
86. Naylor et al., *Simulation Techniques*, p. 333.
87. Ibid., p. 335.
88. Martin Shubik, "Simulation of the Industry and the Firm," *American Economic Review* 50, no. 5 (December 1960): 908-19.
89. Naylor, *Computer Simulation Experiments*, p. 112.
90. Ibid., pp. 112-13.

Chapter 8

1. D. J. Bowersox, "Planning Physical Distribution Operations with Dynamic Simulation," *Journal of Marketing* 36, no. 1 (January 1972): 17-26.
2. Ibid., pp. 22-25.
3. Ibid., pp. 18-19.
4. Ronald H. Ballou, "Multi-Echelon Inventory Control for Interrelated and Vertically Integrated Firms" (Ph.D. dissertation, University Microfilms, Inc., 1965).
5. M. L. Lawrence, "Development of a Dynamic Simulation Model for Planning Physical Distribution Systems: Warehouse Analysis" (Ph.D. dissertation, Michigan State University, 1971).
6. Ronald H. Ballou, "Dynamic Warehouse Location Analysis," pp. 271-76.

7. F. W. Morgan, Jr., "A Simulated Sales Forecasting Model: A Build-up Approach" (Ph.D. dissertation, Michigan State University, 1972).
8. A. H. Packer, "Simulation and Adaptive Forecasting as Applied to Inventory Control," *Operations Research,* July 1967.
9. For results see: Morgan, "Simulated Sales Forecasting Model," chap. 7.
10. Lawrence, "Warehouse Analysis," p. 178.
11. R. Carlson, "Financial Efficiency Model" (Ph.D. dissertation, Michigan State University, 1971).
12. Lawrence, "Warehouse Analysis," p. 178.
13. Ibid., p. 182.
14. Ibid., p. 190.
15. A paper on the conceptual model for the materials input system has been completed by O. K. Helferich and R. M. Monczka, "Development of a Dynamic Simulation Model for Planning Materials Input Systems: Formulation of the Conceptual Model."
16. E. S. Fuggee, *Production-Inventory Systems: Planning and Control* (Homewood, Illinois: Richard D. Irwin, Inc., 1968).
17. C. C. Holt, F. Modigliani, J. F. Muth, and H. A. Simon, *Planning Production, Inventories, and Work Force* (Englewood Cliffs, N.J.: Prentice-Hall, Inc., 1960).
18. Morgan, "Simulated Sales Forecasting Model."
19. Helferich, "Formulation of Mathematical Model," p. 89.
20. S. K. Gupta and J. Rosenhead, "Robustness in Sequential Investment Decisions," *Management Science* 15 (October 1968): pp. 18-29.
21. Lawrence, "Warehouse Analysis," p. 199.
22. Ibid., p. 190.
23. Helferich, "Formulation of Mathematical Model," p. 389.
24. *Comprehensive Studies of Solid Waste Management,* First and Second Annual Reports, U.S. Department of Health, Education, and Welfare, Public Health Service, Environmental Health Service, Bureau of Solid Waste Management, Research Grant No. EC-00260 to the University of California, 1970.
25. W. G. Zikmund and W. J. Stanton, "Recycling Solid Wastes: A Channels-of-Distribution Problem," *Journal of Marketing* 35, no. 3 (July 1971): 34-39.
26. O. K. Helferich, D. E. Gee, and V. R. Hoffner, Jr., "Dynamic Simulation Model for Planning Solid Waste Management." Prepared for presentation to the XIX International TIMS Meeting.
27. Forrester, *Industrial Dynamics.*
28. Heskett, "Missing Link."
29. D. J. Bowersox and E. J. McCarthy, "Strategic Development of Planned Vertical Marketing Systems," in *Vertical Marketing Systems,* edited by Louis P. Bucklin, pp. 64-66 (Glenview, Ill.: Scott, Foresman and Company, 1970).
30. Ibid., p. 66.
31. Morgan, "Simulated Sales Forecasting Model."
32. Helferich, "Formulation of Mathematical Model," pp. 390-91.

SELECTED BIBLIOGRAPHY

Ackoff, R. L., ed. *Progress in Operations Research.* Vol. 1. New York: John Wiley & Sons, Inc., 1961.

Agin, Norman. "A Min-Max Inventory Model." *Management Science* 12, no. 7 (March 1966).

Amstutz, Arnold. *Computer Simulation of Competitive Market Response.* Cambridge, Massachusetts: The M.I.T. Press, Massachusetts Institute of Technology, 1967.

Ansoff, H. Ingor, and Slevin, Dennis P. "Comments on Professor Forrester's 'Industrial Dynamics—After the First Decade.'" *Management Science* 14, no. 9 (May 1968).

Asimow, M. *Introduction to Design.* Englewood Cliffs, New Jersey: Prentice-Hall, Inc., 1962.

Balderston, Frederick E., and Hoggatt, Austin C. *Simulation of Market Processes.* Berkeley, California: Institute of Business and Economic Research, 1962.

———. "Simulation Models: Analytic Variety and the Problem of Model Reduction." *Symposium on Simulation Models.* Cincinnati, Ohio: South-Western Publishing Company, 1963.

Ballou, R. H. "Multi-Echelon Inventory Control for Interrelated and Vertically Integrated Firms." Ph.D. dissertation, Univ. Microfilms, Inc., 1965.

———. "Dynamic Warehouse Location Analysis." *Journal of Marketing Research* 5 (August 1968).

———. "Quantitative Methods—What They Are and How You Can Use Them." In *Readings in Physical Distribution Management,* edited by D. J. Bowersox, B. J. LaLonde, and E. W. Smykay. New York: Macmillan Company, 1969.

Baumol, W. J., and Wolfe, P. "A Warehouse Location Problem." *Operations Research* 6 (March-April 1958).

Bechhofer, R. E. "A Single-Sample Multiple Decision Procedure for Ranking Means of Normal Populations with Known Variances." *Ann. Math. Stat.* 25 (1954).

Bechhofer, R. E., and Blumenthal, S. "A Sequential Multiple-Decision Procedure for Selecting the Best One of Several Normal Populations with a Common Unknown Variance, II: Monte Carlo Sampling Results and New Computing Formulae." *Biometrics* 18 (March 1962): 52-67.

Bechhofer, R. E., and Sobel, M. "A Two-Sample Multiple Decision Procedure for Ranking Means of Normal Populations with a Common Unknown Variance." *Biometrica* 41 (1954).

Bell, Duran. "An Inverse Warehousing Problem for Imperfect Markets." *Management Science* 14, no. 9 (May 1968).

Bellman, R. E., and Dreyfus, S. E. *Applied Dynamic Programming.* Princeton, New Jersey: Princeton University Press, 1962.

Bierman, H.; Bonini, C. P.; and Hausman, W. H. *Quantitative Analysis for Business Decisions.* Homewood, Illinois: Richard D. Irwin, Inc., 1969.

Bonini, Charles P. *Simulation of Information and Decsion Systems in the Firm.* Englewood Cliffs, New Jersey: Prentice-Hall, Inc., 1963.
Boulden, James B., and Buffa, E. S. "Corporate Models: On-line, Real-time Systems." *Harvard Business Review* 48, no. 4 (July-August 1970).
Bowersox, D. J. "An Analytical Approach to Warehouse Location." *Handling & Shipping* 2 (February 1962).
―――――. "Forces Influencing Finished Inventory Distribution." In *Readings in Business Logistics,* edited by D. McConaughy. Homewood, Illinois: American Marketing Association, 1969.
Bowersox, D. J., et al. *Dynamic Simulation of Physical Distribution Systems.* East Lansing, Michigan: Division of Research, Graduate School of Business Administration, Michigan State University, forthcoming.
Bowersox, Donald J., and McCarthy, E. Jerome. "Strategic Development of Planned Vertical Marketing Systems." In *Vertical Marketing Systems,* edited by Louis P. Bucklin, 64-66. Glenview, Ill.: Scott, Foresman and Company, 1970.
Bowersox, D. J.; Smykay, E. W.; and LaLonde, B. J. *Physical Distribution Management.* New York: The Macmillan Company, 1968.
Box, George. "Use of Statistical Methods in the Elucidation of Basic Mechanisms." *Biometrics* 13 (1957).
Box, G. E. P., and Wilson, K. B. "On the Experimental Attainment of Optimum Conditions." *Journal of the Royal Statistical Society* 13B (1951): 1-45.
Branch, M. C. *The Corporate Planning Process.* New York: American Management Association, 1962.
Brown, R. C. *Statistical Forecasting for Inventory Control.* New York: McGraw-Hill, 1959.
―――――. "Information, Decision Rules and Policy for Inventory Management." *Production and Inventory Management* 10, no. 3, Third Quarter (1969): 1-16.
Burdick, Donald S., and Naylor, Thomas H. "Design of Computer Simulation Experiments for Industrial Systems." *Communications of the ACM* 9, no. 5 (May 1966).
―――――. "Response Surface Designs." In *Design of Computer Experiments,* edited by Thomas H. Naylor. Durham, North Carolina: Duke University Press, 1969.
Buxton, J. N., and Laski, J. G. "Control and Simulation Languages." *Computer Journal* 5 (October 1962): 194-200.
Carlson, R. "Financial Efficiency Model." Ph.D. dissertation, Michigan State University, 1971.
Carnap, R. "Testability and Meaning." *Philosophy of Science III,* 1936.
Chew, Victor, ed. *Experimental Design in Industry.* New York: John Wiley & Sons, 1958.
Clarkson, G. P. E. *Portfolio Selection: A Simulation of Trust Investment.* Englewood Cliffs, New Jersey: Prentice-Hall, Inc., 1962.
Clementson, A. T. "Extended Control and Simulation Languages." *Computer Journal* 9, no. 3 (November 1966): 215-20.
Cochran, W. G., and Cox, G. M. *Experimental Designs.* New York: John Wiley & Sons, 1957.
Cohen, Kalman J. *Computer Models of the Shoe, Leather, Hide Sequence.* Englewood Cliffs, New Jersey: Prentice-Hall, Inc., 1960.
Control Data 6400/6500/6600 Computer Systems: FORTRAN Extended Reference Manual. Palo Alto, California: Control Data Corporation, printed in the United States of America, 1969.
Conway, R. W. "Some Tactical Problems in Digital Simulation." *Management Science* 10 (October, 1963).

———. "An Experimental Investigation of Priority Assignment in a Job Shop." RM-3789 (DDC N. Ao429 970). Santa Monica, California: Rand Corp. February 1964.
Conway, R. W.; Johnson, B. M.; and Maxwell, W. L. "Some Problems of Digital Systems Simulation." *Management Science* 6 (October 1959).
Cox, D. R. "A Remark on Multiple Comparisons." *Technometrics* 7 (May 1965).
Cyert, R. M. "A Description and Evaluation of Some Firm Simulations." In *Proceedings of the IBM Scientific Computing Symposium on Simulation Models and Gaming*. White Plains, N.Y.: IBM, 1966.
Cyert, R. M.; Feigenbaum, E. A.; and March, J. G. "Models of a Behavioral Theory of the Firm." *Behavioral Science* 4, no. 2 (April 1959): 81-95.
Cyert, Richard M., and March, James G. *A Behavioral Theory of the Firm*. Englewood Cliffs, New Jersey: Prentice-Hall, Inc., 1963.
Daniel, N. E., and Jones, J. R. *Business Logistics—Concept and Viewpoints*. Boston: Allyn and Bacon, Inc., 1969.
Davies, O. L., ed. *Design and Analysis of Industrial Experiments*. New York: Hafner Publishing Company, 1960.
Day, Ralph L. *Marketing Models*. Scranton, Pennsylvania: International Textbook Company, 1964.
Diegel, A. "A Linear Approach to the Dynamic Inventory Problem." *Management Science* 12, no. 7 (March 1966).
Drucker, P. F. "Long-Range Planning." *Management Science*, April 1959.
Durbin, J., and Watson, G. S. "Testing for Serial Correlation in Least Squares Regression." *Biometrica* 38 (1951).
Efron, R., and Gordon, G. "A General Purpose Digital Simulation-Description." *IBM Systems Journal* 3, no. 1 (1964): 57.
Elison, S., and Elmaleh, J. "Adaptive Limits in Inventory Control." *Management Science* 16, no. 8 (April 1970).
Farrell, J. W. "Distribution Dynamics at Work: Carrier Air Conditioning Company." *Traffic/Physical Distribution Management* 9, no. 6 (June 1970).
Feldman, E.; Lehrer, F. A.; and Ray, T. L. "Warehouse Location Under Continuous Economies of Scale." *Management Science* 12, no. 9 (May 1966).
Fetter, R. B., and Dalleck, W. C. *Decision Models for Inventory Management*. Homewood, Illinois: Richard D. Irwin, 1961.
Fisher, Ronald A. *The Design of Experiments*. London: Oliver and Boyd, 1951.
Fishman, George S. "Problems in the Statistical Analysis of Simulation Experiments: The Comparison of Means and the Length of Sample Records." *Communications of the ACM* 10, no. 2 (February 1967).
Fishman, George S., and Kiviat, Philip J. "Spectral Analysis of Time Series Generated by Simulation Models." RM-4393-PR. Santa Monica, California: Rand Corp., February 1965.
———. "Spectral Analysis of Time Series Generated by Simulation Models." *Management Science* 13 (March 1967).
Flaks, M. "Total Cost Approach to Physical Distribution." *Business Management* 24 (August 1963): 55-61.
Forrester, J. W. *Industrial Dynamics*. Cambridge: The M.I.T. Press, Massachusetts Institute of Technology, 1961.
———. "Industrial Dynamics—A Reply to Ansoff and Slevin." *Management Science* 14, no. 9 (May 1968).
Fuggee, E. S. *Production-Inventory Systems: Planning and Control*. Homewood, Illinois: Richard D. Irwin, Inc., 1968.
Gafarian, A. V., and Ancker, C. I. "Mean Value Estimation from Digital Computer Simulation." SP 2005/000/01. Santa Monica, California: System Development Corporation, 16 July 1965.

Geisler, M. A., and Steger, W. A. "The Combination of Alternative Research Techniques in Logistics Systems Analysis." In *Operations Management Selected Readings*, edited by G. K. Groff and J. F. Muth. Homewood, Illinois: Richard D. Irwin, Inc., 1969.

Gilman, Michael J. "A Brief Survey of Stopping Rules in Monte Carlo Simulations." *Digest of the Second Conference on Applications of Simulation*. 2-4 December 1968.

Gilmour, P. "Development of a Dynamic Simulation Model for Planning Physical Distribution Systems: Validation." Ph.D. dissertation, Michigan State University, 1970.

Granger, C. W. G., and Hatanaka, M. *Spectral Analysis of Economic Time Series*. Princeton, New Jersey: Princeton University Press, 1964.

Gupta, S. K., and Rosenhead, J., Jr. "Robustness in Sequential Investment Decisions." *Management Science* 15, no. 2 (October 1968).

Hadley, C. *Nonlinear and Dynamic Programming*. Reading: Addison-Wesley, 1964.

Hadley, G., and Whitin, T. M. *Analysis of Inventory Systems*. Englewood Cliffs, New Jersey: Prentice-Hall, Inc., 1963.

Hanssmann, Fred. "A Survey of Inventory Theory from the Operations Research Viewpoint." In *Progress in Operations Research*, Vol. I, edited by Russell L. Ackoff. New York: John Wiley & Sons, Inc., 1961.

Hare, Van Court, Jr. *Systems Analysis: A Diagnostic Approach*. New York: Harcourt, Brace & World, Inc., 1967.

Hausman, W. H. "Sequential Decision Problems: A Model to Exploit Existing Forecasters." *Management Science* 16, no. 2 (October 1969).

Hayes, R. H. "Statistical Estimation Problems in Inventory Control." *Management Science* 15, no. 11 (July 1969).

Helferich, O. K. "Development of a Dynamic Simulation Model for Planning Physical Distribution Systems: Formulation of the Mathematical Model." Ph.D. dissertation, Michigan State University, 1970.

Herzberg, A. M., and Cox, D. R. "Recent Work on the Design of Experiments: A Bibliography and a Review." *Journal of the Royal Statistical Society A*. 132 (1969).

Heskett, J. L. "A Missing Link in Physical Distribution System Design." *Journal of Marketing*, October 1966.

Hill, William J., and Hunter, William G. "A Review of Response Surface Methodology: A Literature Survey." *Technometrics* 8 (November 1966).

Hoggatt, A. C. "Statistical Techniques for the Computer Analysis of Simulation Models." In *Studies in a Simulated Market*, by L. E. Preston and N. R. Collins. Berkeley, California: Institute of Business and Economic Research, 1966.

Holstein, W. K., and Berry, W. L. "Work Flow Structure: An Analysis for Planning and Control." *Management Science* 16, no. 6 (February 1970).

Holt, C. C.; Modigliani, F.; Muth, J. F.; and Simon, H. A. *Planning Production, Inventories, and Work Force*. Englewood Cliffs, N.J.: Prentice-Hall, Inc., 1960.

Howard, R. A. "Dynamic Programming." *Management Science* 12, no. 5 (January 1966).

Hunter, J. S., and Naylor, T. H. "Experimental Designs For Computer Simulation Experiments." *Management Science* 16, no. 7 (March 1970).

Ignall, E. "Optimal Continuous Review Policies for Two Product Inventory Systems with Joint Setup Costs." *Management Science* 15, no. 5 (January 1969).

Bibliography

Kaczke, Eugene Edwin. *The Impact of Some Dimensions of Management Climate on the Performance of Industrial Organizations: A Computer Simulation Study.* Ann Arbor, Michigan: Microfilms, Inc. May 1966.

Kiviat, Philip J. *Simulation Language Report Generators.* The Rand Corp. April 1966, pp. 33-49.

──────. *Digital Computer Simulation Modeling Concepts.* Santa Monica, California: The Rand Corporation, 1967.

Kiviat, Philip J., and Pritsker, A. A. B. *Simulation with GASP II: A FORTRAN Based Simulation Language.* Englewood Cliffs, N.J.: Prentice-Hall, Inc., 1969.

Kiviat, Philip J.; Villanueva, R.; and Markowitz, H. M. *SIMSCRIPT II.* Englewood Cliffs, N.J.: Prentice-Hall, Inc., 1968.

Koontz, H., and O'Donnell, C. *Principles of Management.* New York: McGraw-Hill, 1955.

Kotler, P. "Corporate Models: Better Marketing Plans." *Harvard Business Review* 48, no. 4 (July-August 1970).

Kotler, P., and Schultz, R. L. "Marketing Simulations: Review and Prospects." *The Journal of Business* 43, no. 3 (July 1970).

Krasnow, Howard S. "Computer Languages of System Simulation." In *Digital Computer User's Handbook,* edited by Melvin Klerer and Granino Korn, sec. I, pp. 258-77. New York: McGraw Hill Book Co., 1967.

Krasnow, Howard S., and Merikallio, R. A. "The Past, Present and Future of General Simulation Languages." *Management Science* 2 (November 1964): 236-67.

Kuehn, A. A. "Logistics of Physical Facilities in Distribution." In *Readings in Physical Distribution Management,* edited by D. J. Bowersox, B. J. LaLonde, and E. W. Smykay. New York: The Macmillan Company, 1969.

Kuehn, A. A., and Hamburger, M. J. "A Heuristic Program for Locating Warehouses." *Management Science* 9 (July 1963).

Lawrence, M. L. "Development of a Dynamic Simulation Model for Planning Physical Distribution Systems: Warehouse Analysis." Ph.D. dissertation, Michigan State University, 1971.

LeKashman, R., and Stolle, J. F. "The Total Cost Approach to Distribution." *Business Horizons* (Winter 1965): 33-46.

Magee, J. F. *Production Planning and Inventory Control.* New York: McGraw-Hill, 1958.

──────. *Physical Distribution Systems.* New York: McGraw-Hill, 1967.

──────. "Quantitative Analysis of Physical Distribution Systems." In *Readings in Business Logistics,* edited by D. McConaughy for American Marketing Association. Homewood, Illinois: Richard D. Irwin, Inc., 1969.

Marien, E. J. "Development of a Dynamic Simulation Model for Planning Physical Distribution Systems: Formulation of the Computer Model." Ph.D. dissertation, Michigan State University, 1970.

Markowitz, H.; Hausner, B.; and Karr, M. *SIMSCRIPT: A Simulation Programming Language.* Englewood Cliffs, N.J.: Prentice-Hall, Inc., 1963.

Marks, N. E., and Taylor, R. M. *Marketing Logistics Perspectives and Viewpoints.* New York: John Wiley & Sons, 1967.

McConaughy, D., ed. *Readings in Business Logistics.* Homewood, Illinois: Richard D. Irwin, Inc., 1969.

McConaughy, D., and Clawson, C. J., eds. *Business Logistics—Policies and Decisions.* Los Angeles: University of Southern California Graduate School of Business Administration, 1968.

McMillan, C., and Gonzalez, R. R. *Systems Analysis: A Computer Approach to Decision Models.* Homewood, Illinois: Richard D. Irwin, Inc., 1968.

McNeley, J. "Simulation Languages." *Simulation* 9 (August 1967): 95-98.

Meier, Robert C.; Newell, William T.; and Pazer, Harold L. *Simulation in Business and Economics*. Englewood Cliffs, New Jersey: Prentice-Hall, Inc., 1969.

Morgan, Fred. "Development of a Dynamic Simulation Model for Planning Physical Distribution Systems: Forecasting Applications." Ph.D. dissertation, Michigan State University, forthcoming.

Morris, W. T. "On the Art of Modeling." *Management Science* 13, no. 12 (August 1967).

Murray, G. R., and Silver, E. "A Bayesian Analysis of the Style Goods Inventory Policy." *Management Science* 12, no. 11 (July 1966).

Naylor, Thomas H. *The Design of Computer Simulation Experiments*. Durham, North Carolina: Duke University Press, 1969.

──────. *Computer Simulation Experiments with Models of Economic Systems*. New York: John Wiley & Sons, 1971.

Naylor, Thomas H.; Balintfy, J. L.; Burdick, D. S.; and Chu, K. *Computer Simulation Techniques*. New York: John Wiley & Sons, 1966.

Naylor, Thomas H., and Burdick, Donald S. "Response Surface Methods in Economics." *Review of the International Statistical Institute* 37 (1969).

Naylor, Thomas H.; Burdick, Donald S.; and Sasser, W. Earl. "Computer Simulation Experiments with Economic Systems: The Problem of Experimental Design." *Journal of the American Statistical Association* 62 (December 1967).

Naylor, Thomas H., and Finger, J. M. "Verification of Computer Simulation Models." *Management Science* 14 (October 1967): 92-101.

Naylor, Thomas H.; Wallace, William H.; and Sasser, W. Earl. "A Computer Simulation Model of the Textile Industry." *Journal of the American Statistical Association* 62 (December 1967).

Naylor, Thomas H.; Wertz, Kenneth; and Wonnacott, Thomas H. "Methods for Analyzing Data from Computer Simulation Experiments." *Communications of the ACM* 10, no. 11 (November 1967).

──────. "Spectral Analysis of Data Generated by Simulation Experiments with Economic Models." *Econometrica* 37 (April 1969): 333-52.

Overholt, John L. "Factor Selection." In *Design of Computer Experiments*, edited by Thomas H. Naylor. Durham, North Carolina: Duke University Press, 1969.

Packer, A. H. "Simulation and Adaptive Forecasting as Applied to Inventory Control." *Operations Research* 15 (August 1967).

Parente, R. J., and Krasnow, H. S. "A Language for Modeling and Simulating Dynamic Systems." *Communications ACM* 10 (September 1967): 559-60.

Paulson, E. "Sequential Estimation and Closed Sequential Decision Procedures." *The Annals of Mathematical Statistics* 35 (September 1964): 1048-1958.

Popper, K. R. *The Logic of Scientific Discovery*. New York: Basic Books, 1959.

Preston, Lee E., and Collins, Norman R. *Studies in a Simulated Market*. Berkeley: Research Program in Marketing, Graduate School of Business Administration, University of California, 1966.

Sasser, W. E.; Burdick, D. S.; Graham, D. A.; and Naylor, T. H. "The Application of Sequential Sampling to Simulation: An Example Inventory Model." *Communications of the ACM* 13 (May 1970): 287-96.

Scheffé, H. *The Analysis of Variance*. New York: John Wiley & Sons, 1959.

Scott, B. W. *Long-Range Planning in American Industry*. New York: American Management Association, 1965.

Schon, J.; Alexander, M.; and Franco, R. J. *Logistics in Marketing*. New York: Pitman Publishing Corporation, 1969.

Schwartz, B. L. "Optimal Inventory Policies in Perturbed Demand Models." *Management Science* 16, no. 8 (April 1970).

Bibliography

Shubik, Martin. "Simulation of the Industry and the Firm." *American Economic Review* 50, no. 5 (December 1960).

Shycon, H. N., and Maffei, R. B. "Simulation—Tool for Better Distribution." In *Readings in Physical Distribution Management*, edited by D. J. Bowersox, B. J. LaLonde, and E. W. Smykay. New York: The Macmillan Company, 1969.

Sinha, B. K., and Gupta, S. K. "Sensitivity of Cost Functions in Inventory Models." *AIIE Transactions* 1, no. 3 (September 1969): 252-56.

Sorensen, E. E., and Gilheany, J. F. "A Simulation Model for Harvest Operations Under Stochastic Conditions." *Management Science* 16, no. 8 (April 1970).

Starr, M. K. "Evolving Concepts in Production Management." In *Operations Management Selected Readings*, edited by G. K. Groff and J. F. Muth. Homewood, Illinois: Richard D. Irwin, Inc., 1969.

Starr, M. K. "Planning Models." *Management Science* 13, no. 4 (December 1966).

Steiner, G. A. *Top Management Planning*. New York: The Macmillan Company, 1969.

Teichroew, Daniel, and Lubin, J. F. "Computer Simulation—Discussion of Techniques and Comparisons of Languages." *Communications ACM* 10 (October 1966): 732-41.

Teichroew, Daniel; Robichek, A. A.; and Montalbano, M. "An Analysis of Criteria for Investment and Financing Decisions Under Certainty." *Management Science* 12, no. 3 (November 1965).

Teichroew, Daniel; Truitt, T. D.; and Lubin, J. F. "Discussion of Computer Simulation Techniques and Comparison of Languages." *Simulation* 9 (October 1967): 181-90.

Theil, H. *Applied Economic Forecasting*. Amsterdam: The North Holland Publishing Co., 1966.

Tocker, K. D. *The Art of Simulation*. London: The English Universities Press, Ltd., 1963.

―――. "Review of Simulation Languages." *Operations Research Quarterly* 16 (June 1965): 189-218.

Tuason, R. V. "Experimental Simulation on a Pre-Determined Marketing Mix Strategy." Ph.D. dissertation, Northwestern University, 1965.

Tukey, John W. "Discussion Emphasizing the Connection Between Analysis of Variance and Spectral Analysis." *Technometrics* 3 (May 1961).

Turing, A. M. "Can a Machine Think?" In *The World of Mathematics*, edited by J. R. Newman. New York: Simon and Schuster, 1956.

Underwood, R. S., and Sparks, Fred W. *Analytic Geometry*. Boston: Houghton Mifflin Company; Cambridge: The Riverside Press, 1956.

Van Horn, R. "Validation." In *The Design of Computer Simulation Experiments*, edited by Thomas H. Naylor, p. 233. Durham, N.C.: Duke University Press, 1969.

Veinott, A. F. "Optimal Policy for a Multi-Product, Dynamic, Non-stationary Inventory Problem." *Management Science* 12, no. 3 (November 1965).

―――. "The Status of Mathematical Inventory Theory." *Management Science* 12, no. 11 (July 1966).

Voosen, B. J., and Buchanan, M. H. *Planet: Part II—Bench Repair Simulator*. Santa Monica: The Rand Corporation, 1967.

Voosen, B. J.; Buchanan, M. H.; and Glaseman, S. *Planet: Part IV—Depot Repair and Overhaul Simulator*. Santa Monica: The Rand Corporation, 1968.

Voosen, B. J.; Glaseman, S.; Young, R. J.; and Judd, J. *Planet: Part V—Reports and Analysis Library*. Santa Monica: The Rand Corporation, 1969.

Voosen, B. J., and Goldman, D. *Planet: Part I—Availability and Base Cadre Simulator*. Santa Monica: The Rand Corporation, 1967.

Wagner, H. M. *Principles of Operations Research.* Englewood Cliffs, New Jersey: Prentice-Hall, Inc., 1969.
Wald, A. *Sequential Analysis.* New York: John Wiley & Sons, 1947.
Watts, Donald. "Time Series Analysis." In *The Design of Computer Simulation Experiments,* edited by Thomas H. Naylor. Durham, North Carolina: Duke University Press, 1969.
Winer, B. J. *Statistical Principles in Experimental Design.* New York: McGraw-Hill Book Company, 1962.
Yance, J. V. "A Model of Price Flexibility." *American Economic Review* 50 (June 1960).
Yurow, Jerome A. "Analysis and Computer Simulation of the Production and Distribution Systems for a Tufted Carpet Mill." *Journal of Industrial Engineering* 18 (January 1967).
Zikmund, W. G., and Stanton, W. J. "Recycling Solid Wastes: A Channels-of-Distribution Problems." *Journal of Marketing* 35, no. 3 (July 1971): 34-39.